Study Guide

Henry Borne

SOCIOLOGY
Ninth Edition

JOHN J. MACIONIS

Prentice Hall, Upper Saddle River, New Jersey 07458

©2003 by PEARSON EDUCATION, INC.
Upper Saddle River, New Jersey 07458

10 9 8 7 6 5 4 3

ISBN 0-13-098816-2

Printed in the United States of America

Table of Contents

Preface

This study guide has been written to enhance the foundation of sociological ideas and issues that are presented in the text, *Sociology 9/e* by John Macionis. To help you review and think about the material found in the text, the study guide has been organized into several different sections to accompany each chapter in the text.

Part I provides a ***Chapter Outline*** the student using the study guide to organize segments of information from each chapter in the text. Part II on ***Learning Objectives*** identifies the basic knowledge, explanations, comparisons, and understandings students should have after reading and reflecting upon each chapter. Part III is entitled ***Key Concepts*** and has the important concepts the chapter defined. The student is asked to write the appropriate concept in the blank space found in each definition. Part IV, ***Important Researchers*** cites many of the researchers cited in the text, with space provided for students to write out important ideas, findings, etc. Part V provides ***Study Questions***, including true-false, multiple-choice, matching, fill-in, and discussion type questions. They are followed by Part VI ***Answers to Study Questions***, which includes a list of the page numbers where the answers to these questions can be found. Part VII, ***In Focus—Major Issues***, provides the student an opportunity to answer questions relating to some of the more important concepts and ideas presented in each chapter.

This study guide is intended as a learning tool to accompany the text *Sociology 9/e*. It will hopefully provide the student with the opportunity to gain more knowledge of sociology as it is presented by the author, who discusses the social issues and problems confronting us today.

On a personal note, I want to once again congratulate Dr. Macionis for writing such an excellent and engaging sociology text. He offers students a very meaningful perspective on many important issues confronting our society and the world. I believe students will be excited by this text, and rewarded by what it has to offer them both personally and academically. It has been a pleasure for me to write this Study Guide. I would also like to praise Senior Acquisitions Editor Christopher DeJohn for his ability to find and keep such outstanding scholars like Dr. Macionis writing textbooks for Prentice Hall. I would like to thank Nancy Roberts, Publisher, Sociology/Anthropology of Prentice Hall for all of her dedicated and work and creativity. I would most like to give my sincere appreciation to Christina Scalia, Assistant Editor, Sociology for all her effort, insight, and guidance during this project. It is a joy working with all of these outstanding people. Heart felt thanks to the proof reader of my last draft of this study guide. Finally, my love to my family—Cincy, Ben, and Abby—for their support and love.

HB

Chapter	The Sociological
1	Perspective

PART I: CHAPTER OUTLINE

I.   The Sociological Perspective
    A.   Seeing the General in the Particular
    B.   Seeing the Strange in the Familiar
    C.   Individuality in Social Context
II. The Importance of Global Perspective
III. Applying the Sociological Perspective
    A.   Sociology and Social Marginality
    B.   Sociology and Social Crisis
    C.   Benefits of the Sociological Perspective
    D.   Sociology, Policy, and Careers
IV. The Origins of Sociology
    A.   Social Change and Sociology
          1.   A New Industrial Economy
          2.   The Growth of Cities
          3.   Political Change
          4.   A New Awareness of Society
    B.   Science and Sociology
    C.   Gender and Race: Marginal Voices
V.   Sociological Theory
    A.   The Structural-Functional Paradigm
    B.   The Social-Conflict Paradigm
    C.   The Symbolic-Interaction Paradigm
    D.   Applying the Paradigms: The Sociology of Sport
          1.   The Functions of Sports
          2.   Sports and Conflict
          3.   Sports as Interaction

PART II: LEARNING OBJECTIVES

- To be able to define sociology and understand the basic components of the sociological perspective.
- To be able to provide examples of the ways in which social forces affect our everyday lives.
- To recognize the importance of taking a global perspective in order to recognize the interdependence of our world's nations and people.
- To begin to recognize factors in society that encourage people to perceive the world sociologically.
- To be able to recognize the benefits of using the sociological perspective.
- To be able to identify important historical factors in the development of the discipline of sociology as a science.
- To be able to identify and discuss the differences between the three major theoretical paradigms used by sociologists in the analysis of society.

PART III: KEY CONCEPTS

Fill in the following blank spaces with the appropriate concept.

1. _____ is the systematic study of human society.
2. Studying the larger world and our society's place in it refers to taking a _____ _____.
3. _____ *countries* are nations with very productive economic systems in which most people have relatively high incomes.
4. The world's _____ *countries* are nations with moderately productive economic systems in which people's incomes are about the global average.
5. About one half the world's population live in the sixty _____ *countries*, nations with less productive economic systems in which most people are poor.
6. A way of understanding based on science is known as _____.
7. A _____ is a statement of how and why specific facts are related.
8. A _____ _____ is a basic image of society that guides thinking and research.
9. The _____ *paradigm* is a framework for building theory that sees society as a complex system whose parts work together to promote solidarity and stability.
10. The term _____ _____ refers to any relatively stable pattern of social behavior.
11. The consequences of any social pattern for the operation of society refer to _____ _____.
12. _____ _____ are the recognized and intended consequences of any social pattern.
13. _____ _____ are consequences that are largely unrecognized and unintended.

14. The undesirable consequences of any social pattern for the operation of society refer to _____ _____.

15. The _____ *paradigm* is a framework for building theory that sees society as an arena of inequality that generates conflict and change.

16. A _____ *orientation* refers to a concern with broad patterns that shape society as a whole.

17. A _____ *orientation* refers to a close-up focus on social interaction in specific situations.

18. The _____ *paradigm* is a framework for building theory that sees society as the product of the everyday interactions of individuals.

19. _____ refer to exaggerated descriptions applied to every person in some category.

PART IV: IMPORTANT RESEARCHERS

In the space provided below each of the following researchers, write two or three sentences to help you remember his or her respective contributions to sociology.

Jane Addams   Herbert Spencer

Emile Durkheim   Karl Marx

Max Weber   Robert Merton

Peter Berger   C. Wright Mills

Lenore Weitzman   W.E.B. Du Bois

Harriet Martineau   Auguste Comte

PART V: STUDY QUESTIONS

True-False

1. T   F   Emile Durkheim's research on *suicide* illustrates the point that not all aspects of social life can be meaningfully studied using the sociological perspective.
2. T   F   African Americans and females have *higher suicide rates* than whites and males.
3. T   F   The *middle-income countries* of the world are primarily found in Latin America, Eastern Europe, and much of southern Africa.
4. T   F   A *New Industrial economy, the growth of cities,* and *new ideas about democracy and political freedom*s are identified as factors that helped people to view the world sociologically.
5. T   F   For Auguste Comte sociology was the product of a three-stage historical process, including the *theological stage,* the *metaphysical stage*, and the *scientific stage.*
6. T   F   *Positivism* is an approach to understanding the world based on metaphysics.
7. T   F   A *theory* is a statement of how and why specific facts are related.
8. T   F   *Latent functions* refer to social processes which appear on the surface to be functional for society, but which are actually detrimental.
9. T   F   The *symbolic-interactionist* paradigm presents society less in terms of abstract generalizations and more as everyday experiences.
10. T   F   A *generalization* is defined as an exaggerated description that one applies to all people in some category.

Multiple Choice

1. According to the author, some forty million young people in the United States—about three out of four—

    (a)   have committed at least one felony crime.
    (b)   drink alcohol.
    (c)   use illicit drugs.
    (d)   participate in organized sports.

2. What is the *essential wisdom* of sociology?

    (a)   Patterns in life are predestined.
    (b)   Society is essentially nonpatterned.
    (c)   Surrounding society affects our actions, thoughts, and feelings.
    (d)   Common sense needs to guide sociological investigations.

3. The sociological perspective involves *seeing the strange in the familiar*. Which of the following best provides the essential meaning of this phrase?

    (a) Sociology interprets social life primarily relying on common sense.
    (b) Sociologists believe intuition rather than logic is the preferred way to study society.
    (c) Sociologists focus on the bizarre behaviors that occur in society.
    (d) Sociologists work to avoid the assumption that human behavior is simply a matter of what people decide to do.

4. Which sociologist, in a systematic empirical study, linked the incidence of *suicide* to the degree of *social integration* of different categories of people?

    (a) Emile Durkheim
    (b) Max Weber
    (c) Robert Merton
    (d) C. Wright Mills

5. *Low-income countries* are described as

    (a) nations with little industrialization and severe poverty.
    (b) nations with limited natural resources and large populations.
    (c) nations with per capita incomes of less than $15,000.
    (d) nations with no industrialization and limited natural resources.

6. Which of the following is *not* identified as a reason a *global perspective* is so important?

    (a) Societies the world over are increasingly interconnected.
    (b) Many problems that we face in the United States are not found in other societies.
    (c) Thinking globally is a good way to learn more about ourselves.
    (d) All of the above are identified as reasons why a global perspective is so important.

7. Which of the following is *not* identified as situations that simulate *sociological thinking*?

    (a) encountering people who are different from us
    (b) social stability
    (c) social marginality
    (d) social crisis

8. Learning to understand our individual lives in terms of the social forces that have shaped them is a state of mind that C. Wright Mills called

    (a) science.
    (b) hypothesis testing.
    (c) the sociological imagination.
    (d) positivism.

9. The benefits of sociology go well beyond personal growth. Sociologists have helped shape public policy and law in countless ways. To illustrate this, the work by Lenore Weitzman on _____ had a real impact on public policy and resulted in the passage of several laws in California.

    (a)   macro-level forces affecting suicide rates
    (b)   date rape
    (c)   financial hardships facing women after a divorce
    (d)   standardized educational assessment measures

10. The term *sociology* was coined in 1838 by

    (a)   Auguste Comte.
    (b)   Karl Marx.
    (c)   Herbert Spencer.
    (d)   Emile Durkheim.

11. According to Auguste Comte, the key to understanding society was to look at it

    (a)   using common sense.
    (b)   using intuition.
    (c)   theologically.
    (d)   metaphysically.
    (e)   scientifically.

12. *Positivism* is the idea that _____, rather than any other type of human understanding, is the path to knowledge.

    (a)   common sense
    (b)   science
    (c)   faith
    (d)   optimism

13. A *basic image* of society that guides thinking and research is the definition for

    (a)   a theoretical paradigm.
    (b)   manifest functions.
    (c)   social marginality.
    (d)   positivism.

14. Any relatively stable pattern of social behavior refers to

    (a)   social functions.
    (b)   theories.
    (c)   social structure.
    (d)   positivism.

15. Consequences of social structure which are largely *unrecognized* and *unintended* are called

    (a) paradigms.
    (b) latent functions.
    (c) manifest functions.
    (d) social integration.

16. Which of the following is a criticism of *structural-functionalism*?

    (a) This theoretical paradigm focuses too much attention on social conflict.
    (b) This theoretical paradigm attends to questions concerning how life is experienced by individuals on a day-to-day basis while ignoring larger social structures.
    (c) This theoretical paradigm tends to ignore inequalities which can generate tension and conflict.
    (d) This theoretical paradigm stresses the functional value of social change, while ignoring the integrative qualities of different social institutions.

17. Which theoretical perspective is best suited for analysis using a *macro-level* orientation?

    (a) dramaturgical analysis
    (b) social exchange theory
    (c) symbolic-interactionist paradigm
    (d) ethnomethodology
    (e) social-conflict paradigm

18. _____ did not see sociology as a dry, academic discipline. On the contrary, he wanted to apply sociology to solving the pressing problems of his time (1868-1963), especially racial inequality.

    (a) Karl Marx
    (b) Auguste Comte
    (c) Herbert Spencer
    (d) W.E.B. Du Bois

19. The questions "How is society experienced?" and, "How do individuals attempt to shape the reality perceived by others?" are most likely asked by a researcher following which theoretical paradigms?

    (a) structural-functional
    (b) symbolic-interaction
    (c) social Darwinism
    (d) social-conflict

20.   Sociology is not involved in *stereotyping* because

(a)   sociology makes generalizations about categories of people, not stereotypes.
(b)   sociologists base their generalizations on research.
(c)   sociologists strive to be fair-minded.
(d)   all of the above

Matching

1.   ___   The study of the larger world and our society's place in it.
2.   ___   Nations with limited industrialization and moderate personal income.
3.   ___   Says we need to turn personal problems into public issues to view the world sociologically.
4.   ___   An approach to studying the world based on science.
5.   ___   A statement of how and why specific facts are related.
6.   ___   A framework for building theory based on the assumption that society is a complex system whose parts work together to promote solidarity and stability.
7.   ___   Relatively stable patterns of social behavior.
8.   ___   The largely unrecognized and unintended consequences of social structure.
9.   ___   A framework for building theory that sees society as an arena of inequality that generates conflict and change.
10.   ___   An exaggerated description applied to all people in some category.

a.	C. Wright Mills	f.	stereotype
b.	theory	g.	middle-income countries
c.	social-conflict paradigm	h.	latent functions
d.	positivism	i.	global perspective
e.	structural-functional paradigm	j.	social structure

Fill-In

1.   The systematic study of human society is the general definition for _____.
2.   Emile Durkheim reasoned that the variation in *suicide rates* between different categories of people had to do with *social* _____.
3.   A _____ _____ is a view of the larger world and our society's place in it.
4.   The United States, Canada, and most of the nations of Western Europe are classified in terms of economic development as being the _____-*income countries.*
5.   Three important reasons for taking a *global perspective* include: where we live makes a great difference in _____ our lives, societies around the world are increasingly _____, many human problems that we face in the United States are far more _____ elsewhere, and it is a good way to learn more about _____.
6.   According to C. Wright Mills, using the *sociological* _____ can transform individual lives as it transforms society. Further, as we see others grapple with the same problems we do enables us to join together and turn *personal* _____ into *public* _____.

7.   Three changes are especially important to the development of sociology in Europe during the nineteenth century, including: a new _____ *economy*, a growth of _____, and _____ change.

8.   Auguste Comte asserted that scientific sociology was a result of a progression throughout history of thought and understanding in *three stages*: the _____, _____, and _____.

9.   A _____ is a statement of how and why specific facts are related.

10. _____ _____ are consequences for the operation of society as a whole.

Discussion

1.   Differentiate between the concepts *manifest* and *latent functions* and provide an illustration for each.

2.   Discuss Emile Durkheim's explanation of how *suicide rates* vary between different categories of people. Explain how this research demonstrates the application of the *sociological perspective*.

3.   What are the three types of countries identified in the text as measured by their level of *economic development*? What are the characteristics of the countries that represent each of the three types?

4.   What are the three major reasons why a *global perspective* is so important today?

5.   What are the three major components of the *sociological perspective*? Describe and provide an illustration for each.

6.   What are the three major *theoretical paradigms* used by sociologists? Identify two key questions raised by each in the analysis of society. Identify one weakness for each of these paradigms for understanding the nature of human social life.

7.   What are three reasons why sociology is *not to be considered* nothing more than *stereotyping*?

8.   What are the four *benefits* of using the sociological perspective? Provide an illustration for two of these.

9.   What does C. Wright Mills mean by turning *personal problems* into *public issues*? Provide an illustration.

10. Based on what you have read in the text so far, what is you interpretation of *sociology* as a disciple of study?

PART VI: ANSWERS TO STUDY QUESTIONS

Key Concepts

1.   Sociology (p. 1)
2.   global perspective (p. 5)
3.   High-income (pp. 5-7)
4.   middle-income (p. 7)
5.   low-income (p. 7)
6.   positivism (p. 12)
7.   theory (p. 13)
8.   theoretical paradigm (p. 13)
9.   structural-functionalism (p. 14)
10. social structure (p. 14)
11. social functions (p. 16)
12. Manifest functions (p. 14)
13. Latent functions (p. 14)
14. social dysfunctions (p. 15)
15. social-conflict (p. 15)
16. macro-level (p. 17)
17. micro-level (p. 17)
18. symbolic-interactionism (p. 17)
19. Stereotypes (p. 21)

True-False

1.	F	(p. 3)		6.	F	(p. 12)
2.	F	(p. 3)		7.	T	(p. 13)
3.	T	(pp. 6-7)		8.	F	(p. 14)
4.	T	(p. 10)		9.	T	(p. 17)
5.	T	(p. 12)		10.	F	(p. 21)

Multiple Choice

1.	d	(p. 1)		11.	e	(p. 12)
2.	c	(p. 3)		12.	b	(p. 12)
3.	d	(pp. 2-3)		13.	a	(pp. 13-14)
4.	a	(p. 3)		14.	c	(p. 14)
5.	a	(p. 7)		15.	b	(p. 14)
6.	b	(pp. 7-8)		16.	d	(p. 15)
7.	b	(p. 8)		17.	e	(p. 16)
8.	c	(p. 8)		18.	d	(p. 16)
9.	c	(p. 10)		19.	b	(p. 19)
10.	a	(p. 12)		20.	d	(p. 21)

Matching

1.	i	(p. 5)		6.	m	(p. 14)
2.	g	(pp. 6-7)		7.	j	(p. 14)
3.	k	(p. 9)		8.	h	(p. 14)
4.	l	(p. 12)		9.	c	(p. 15)
5.	b	(p. 13)		10.	p	(p. 21)

Fill-In

1. sociology (p. 1)
2. integration (p. 3)
3. global perspective (p. 5)
4. high (pp. 6-7)
5. shaping, interconnected, serious, ourselves (pp. 8-9)
6. imagination, problems, issues (p. 9)
7. industrial, cities, political (p. 10)
8. theological, metaphysical, scientific (p. 12)
9. theory (p. 13)
10. Social functions (p. 14)

PART VII: IN FOCUS--IMPORTANT ISSUES

- The Sociological Perspective

  Define and illustrate each of the three *components of the sociological perspective.*

    seeing the general in the particular

    seeing the strange in the familiar

    seeing individuality in social context

- The Importance of Global Perspective

  What are the four reasons why a *global perspective* is so important?

- Applying the Sociological Perspective

  Provide an example of how each of the following encourages the application of the sociological perspective.

    encountering people who are different from us

    social marginality

    social crisis

  What are the four *benefits* of using the sociological perspective?

- The Origins of Sociology

  What were the three striking *transformations* in Europe during the eighteenth and nineteenth centuries that were especially important for the emergence of sociology?

  Auguste Comte saw sociology as the product of a three-stage historical development. Define each of them.

  theological stage

  metaphysical stage

  scientific stage

- Sociological Theory

  Define each of the following *theoretical paradigms*.

  structural-functionalism

  social-conflict

  symbolic-interactionism

  Identify one *strength* and one *weakness* for each of the following theoretical paradigms.

  structural-functionalism

  strength

  weakness

social-conflict

    strength

    weakness

symbolic-interactionism

    strength

    weakness

What do structural-functionalists mean by the *functions of sports*? Provide an illustration.

What do social-conflict theorists mean by stating that sports are closely linked to *social inequality*? Provide two illustrations.

What points are being made by symbolic-interactionists about sports as *interaction*?

Provide an example from this chapter illustrating the point that sociological thinking involves *generalizations*, not stereotypes.

<table>
<tr><td>Chapter</td><td rowspan="2"></td></tr>
<tr><td>2</td></tr>
</table>

Sociological Investigation

PART I: CHAPTER OUTLINE

I.   The Basics of Sociological Investigation
    A.   Science As One Form of "Truth"
    B.   Common Sense Versus Scientific Evidence

II.   Science: Basic Elements and Limitations
    A.   Concepts, Variables, and Measurement
        1.   Defining Concepts
        2.   Reliability and Validity
        3.   Relationships between Variables
    B.   The Ideal of Objectivity
        1.   Max Weber: Value-Free Research
    C.   Some Limitations of Scientific Sociology
    D.   A Second Framework: Interpretive Sociology
    E.   A Third Framework: Critical Sociology
    F.   Gender and Research
    G.   Research Ethics

III.   The Methods of Sociological Research
    A.   Testing a Hypothesis: The Experiment
        1.   The Hawthorne Effect
        2.   An Illustration: The Stanford County Prison
    B.   Asking Questions: Survey Research
        1.   Population and Sample
        2.   Using Questionnaires
        3.   Conducting Interviews
        4.   An Illustration: Studying the African American Elite
    C.   In the Field: Participant Observation
        1.   An Illustration: Street Corner Society
    D.   Using Available Data: Secondary and Historical Analysis
        1.   An Illustration: A Tale of Two Cities
    E.   The Interplay of Theory and Method
    F.   Putting It All Together: Ten Steps in Sociological Investigation

IV.   Summary

V.   Key Concepts

VI.   Critical-Thinking Questions

VII.   Applications and Exercises

VIII.   Sites to See

PART II: LEARNING OBJECTIVES

- To review the fundamental requirements for engaging in scientific investigation using the sociological perspective.
- To become familiar with the basic elements of science and how they are used in sociological investigation.
- To see how research is affected by politics and gender.
- To begin to view ethical considerations involved in studying people.
- To become familiar with research methods used by sociologists in the investigation of society.
- To begin to understand the interplay of theory and method.
- To be able to identify and describe each of the ten steps in sociological research.

PART III: KEY CONCEPTS

Fill in the following blank spaces with the appropriate concept.

1. _____ is a logical system that bases knowledge on direct, systematic observation.
2. The study of society based on systematic observation of social behavior refers to _____ _____.
3. Information that we can verify with our senses refers to _____ _____.
4. A _____ is a mental construct that represents some part of the world in a simplified form.
5. _____ are concepts whose values change from case to case.
6. A procedure for determining the value of a variable in a specific case is known as _____.
7. _____ ____ _____ means specifying exactly what one is to measure before assigning a value to a variable.
8. _____ refers to consistency in measurement.
9. _____ refers to precision in measuring exactly what one intends to measure.
10. A relationship in which change in one variable (the independent variable) causes change in another (the dependent variable) is known as _____ _____ _____.
11. An _____ _____ is a variable that causes change in another (dependent) variable.
12. A variable that is changed by another (independent) variable is known as a _____ _____.
13. A _____ refers to a relationship by which two (or more) variables change together.
14. A _____ _____ is an apparent, although false, relationship between two (or more) variables caused by some other variable.
15. A technique used for unmasking spurious correlations called _____ refers to holding constant all variables except one in order to see clearly the effect of that variable.
16. Science demands that researchers strive for _____, a state of personal neutrality in conducting research.
17. One way to limit distortion caused by personal values is _____, repetition of research by other investigations.
18. _____ _____ is the study that focuses on the meanings people attach to their social world.
19. _____ _____ is the study of society that focuses on the needs for social change.
20. In recent years sociologists have become aware of the fact that research is affected by _____, the personal traits and social positions that members of a society attach to being female or male.

21. A _____ _____ is a systematic plan for conducting research.
22. A research method for investigating cause and effect under controlled conditions refers to an _____.
23. A _____ is an unverified statement of a relationship between variables.
24. The _____ _____ refers to a change in a subject's behavior caused simply by the awareness of being studied.
25. A _____ is a research method in which subjects respond to a series of statements or questions in a questionnaire or an interview.
26. The people who are the focus of research are known as the _____.
27. A _____ refers to a part of the population that represents the whole.
28. A _____ is a series of written questions a researcher presents to subjects.
29. An_____ is a series of questions a researcher administers in person to respondents.
30. _____ _____ is a research method in which investigators systematically observe people while joining in their routine activities.
31. _____ _____ refers to a research method in which a researcher uses data collected by others.
32. Reasoning that transforms general theory into specific observations into general observations is known as _____ _____.
33. Reasoning that transforms general theory into specific hypotheses suitable for testing refers to _____ _____.

PART IV: IMPORTANT RESEARCHERS

In the space provided below each of the following researchers, write two or three sentences to help you remember his or her respective contributions to sociology.

Max Weber   Alvin Gouldner

Philip Zimbardo   Lois Benjamin

William F. Whyte   E. Digby Baltzell

PART V: STUDY QUESTIONS

True-False

1. T   F   Research by Lois Benjamin focused on *uneducated, lower-class* African Americans and how they deal with racism.
2. T   F   *Science* is a logical system that bases knowledge on direct, systematic observation.
3. T   F   A major strength of sociology is that it is basically just like using *common sense*.
4. T   F   A *concept* refers to the process of determining the value of a variable in a specific case.
5. T   F   Max Weber said that people doing scientific research must strive to be *value-free*.
6. T   F   *Androcentricity* refers to approaching an issue from a male perspective.
7. T   F   The *Hawthorne Effect* refers to a change in a subject's behavior caused simply by the awareness of being studied.
8. T   F   A *sample* refers to a research method in which subjects respond to a series of statements or questions in a questionnaire or an interview.
9. T   F   *Inductive logical thought* is reasoning that transforms general theory into specific hypotheses suitable for testing.
10. T   F   The first step in the scientific research process should always be to determine what research design will be used to obtain the data.

Multiple Choice

1. _____ *evidence* is information we can verify with our senses.

    (a)   Consensual
    (b)   Common sense
    (c)   Intrapsychic
    (d)   Holistic
    (e)   Empirical

2. _____ is a logical system that bases knowledge on direct, systematic observation.

    (a)   A research method
    (b)   Critical sociology
    (c)   A hypothesis
    (d)   Science
    (e)   A theory

3. Specifying exactly what one is to measure before assigning a value to a variable is called

    (a)   validity.
    (b)   objectivity.
    (c)   operationalizing a variable.
    (d)   reliability.

4. The *descriptive statistic* representing the value occurring *midway* in a series of numbers is called the

   (a) median.
   (b) correlation.
   (c) mode.
   (d) norm.
   (e) mean.

5. The quality of *consistency* in measurement is known as

   (a) spuriousness.
   (b) reliability.
   (c) empirical evidence.
   (d) objectivity.
   (e) validity.

6. Measuring what one *intends* to measure is the quality of measurement known as

   (a) reliability.
   (b) operationalization.
   (c) validity.
   (d) objectivity.

7. An apparent, although false, relationship between two (or more) variables caused by some other variable refers to

   (a) a deductive correlation.
   (b) an inductive correlation.
   (c) a replicated correlation.
   (d) a operationalized correlation
   (e) a spurious correlation.

8. A state of personal neutrality in conducting research is known as

   (a) subjective interpretation.
   (b) objectivity.
   (c) a control variable.
   (d) validity.

9. The study of society that focuses on the meanings people attach to their social world refers to

   (a) critical sociology.
   (b) quantitative sociology.
   (c) residual sociology.
   (d) interpretive sociology.

10. _____ is the study of society that focuses on the need for social change.

   (a) Androcentricity
   (b) Qualitative research
   (c) Critical sociology
   (d) Interpretive sociology

11. A _____ is a systematic plan for conducting research.

   (a) hypothesis
   (b) research method
   (c) sample
   (d) replication

12. An unverified statement of a relationship between variables is a(n)

   (a) correlation.
   (b) logical deduction.
   (c) hypothesis.
   (d) logical induction.
   (e) theory.

13. Which *research method* is explanatory and is usually used to test hypotheses?

   (a) the survey
   (b) participant observation
   (c) the experiment
   (d) the use of existing sources
   (e) the interview

14. A change in a subject's behavior caused simply by the awareness of being studied refers to

   (a) the Hawthorne effect.
   (b) androcentricity.
   (c) replication.
   (d) objectivity.
   (e) control.

15. Phillip Zimbardo's *prison study* is used in the text to illustrate which of the research designs?

   (a) participant observation
   (b) survey--using questionnaires
   (c) survey--using interviews
   (d) the experiment
   (e) secondary analysis

16. A disadvantage of the *interview* type of survey is that

    (a)   it does not permit follow-up questions.
    (b)   the subjects' answers cannot be clarified.
    (c)   a person is less likely to complete a survey if contacted personally.
    (d)   the researcher may inadvertently influence the subject.

17. A type of sampling in which the researcher starts out with people she knows and asks them to suggest others is know as

    (a)   residual sampling.
    (b)   snowball sampling.
    (c)   consensus sampling.
    (d)   contact sampling.

18. _____ *analysis* is a research method in which a researcher uses data collected by others.

    (a)   Secondary
    (b)   Residual
    (c)   Marginal
    (d)   Ethnographic

19. E. Digby Baltzell's study of important and successful Americans, comparing Puritans and Quakers, is an example of which research method?

    (a)   experiment
    (b)   participant observation
    (c)   secondary analysis
    (d)   survey--questionnaire
    (e)   survey--interview

20. If a researcher begins a sociological investigation with general ideas about the world which then are used to produce specific hypotheses suited for scientific testing, the process is known as

    (a)   inductive logical thought.
    (b)   a qualitative methodology.
    (c)   empirical analysis.
    (d)   deductive logical thought.
    (e)   speculative reasoning.

Matching

1. ___ A mental construct that represents an aspect of the world, inevitably in a somewhat simplified way.
2. ___ The quality of measurement gained by measuring precisely what one intends to measure.
3. ___ A relationship in which two (or more) variables change together.
4. ___ An apparent, although false, relationship between two (or more) variables caused by some other variable.
5. ___ A state of personal neutrality in conducting research.
6. ___ A systematic plan for conducting research.
7. ___ A part of a population that represents the whole.
8. ___ A research method in which subjects respond to a series of statements and questions in a questionnaire or interview.
9. ___ A series of written questions a researcher presents to subjects.
10. ___ The study *Street Corner Society* by William Foote Whyte illustrates this research method.

a.	objectivity	f.	participant observation
b.	correlation	g.	sample
c.	research method	h.	spurious correlation
d.	survey	i.	questionnaire
e.	concept	j.	validity

Fill-In

1. _____ _____ is the study of society based on systematic observation of social behavior.
2. The term _____ refers to a procedure for determining the value of a variable in a specific case.
3. _____ refers to two variables that *vary together*, such as the extent of crowding and juvenile delinquency.
4. _____ refers to *repetition of research* by other researchers.
5. Five ways in which *gender* can jeopardize good research include: _____, _____, _____, gender _____, _____ standards, and _____.
6. In an *experiment*, controlling outside influences often involves dividing subjects into an _____ group and a _____ group.
7. Two types of surveys include _____ and _____.
8. *Fieldwork, ethnographies,* and *case studies* are all examples of _____ _____ research.
9. William Foote Whyte's relationship with *Doc* in his study *Street Corner Society* illustrates the importance of a _____ _____ in participant observation research.
10. E. Digsby Baltzell's research using secondary analysis focused on the *Puritans* of the Boston area and the *Quakers* of the Philadelphia area. He argues that the former group respected _____ and the latter group believed in _____, which he argued explained in part why the number of "famous people" from each group is so different.

Discussion

1. What are the three factors which must be determined to conclude that a *cause and effect* relationship between two variables may exist?
2. Margaret Eichler identifies five dangers to research that involves *gender*. Identify and define each.
3. Define the concept *hypothesis*. Further, write your own hypothesis and operationalize the variables.
4. Identify two advantages and two disadvantages for each of the four major *research methods* used by sociologists. Further, identify four *limitations* of scientific sociology.
5. Three illustrations are provided to show that *common sense* does not always guide us to a meaningful sense of reality. What two examples can you give concerning common sense not paving the way toward our understanding of what is really happening in social life?
6. Differentiate between the viewpoints of Max Weber and Alvin Gouldner concerning *objectivity* in social science research. Whose argument do you agree with more? What is your reasoning for having this opinion?
7. What are the basic guidelines for *research ethics* in sociological research? What other guidelines do you think might be important or necessary to have in place?
8. What sorts of questions about society are being asked by researchers using *critical sociology*?
9. Explain why Phillip Zimabardo's prison research is an example of *deductive logical thought*.
10. What are three ways in which people can *lie with statistics*? Find an example of one of these ways in a popular magazine or newspaper.

PART VI: ANSWERS TO STUDY QUESTIONS

Key Concepts

1. Science (p. 26)
2. scientific sociology (p. 26)
3. empirical evidence (p. 26)
4. concept (p. 28)
5. Variables (p. 28)
6. measurement (p. 28)
7. Operationalizing a variable (p. 29)
8. Reliability (p. 29)
9. Validity (p. 29)
10. cause and effect (p. 30)
11. independent variable (p. 30)
12. dependent variable (p. 30)
13. correlation (p. 31)
14. spurious correlation (p. 31)
15. control (p. 31)
16. objectivity (p. 32)
17. replication (p. 33)
18. Interpretive sociology (p. 34)
19. Critical sociology (p. 34)
20. gender (p. 35)

21.   research method (p. 36)
22.   experiment (p. 36)
23.   hypothesis (p. 36)
24.   Hawthorne effect (p. 38)
25.   survey (p. 39)
26.   population (p. 39)
27.   sample (p. 39)
28.   questionnaire (p. 39)
29.   interview (p. 41)
30.   Participant observation (p. 43)
31.   Secondary analysis (p. 45)
32.   inductive logical thought (p. 47)
33.   deductive logical thought (p. 48)

True-False

1.	F	(p. 25)	6.	T	(p. 35)
2.	T	(p. 26)	7.	T	(p. 38)
3.	F	(p. 27)	8.	F	(p. 39)
4.	F	(p. 28)	9.	F	(p. 47)
5.	T	(p. 32)	10.	F	(p. 49)

Multiple Choice

1.	e	(p. 26)	11.	b	(p. 36)
2.	d	(p. 26)	12.	c	(p. 36)
3.	c	(p. 29)	13.	c	(p. 36)
4.	a	(p. 29)	14.	a	(p 38)
5.	b	(p. 29)	15.	d	(p. 38)
6.	c	(p. 29)	16.	d	(p. 41)
7.	e	(p. 31)	17.	b	(p. 42)
8.	b	(p. 32)	18.	a	(p. 45)
9.	d	(p. 34)	19.	c	(p. 46)
10.	c	(p. 34)	20.	d	(p. 48)

Matching

1.	e	(p. 28)	6.	c	(p. 36)
2.	j	(p. 29)	7.	g	(p. 39)
3.	b	(p. 31)	8.	d	(p. 39)
4.	h	(p. 31)	9.	i	(p. 39)
5.	a	(p. 32)	10.	f	(p. 44)

<u>Fill-In</u>

1. Scientific sociology (p. 26)
2. measurement (p. 28)
3. Correlation (p. 30)
4. Replication (p. 3)
5. androcentricity, overgeneralizing, blindness, double, interference (p. 35)
6. experimental, control (p. 37)
7. questionnaires, interviews (p. 39)
8. participant observation (p. 43)
9. key informant (p. 45)
10. achievement, equality (p. 47)

PART VII: IN FOCUS—IMPORTANT ISSUES

- The Basics of Sociological Investigation

    Sociological investigation starts with two simple *requirements*. What are these? What do these to requirements mean to you?

    Provide three examples of why *common sense* is challenged by scientific evidence. Two of these are to be from the text, and one from your own inquiry.

- Science: Basic Elements and Limitations

  Define and illustrate each of the following *elements of science*.

    concept

    variable

    measurement

    reliability

    validity

    correlation

    cause and effect

    objectivity

  What are the four *limitations* of scientific sociology?

  What are five important *ethical considerations* involved in sociological research?

- What is a *research method*?

  Describe each of the following research methods.

  experiment

  survey

  participant observation

  secondary analysis

- List the ten basic steps in *sociological investigation.*

Chapter 3 — Culture

PART I: CHAPTER OUTLINE

I. What is Culture?
   A. Culture and Human Intelligence
   B. Culture, Nation, and Society
II. The Components of Culture
   A. Symbols
   B. Language
      1. Language: Only for Humans?
      2. Does Language Shape Reality?
   C. Values and Beliefs
      1. Key Values of U.S. Culture
      2. Values: Sometimes in Conflict
   D. Norms
      1. Mores and Folkways
      2. Social Control
   E. "Ideal" and "Real" Culture
   F. Material Culture and Technology
   G. New Information Technology and Culture
III. Cultural Diversity: Many Ways of Life In One World
   A. High Culture and Popular Culture
   B. Subculture
   C. Multiculturalism
   D. Counterculture
   E. Cultural Change
      1. Cultural Lag
      2. Causes of Cultural Change
   F. Ethnocentrism and Cultural Relativity
   G. A Global Culture?
IV. Theoretical Analysis of Culture
   A. Structural-Functional Analysis
   B. Social-Conflict Analysis
   C. Sociobiology
V. Culture and Human Freedom
   A. Culture as Constraint
   B. Culture as Freedom

VI. Summary
VII. Key Concepts
VIII. Critical-Thinking Questions
IX. Applications and Exercises
X. Sites to See

PART II: LEARNING OBJECTIVES

- To begin to understand the sociological meaning of the concept of culture.
- To consider the relationship between human intelligence and culture.
- To know the components of culture and to be able to provide examples of each.
- To consider the current state of knowledge about whether language is uniquely human.
- To consider the significance of symbols in the construction and maintenance of social reality.
- To identify the dominant values in our society and to recognize their interrelationships with one another and with other aspects of our culture.
- To be able to provide examples of the different types of norms operative in a culture, and how these are related to the process of social control.
- To be able to explain how subcultures and countercultures contribute to cultural diversity.
- To begin to develop your understanding of multiculturalism.
- To be able to differentiate between ethnocentrism and cultural relativism.
- To be able to compare and contrast analyses of culture using structural-functional, social-conflict, and sociobiological paradigms.
- To be able to identify the consequences of culture for human freedom and constraint.

PART III: KEY CONCEPTS

Fill in the following blank spaces with the appropriate concept.

1. The term _____ refers to the values, beliefs, behavior, and material objects that, together, form a people's way of life.
2. _____ _____ refers to the intangible world of ideas created by members of a society.
3. _____ _____ refers to the tangible things created by members of a society.
4. Going to another culture can cause _____ _____, or personal disorientation when experiencing another way of life.
5. _____ are anything that carries a particular meaning recognized by people who share a culture.
6. A system of symbols that allows people to communicate with one another is known as a _____.
7. _____ _____ refers to the process by which one generation passes culture to the next.
8. The _____ _____ states that people perceive the world through the cultural lens of language.
9. _____ are culturally defined standards by which people assess desirability, goodness, and beauty and that serve as broad guidelines for social living.
10. _____ are specific statements that people hold to be true.

28

11. _____ refer to rules and expectations by which a society guides the behavior of its members.
12. Norms that are widely observed and have great moral significance are called _____.
13. _____ are norms for routine, casual interaction.
14. _____ _____ refers to the various means by which members of a society encourage conformity to norms.
15. _____ refers to knowledge that people use to make a way of life in their surroundings.
16. Cultural patterns that distinguishes a culture's elite is known as _____ _____.
17. _____ _____ refers to cultural patterns that are widespread among a society's population.
18. The term _____ refers to cultural patterns that set apart some segment of a society's population.
19. _____ is an educational program recognizing the cultural diversity of the United States and promoting the equality of all cultural traditions.
20. _____ refers to the dominance of European (especially English) cultural patterns.
21. _____ refers to the dominance of African cultural patterns.
22. A _____ refers to cultural patterns that strongly oppose those widely accepted within a society.
23. _____ _____ refers to the close relationships among various elements of a cultural system.
24. The fact that some cultural elements change more quickly than others, which may disrupt a cultural system is known as _____ _____.
25. The practice of judging another culture by the standards of one's own culture is known as _____.
26. _____ _____ refers to the practice of evaluating a culture by its own standards.
27. Traits that are part of every known culture are referred to as _____ _____.
28. _____ is a theoretical paradigm that explores ways in which human biology affects how we create culture.

PART IV: IMPORTANT RESEARCHERS

In the space provided below each of the following researchers, write two or three sentences to help you remember his or her respective contributions to sociology.

Napoleon Chagnon   Edward Sapir and Benjamin Whorf

Charles Darwin   George Peter Murdock

Marvin Harris   Robin Williams

PART V: STUDY QUESTIONS

<u>True-False</u>

1.	T	F	*Nonmaterial culture* refers to the intangible world of ideas created by members of a society.
2.	T	F	The term *society* refers to a shared way of life.
3.	T	F	*Values* are defined as rules and expectations by which society guides the behavior of its members.
4.	T	F	*Mores* are norms which have little moral significance within a culture.
5.	T	F	Social *sanctions*, operating as a system of social control, can involve rewards or punishments.
6.	T	F	*Technology* is defined as the knowledge that people apply to the task of living in their surroundings.
7.	T	F	*Virtual culture* refers to the gap between "ideal" and "real" culture.
8.	T	F	During the last decade, most *immigrants* to the United States have come from Asia and Latin America.
9.	T	F	The practice of judging any culture by its own standards is referred to as *ethnocentrism*.
10.	T	F	*Structural-functionalists* argue that there are no *cultural universals*.

<u>Multiple-Choice</u>

1. *Culture* is

    (a)   the process by which members of a culture encourage conformity to social norms.
    (b)   the beliefs, values, behavior, and material objects that constitute a people's way of life.
    (c)   the practice of judging another society's norms.
    (d)   a group of people who engage in interaction with one another on a continuous basis.

2. The personal disorientation that accompanies exposure to an unfamiliar way of life is termed

    (a)   anomie.
    (b)   alienation.
    (c)   cultural relativism.
    (d)   culture shock.
    (e)   cultural transmission.

30

3. The *Yanomamo* are

    (a)   a small tribal group of herders living in Eastern Africa.
    (b)   a technologically primitive horticultural society living in South America.
    (c)   a nomadic culture living above the Arctic circle as hunters.
    (d)   a small, dying society living as farmers in a mountainous region of western Africa.
    (e)   a people who until very recently were living in complete isolation from the rest of the world in a tropical rain forest in Malaysia.

4. Studying *fossil records*, scientists have concluded that the first creatures with clearly human characteristics, setting the human line apart from that of the great apes, existed about ___ years ago.

    (a)   2 million
    (b)   12 thousand
    (c)   40 million
    (d)   60 thousand
    (e)   12 million

5. *Homo sapiens* is a Latin term that means

    (a)   thinking person.
    (b)   to walk upright.
    (c)   evolving life form.
    (d)   dependent person.

6. The organized interaction of people in a nation or within some other boundary is the definition for

    (a)   culture.
    (b)   social structure.
    (c)   enculturation.
    (d)   socialization.
    (e)   society.

7. Which of the following identifies two of the *components of culture*?

    (a)   values and norms
    (b)   social change and social statics
    (c)   social structure and social function
    (d)   people and the natural environment

8. A system of *symbols* that allows members of a society to communicate with one another is the definition of

   (a) language.
   (b) cultural relativity.
   (c) cultural transmission.
   (d) values.

9. The *Sapir-Whorf thesis* relates to

   (a) human evolution.
   (b) language and cultural relativity.
   (c) social sanctions.
   (d) victimization patterns.

10. Culturally defined *standards* of desirability, goodness, and beauty, which serve as broad guidelines for social living, is the definition for

    (a) norms.
    (b) mores.
    (c) beliefs.
    (d) sanctions.
    (e) values.

11. Progress and freedom are examples of U.S.

    (a) norms.
    (b) sanctions.
    (c) values.
    (d) beliefs.

12. Specific statements that people hold to be true refer to

    (a) norms.
    (b) values.
    (c) sanctions.
    (d) technology.
    (e) beliefs.

13. Rules and expectations by which a society guides the behavior of is members refers to

    (a) norms.
    (b) values.
    (c) sanctions.
    (d) beliefs.

14. The old adage "Do as I say, not as I do" illustrates the distinction between

    (a)   ideal and real culture.
    (b)   the Sapir-Whorf hypothesis and "real" culture.
    (c)   cultural integration and cultural lag.
    (d)   folkways and mores.
    (e)   subcultures and countercultures.

15. Knowledge that people apply to the task of living in their surroundings refers to

    (a)   social control.
    (b)   technology.
    (c)   real culture.
    (d)   ideal culture.

16. Cultural patterns that set apart some segment of a society's population is termed

    (a)   social stratification.
    (b)   social differentiation.
    (c)   counterculture.
    (d)   cultural lag.
    (e)   subculture.

17. Inconsistencies within a cultural system resulting from the unequal rates at which different cultural elements change is termed

    (a)   cultural lag.
    (b)   counterculture.
    (c)   culture shock.
    (d)   cultural relativity.

18. The spread of cultural elements from one society to another is called

    (a)   invention.
    (b)   integration.
    (c)   diffusion.
    (d)   discovery.

19. The philosophical doctrine of *materialism* is utilized in the analysis of culture by proponents of which theoretical paradigm?

    (a)   sociobiologists
    (b)   cultural ecology
    (c)   social-conflict
    (d)   structural-functionalism

20.   In studying the cultural differences in *values* between Canada and the United States, *individualism* was found to be stronger in the U.S. and _____ was found to be stronger in Canada.

    (a)   self-reliance
    (b)   instrumentalism
    (c)   patriotism
    (d)   collectivism

Matching

1.   ___   The intangible world of ideas created by members of society.
2.   ___   Anything that carries a particular meaning recognized by people who share a culture.
3.   ___   States that people perceive the world through the cultural lens of language.
4.   ___   Rules and expectations by which a society guides the behavior of its members.
5.   ___   Takes the form of rewards and punishments.
6.   ___   Knowledge that people use to make a way of life in their surroundings.
7.   ___   An educational program recognizing past and present diversity in U.S. society and promoting the equality of all cultural traditions.
8.   ___   Cultural patterns that strongly oppose those widely accepted within a society.
9.   ___   The fact that cultural elements change at different rates, which may disrupt a cultural system.
10.   ___   The practice of judging another culture by the standards of one's own culture.

    a.   sanctions   f.   nonmaterial culture
    b.   multiculturalism   g.   technology
    c.   counterculture   h.   norms
    d.   cultural lag   i.   symbol
    e.   Sapir-Whorf thesis   j.   ethnocentrism

Fill-In

1.   _____ are the biological programming over which animals have no control.
2.   Worldwide, experts have documented the existence of over _____ languages.
3.   While _____ are broad guidelines for social living, _____ are statements that people hold to be true.
4.   _____ *norms* tell us what we *should do*, while _____ *norms* tell us what we *should not do*.
5.   Knowledge that people apply to the task of living in their surroundings refers to _____.
6.   Sociologists use the term _____ *culture* to refer to cultural patterns that distinguish a society's elite; _____ *culture* designates cultural patterns that are widespread among a society's population.
7.   _____ refers to an educational program recognizing the cultural diversity of the United States and promoting the equality of all cultural traditions.

8. Women's increased participation in the labor force parallels many changing family patterns, including first marriages at a later age and a rising divorce rate. Such patterns illustrate _____ _____, the close relationship among various elements of a cultural system.

9. The fact that some cultural elements change more quickly than others, which may disrupt a cultural system, is known as _____ _____.

10. Today, more than ever before, we can observe many of the same cultural practices the world over. This *global culture* is evidenced by the presence of a global _____, global _____, and global _____.

Discussion

1. Discuss the research presented in the text concerning the uniqueness of *language* to humans. What are your opinions on this issue?

2. Describe the process of *natural selection*.

3. What are the basic qualities of the *Yanomamo* culture? What factors do you think may explain why they are so aggressive? To what extent are you able to view these people from a *cultural relativistic* perspective?

4. What is the basic position being taken by *sociobiologists* concerning the nature of culture? What are three examples used by sociobiologists to argue that human culture is determined by biology? To what extent do you agree or disagree with their position? Explain.

5. What is the *Sapir-Whorf thesis*? What evidence supports it? What evidence is inconsistent with this hypothesis?

6. In what ways are we *globally connected?* Illustrate two of these.

7. Write a paragraph in which you express your opinions about the issue of multiculturalism in our society. Address the benefits of this perspective being suggested by proponents of multiculturalism, as well as the potential problems with this perspective suggested by its critics.

8. Provide two examples of how culture *constrains* us (limits our freedom).

9. What conclusions do you make about immigration concerning the data presented in *Figure 3-2*?

10. Review the list of *core values* of our culture in the United States. Rank order the ten identified in the text in terms of how important they are in our society from your point of view. What values, if any, do you believe should be included in the "top ten" list? Do you feel any of those listed should not be on the list?

PART VI: ANSWERS TO STUDY QUESTIONS

Key Concepts

1. culture (p. 61)
2. Nonmaterial culture (p. 61)
3. Material culture (p. 61)
4. culture shock (p. 61)
5. Symbols (p. 63)
6. language (p. 65)

True-False

1.	T	(p. 61)	6.	T	(p. 71)
2.	F	(p. 63)	7.	F	(p. 72)
3.	F	(p. 67)	8.	T	(p. 73)
4.	F	(p. 70)	9.	F	(p. 79)
5.	T	(p. 70)	10.	F	(p. 82)

Multiple Choice

1.	b	(p. 61)	11.	c	(p. 67)
2.	d	(p. 61)	12.	e	(p. 67)
3.	b	(p. 62)	13.	a	(p. 69)
4.	e	(p. 63)	14.	a	(p. 70)
5.	a	(p. 63)	15.	b	(p. 71)
6.	e	(p. 63)	16.	e	(p. 74)
7.	a	(p. 63)	17.	a	(p. 78)
8.	a	(p. 65)	18.	c	(p. 78)
9.	b	(p. 65)	19.	c	(p. 82)
10.	e	(p. 67)	20.	d	(p. 84)

<u>Matching</u>

1.	f	(p. 61)	6.	g	(p. 71)
2.	i	(p. 63)	7.	b	(p. 75)
3.	e	(p. 65)	8.	c	(p. 77)
4.	h	(p. 69)	9.	d	(p. 78)
5.	a	(p. 70)	10.	j	(p. 79)

<u>Fill-In</u>

1. Instincts (p. 62)
2. 5000 (p. 63)
3. values, beliefs (p. 66)
4. prescriptive, proscriptive (p. 70)
5. technology (p. 71)
6. high, popular (p. 73)
7. Multiculturalism (p. 75)
8. cultural integration (p. 77)
9. cultural lag (p. 78)
10. economy, communication, migration (p. 81)

PART VII: IN FOCUS--IMPORTANT ISSUES

- What is Culture?

  Illustrate each of the following.

  nonmaterial culture

  material culture

  What is meant by the author that no way of life is "natural" to humanity?

  Briefly recount the evolutionary background of human beings.

Differentiate between the following terms.

    culture

    nation

    society

- The Components of Culture

Define and illustrate each of the following *components of culture.*

    symbols

    language

    values

    beliefs

    norms

    social control

List the ten *key values of U.S. culture* as identified in the text.

Provide an illustration of *"values in conflict."*

- Cultural Diversity: Many Ways of Life In One World

  Identify and describe an example for each of the following terms.

  counterculture

  subculture

  multiculturalism

  cultural lag

  ethnocentrism

  cultural relativism

  What are three reasons given in the text for the existence of a *global culture*?

- Theoretical Analysis of Culture

  Briefly describe each how each of the following *theoretical approaches* helps us understand cultural uniformity and diversity.

  structural-functionalism

  social-conflict analysis

  sociobiology

- Culture and Human Freedom

  In what ways does culture *constrain* us?

  In what ways does culture offer us *freedom*?

Chapter 4 Society

PART I: CHAPTER OUTLINE

PART II: LEARNING OBJECTIVES

- To be able to differentiate between the four "visions" of society offered by sociologists.
- To learn about the ideas of Gerhard and Jean Lenski, Karl Marx, Max Weber, and Emile Durkheim concerning the structure of society and social change.
- To be able to identify and describe the different types of society as distinguished by their level of technology.

PART III: KEY CONCEPTS

Fill in the blank spaces below with the appropriate concept.

1. The term _____ refers to people who interact in a defined territory and share culture.
2. _____ _____ refers to Lenski's term for the changes that occur as a society acquires new technology.
3. _____ _____ refers to the use of simple tools to hunt animals and gather vegetation.
4. The use of hand tools to raise crops refers to _____.
5. _____ refers to the domestication of animals.
6. Large-scale cultivation using plows harnessed to animals or more powerful energy sources refers to _____.
7. _____ refers to the production of goods using advanced sources of energy to drive large machinery.
8. _____ is a technology that supports an information-based economy.
9. _____ _____ refers to the struggle between segments of society over valued resources.
10. People who own and operate factories and other businesses in pursuit of profits are known as _____.
11. People who sell their productive labor for wages are known as _____.
12. _____ _____ are the major spheres of social life, or societal subsystems, organized to meet human needs.
13. Marx's term for explanations of social problems as shortcomings of individuals rather than the flaws of society is known as _____ _____.
14. _____ _____ refers to conflict between entire classes of the distribution of society's wealth and power.
15. Marx's term for workers' recognition of themselves as a class unified by opposition to capitalists and, ultimately, to Capitalism itself is known as _____ _____.
16. _____ is the experience of isolation and misery resulting from powerlessness.
17. An _____ _____ is an abstract statement of the essential characteristics of any social phenomenon.
18. _____ refers to sentiments and beliefs passed from generation to generation.
19. _____ refers to deliberate, matter-of-fact calculation of the most efficient means to accomplish a particular task.
20. The _____ _____ is Weber's term for the historical change from tradition to rationality as the dominant mode of human thought.

21. _____ is Durkheim's term for a condition in which society provides little moral guidance to individuals.

22. _____ _____ is Durkheim's term for social bonds based on common sentiments and shared moral values that are strong among members of preindustrial societies.

23. _____ _____ is Durkheim's term for social bonds based on specialization and interdependence that are strong among members of industrial society.

24. The _____ ____ _____ refers to the specialization of economic activity.

PART IV: IMPORTANT RESEARCHERS

In the space provided below each of the following researchers, write two or three sentences to help you remember his or her respective contributions to sociology

Gerhard and Jean Lenski   Max Weber

Karl Marx   Emile Durkheim

PART V: STUDY QUESTIONS

True-False

1. T F As used sociologically, the concept of *society* refers to people who interact in a defined territory and share a culture.

2. T F A criticism of the Lenskis' concept of *sociocultural evolution* is that it doesn't take technology into account when being used to explain social change.

3. T F *Hunting and gathering* societies tend to be characterized by more social inequality than horticultural or agrarian societies.

4. T F For Karl Marx, the most significant form of *social conflict* arises from the way society produces material goods.

5. T F According to the theory of Karl Marx, social institutions like the family and religion comprise an important component of society's *infrastructure*.

6. T F In line with the philosophical doctrine of *idealism*, Max Weber emphasized how human ideas shape society.

7. T F An *ideal type* is defined as an abstract statement of the essential characteristics of any social phenomenon.

8. T F *Anomie* is the experience of isolation and misery resulting from powerlessness.

9. T F According to Emile Durkheim, *organic solidarity* characterizes preindustrial societies.

10.   T   F   For Emile Durkheim, the key to change in a society is the expanding *division of labor*.

<u>Multiple-Choice</u>

1.   The _____ nomads who wander the vastness of the Sahara in western Africa, north of the city of Timbuktu in the nation of Mali, are known as the "blue men of the desert."

   (a)   Tasaday
   (b)   !Kung
   (c)   BaMbuti
   (d)   Tuaregs

2.   People who interact in a defined territory and share a culture refers to the concept of

   (a)   culture.
   (b)   social organization.
   (c)   social structure.
   (d)   society.

3.   Gerhard and Jean Lenski focus on which factor as a major determinant of social change?

   (a)   human ideas
   (b)   technology
   (c)   social conflict
   (d)   social solidarity
   (e)   religious doctrine

4.   The key organizational principle of *hunting and gathering* societies is

   (a)   politics.
   (b)   religion.
   (c)   health.
   (d)   kinship.

5.   Which of the following is/are characteristic of *hunting and gathering societies*?

   (a)   Hunters and gatherers have little control over their environment.
   (b)   Hunting and gathering societies are built on kinship.
   (c)   Hunting and gathering societies are nomadic.
   (d)   Hunting and gathering societies have few formal leaders and are egalitarian.
   (e)   all of the above

6. A settlement of several hundred people who use hand tools to cultivate plants, is family-centered, and came into existence 10-12,000 years ago is a(n)

    (a) hunting and gathering society.
    (b) horticultural society.
    (c) pastoral society.
    (d) agrarian society.

7. *Agrarian* societies first emerged about _____ years ago.

    (a)   1,000
    (b) 12,000
    (c) 25,000
    (d) 50,000
    (e)   5,000

8. The development of metal for use in agrarian societies

    (a) increased the status of women in society.
    (b) lowered the status of males in society.
    (c) had little effect on the status of either men or women.
    (d) lowered the status of females in society.

9. Which of the following is/are accurate statements concerning *industrial society*?

    (a) The industrial era began about 1750.
    (b) With industrial technology, societies began to change faster than ever before.
    (c) Occupational specialization became more pronounced than ever in industrial society.
    (d) Industrial technology recast the family, lessening its traditional significance as the center of social life.
    (e) all of the above

10. *Postindustrial* society is _____-based.

    (a) family
    (b) labor
    (c) gender
    (d) leisure
    (e) information

11. For Karl Marx, ideas, values, and social institutions like *religion, education,* and the *family* are part of the _____ of society.

   (a) superstructure
   (b) predestination
   (c) rationality
   (d) infrastructure
   (e) ideal type

12. _____ refer(s) to the major spheres of social life, or societal subsystems, organized to meet human needs.

   (a) Social structure
   (b) Social organization
   (c) Social institutions
   (d) Culture

13. Which social institution did Karl Marx argue dominated all the others?

   (a) family
   (b) economy
   (c) politics
   (d) religion

14. According to Karl Marx, the *capitalists* controlled the means of production in society. As new productive forces eroded the feudal order, a new class of merchants and skilled crafts workers emerged, known as the *bourgeoisie*. This terms means:

   (a) "the exploited."
   (b) "the workers."
   (c) "of the town."
   (d) "the tyrannical."

15. *Alienation* is defined as

   (a) the experience of isolation and misery resulting from powerlessness.
   (b) deliberate, matter-of-fact calculation of the most efficient means to accomplish a particular goal.
   (c) a condition in which society provides little moral guidance to individuals.
   (d) social bonds, based on specialization, that unite members of a society.

16. Max Weber's analysis of society reflects the *philosophical approach* known as

    (a) materialism.
    (b) idealism.
    (c) cultural ecology.
    (d) egalitarianism.

17. A(n) _____ is an abstract statement of the essential characteristics of any social phenomenon.

    (a) concept
    (b) ideal type
    (c) superstructure
    (d) social fact

18. Max Weber's "great thesis" concerned the relationship between

    (a) conflict and change.
    (b) technology and ideas.
    (c) Protestantism and capitalism.
    (d) alienation and powerlessness.
    (e) social order and social facts.

19. A condition in which society provides little moral guidance to individuals is the definition for

    (a) anomie.
    (b) alienation.
    (c) mechanical solidarity.
    (d) rationality.

20. For Emile Durkheim, the key dimension of cultural change is society's expanding

    (a) mechanical solidarity.
    (b) false consciousness.
    (c) division of labor.
    (d) infrastructure.

Matching

1. ___ The aspect of society focused on by Gerhard and Jean Lenski.
2. ___ The technology of using hand tools to cultivate plants.
3. ___ Technology that supports an information-based economy.
4. ___ Major spheres of social life, or society's subsystems, organized to meet basic human needs.
5. ___ According to Karl Marx, the economic system represents a society's _____.

47

6.   ___   The experience of isolation and misery resulting from powerlessness.
7.   ___   An abstract statement of the essential characteristics of any social phenomenon.
8.   ___   A condition in which society provides little moral guidance to individuals.
9.   ___   Social bonds, based on shared morality, that unites members of preindustrial societies.
10.   ___   Social bonds, based on specialization, that unites members of industrial societies.

a.   postindustrialism   f.   anomie
b.   ideal type   g.   horticulture
c.   social institutions   h.   mechanical solidarity
d.   infrastructure   i.   technology
e.   alienation   j.   organic solidarity

Fill-In

1. While Gerhard and Jean Lenski focused on how _____ shapes society, Max Weber investigated the influence of _____ on society.
2. _____ *evolution* refers to the changes that occur as a society gains new technology.
3. The key to Marx's thinking is the idea of _____ _____, or the struggle between segments of society over valued resources.
4. Karl Marx referred to those who *own* the means of production as the _____, and those who provide the *labor* for its operation as the _____.
5. _____ _____ refers to explanations of social problems grounded in the shortcomings of individuals rather than the flaws of society.
6. Karl Marx cited four ways in which capitalism *alienates* workers, including alienation from the act of _____, from the _____ of work, from other _____, and from _____ potential.
7. By _____ Max Weber meant sentiments and beliefs passed from generation to generation.
8. According to Max Weber, *rational social organization* has seven distinctive characteristics, including: distinctive _____ _____, _____ organizations, _____ tasks, _____ discipline, awareness of _____, _____ competence, and _____.
9. Any part of society that is argued to have an objective existence apart from the individual Emile Durkheim called a _____ _____.
10. Emile Durkheim acknowledged the advantages of modern-day freedom, but he warned of increased _____, or a condition in which society provides little moral guidance to individuals.

Discussion

1. How do the Lenskis define *sociocultural evolution*? What are the basic *types of societies* identified by the Gerhard and Jean Lenski? What are three general characteristics of each?
2. What is meant by the term *material surplus*? What are its effects on society?
3. What is the meaning of the philosophy of *idealism*? *Materialism*?

4. According to Karl Marx, what are the four ways in which industrial capitalism *alienates* workers? Provide an illustration for each.
5. Differentiate between Karl Marx's concepts *infrastructure* and *superstructure*.
6. According to Max Weber, what are the roots of *rationality* in modern society?
7. For Max Weber, what are the characteristics of *rational social organization*? Provide illustrations..
8. What concerned Max Weber about *rationality*? Provide an illustration.
9. What does Emile Durkheim mean by suggesting that society has an *objective existence* apart from individuals? Provide an illustration.
10. Summarize the basic similarities and differences between the views of Gerhard and Jean Lenski, Karl Marx, Max Weber, and Emile Durkheim on modern society. Which theorist most impresses you in terms of explaining what holds a society together? What about how a society changes?

PART VI: ANSWERS TO STUDY QUESTIONS

Key Concepts

1. society (p. 89)
2. Sociocultural evolution (p. 90)
3. Hunting and gathering (p. 90)
4. horticulture (p. 91)
5. Pastoralism (p. 91)
6. agriculture (p. 92)
7. Industrialism (p. 93)
8. Postindustrialism (p. 95)
9. Social conflict (p. 97)
10. capitalists (p. 97)
11. proletarians (p. 97)
12. Social institutions (p. 98)
13. false consciousness (p. 99)
14. Class conflict (p. 99)
15. class consciousness (p. 99)
16. Alienation (p. 100)
17. ideal type (p. 102)
18. Tradition (p. 102)
19. Rationality (p. 102)
20. rationalization of society (p. 103)
21. Anomie (p. 108)
22. Mechanical solidarity (p. 108)
23. Organic solidarity (p. 108)
24. division of labor (p. 109)

True-False

1.	T	(p.	89)		6.	T	(p.	102)
2.	F	(p.	89)		7.	T	(p.	102)
3.	F	(p.	89)		8.	F	(p.	102)
4.	T	(p.	90)		9.	F	(p.	108)
5.	F	(p.	90)		10.	T	(p.	109)

Multiple-Choice

1.	d	(p.	89)		11.	a	(p.	98)
2.	d	(p.	89)		12.	c	(p.	98)
3.	b	(p.	90)		13.	b	(p.	98)
4.	d	(p.	90)		14.	c	(p.	99)
5.	e	(p.	90)		15.	a	(p.	100)
6.	b	(p.	91)		16.	b	(p.	102)
7.	e	(pp.	91-92)		17.	b	(p.	102)
8.	d	(p.	93)		18.	c	(p.	103)
9.	e	(pp.	93-94)		19	a	(p.	108)
10.	e	(p.	94)		20.	c	(p.	109)

Matching

1.	i	(p.	89)		6.	e	(p.	100)
2.	g	(p.	90)		7.	b	(p.	102)
3.	a	(p.	95)		8.	f	(p.	108)
4.	c	(p.	98)		9.	h	(p.	108)
5.	d	(p.	98)		10.	j	(p.	108)

Fill-In

1. technology, ideas (p. 89)
2. Sociocultural (p. 90)
3. social conflict (p. 97)
4. capitalists, proletariat (p. 97)
5. false consciousness (p. 98)
6. working, products, workers, human (p. 100)
7. tradition (p. 102)
8. Social institutions, large-scale, specialized, personal, time, technical, impersonality (p. 105)
9. social facts (p. 107)
10. anomie (p. 108)

PART VII: IN FOCUS--IMPORTANT ISSUES

- Gerhard Lenski and Jean Lenski: Society and Technology

  Describe each of the following types of societies based on their respective *level of technological development.*

  > hunting and gathering societies

  > horticultural societies

  > agrarian societies

  > pastoral societies

  > industrial societies

  > postindustrial societies

  What are the benefits of the advancements in *technology* in industrial and postindustrial societies? What are the problems caused by these advancements?

- Karl Marx: Society and Conflict

  Summarize one important point concerning Karl Marx's views on each of the following.

  > society and production

  > conflict and history

  > capitalism and class conflict

  > capitalism and alienation

  > revolution

- Max Weber: The Rationalization of Society

Differentiate between the two following world views.

    tradition

    rationality

Summarize Max Weber's great thesis.

Describe each of the following characteristics of *rational social organization*.

    distinctive social institutions

    large-scale organizations

    specialized tasks

    personal discipline

    awareness of time

    technical competence

    impersonality

According to Max Weber, what is the relationship between *rationality* and *alienation*?

- Emile Durkheim: Society and Function

What did Emile Durkheim mean by saying society exists beyond ourselves (society as structure)?

Why did Emile Durkheim suggest *crime* is not "pathological" (function: society as system)?

What evidence was used by Emile Durkheim to suggest that society is not merely "beyond ourselves," but also "in ourselves?"

Describe the following two forms of the *division of labor*.

mechanical solidarity

organic solidarity

- Critical Evaluation: Four Visions of Society

What holds society together?

    According to Gerhard Lenski and Jean Lenski

    According to Karl Marx

    According to Max Weber

    According to Emile Durkheim

How and why have societies changed?

    According to Gerhard Lenski and Jean Lenski

    According to Karl Marx

    According to Max Weber

    According to Emile Durkheim

Chapter 5 Socialization

PART I: CHAPTER OUTLINE

I. Social Experience: The Key to Our Humanity
   A. Human Development: Nature and Nurture
      1. Charles Darwin: The Role of Nature
      2. The Social Sciences: The Role of Nurture
   B. Social Isolation
      1. Studies of Nonhuman Primates
      2. Studies of Isolated Children
II. Understanding Socialization
   A. Sigmund Freud: The Elements of Personality
      1. Basic Human Needs
      2. Freud's Model of Personality
      3. Personality Development
   B. Jean Piaget: Cognitive Development
      1. The Sensorimotor Stage
      2. The Preoperational Stage
      3. The Concrete Operational Stage
      4. The Formal Operational Stage
   C. Lawrence Kohlberg: Moral Development
   D. Carol Gilligan: Bringing In Gender
   E. George Herbert Mead: The Social Self
      1. The Self
      2. The Looking-Glass Self
      3. The I and the Me
      4. Development of the Self
   F. Erik H. Erikson: Eight Stages of Development
III. Agents of Socialization
   A. The Family
   B. The School
   C. Peer Groups
   D. The Mass Media
IV. Socialization and the Life Course
   A. Childhood
   B. Adolescence

PART II: LEARNING OBJECTIVES

- To understand the "nature-nurture" debate regarding socialization and personality development.
- To become aware of the effects of social isolation on humans and other primates.
- To become aware of the key components of Sigmund Freud's model of personality.
- To be able to identify and describe the four stages of Jean Piaget's cognitive development theory.
- To be able to identify and describe the stages of moral development as identified by Lawrence Kohlberg.
- To analyze Carol Gilligan's critique of Kohlberg's moral development model.
- To be able to identify and describe Erik H. Erikson's stages of personality development.
- To consider the contributions of George Herbert Mead to the understanding of personality development.
- To be able to compare the spheres of socialization (family, school, etc.) in terms of their effects on an individual's socialization experiences.
- To develop a life-course perspective of the socialization experience.
- To begin to understand the cross-cultural and historical patterns of death and dying.
- To be able to discuss the sociological perspective on socialization as a constraint to freedom.

PART III: KEY CONCEPTS

Fill in the following blank spaces write the appropriate concepts.

1. _____ refers to the lifelong social experience by which people develop their human potential and learn culture.
2. A person's fairly consistent patterns of acting, thinking, and feeling refers to their _____.
3. According to Sigmund Freud, the _____ represents the human being's basic drives, which are unconscious and demand immediate satisfaction.
4. According to Sigmund Freud, the _____ is a person's conscious efforts to balance innate pleasure-seeking drives with the demands of society.
5. Freud's term for the cultural values and norms internalized by an individual is known as the _____.

6. The _____ _____ refers to Piaget's term for the level of human development at which individuals experience the world only through their senses.

7. The _____ _____ refers to Piaget's term for the level of human development at which individuals first use language and other symbols.

8. The _____ _____ _____ refers to Piaget's term for the level of human development at individuals first perceive causal connections in their surroundings.

9. The _____ _____ _____ refers to Piaget's term for the level of human development at which individuals think abstractly and critically.

10. The _____ refers to George Herbert Mead's term for the part of an individual's personality composed of self-awareness and self-image.

11. The _____ _____ refers to Cooley's term for self-image based on how we think others see us.

12. The _____ _____ refers to George Herbert Mead's term for the widespread cultural norms and values we use as a reference in evaluating others.

13. A _____ _____ is a group whose members have interests, social position, and age in common.

14. _____ _____ refers to learning that helps a person achieve a desired position.

15. The _____ _____ refers to the impersonal communications aimed at a vast audience.

16. A _____ is a category of people with a common characteristic, usually their age.

17. A _____ refers to a setting in which people are isolated from the rest of society and manipulated by an administrative staff.

18. _____ refers to radically changing an inmate's personality by carefully controlling the environment.

PART IV: IMPORTANT RESEARCHERS

Identified below are some of the more important sociologists and other social and behavioral scientists discussed in this chapter. In the space provided under each name write two or three sentences to help you remember their important contributions to sociology.

Kingsley Davis   John Watson

Harry and Margaret Harlow   Sigmund Freud

Jean Piaget   Lawrence Kohlberg

Carol Gilligan   Erik H. Erikson

Charles Horton Cooley   George Herbert Mead

Elizabeth Kubler-Ross

PART V: STUDY QUESTIONS

True-False

1.   T   F   John Watson was a nineteenth-century psychologist who argued that human behavior was largely determined by *heredity*.
2.   T   F   The cases of *Isabelle, Anna,* and *Genie* support the arguments made by naturalists that certain personality characteristics are determined by heredity.
3.   T   F   Sigmund Freud envisioned *biological factors* as having little or no influence on personality development.
4.   T   F   The *id* in Freud's psychoanalytic theory represents the human being's basic needs which are unconscious and demand immediate satisfaction.

5. T   F   The first stage in Jean Piaget's *cognitive development* theory is referred to as the *preoperational stage*.

6. T   F   According to Lawrence Kohlberg, during the *conventional stage* of moral development, a person takes behavior at face value rather than trying to infer a person's intention in making a moral judgement.

7. T   F   According to Carol Gilligan, taking a *rule-based* approach to moral reasoning is superior to taking a *person-based* approach.

8. T   F   George Herbert Mead refers to *taking the role of the other* as the interplay between the *I* and *me*.

9. T   F   According to Erik H. Erikson's theory of personality development, the first challenge faced in life is *intimacy* versus *isolation*.

10. T   F   A *cohort* is a setting in which people are isolated from the rest of society and manipulated by an administrative staff.

Multiple Choice

1. _____ holds that behavior is not instinctual but learned.

    (a)   The theory of natural selection
    (b)   Behaviorism
    (c)   Sociobiology
    (d)   Evolutionary theory

2. The story of *Anna* illustrates the significance of _____ in personality development.

    (a)   heredity
    (b)   social interaction
    (c)   physical conditions
    (d)   ecology

3. What did the experiments on social isolation among rhesus monkeys show?

    (a)   Artificial wire monkeys provided sufficient contact for young monkeys to develop normally.
    (b)   The behavior of rhesus monkey infants is totally dissimilar to human infants.
    (c)   Deprivation of social experience, rather than the absence of a specific parent, has devastating effects.
    (d)   Genes found in rhesus monkeys cushion them from the negative effects of social isolation.

4. Which of the following is representative of *Sigmund Freud's* analysis of personality?

    (a)   Biological forces play only a small role in personality development.
    (b)   The term instinct is understood as very general human needs in the form of urges and drives.
    (c)   The most significant period for personality development is adolescence.
    (d)   Personality is best studied as a process of externalizing social forces.

5. Sigmund Freud theorized that humans have two basic needs. First, the need for bonding, which Freud called the life instinct, or *eros*. Second, is an aggressive drive he called the *death instinct*, or

    (a)   storge.
    (b)   philos.
    (c)   agape.
    (d)   the superego.
    (e)   thanatos.

6. *Sigmund Freud's* model of personality does *not* include which of the following elements?

    (a)   superego
    (b)   id
    (c)   self
    (d)   ego

7. Culture existing within the individual was what *Sigmund Freud* called

    (a)   thanatos.
    (b)   eros.
    (c)   the ego.
    (d)   the id.
    (e)   the superego.

8. In Sigmund Freud's model of personality, what balances the innate pleasure-seeking drive with the demands of society?

    (a)   id
    (b)   ego
    (c)   superego
    (d)   thanatos

9. Jean Piaget's focus was on

    (a)   how children develop fine motor skills.
    (b)   how children are stimulated by their environment.
    (c)   cognition--how people think and understand.
    (d)   the role of heredity in determining human behavior.

10. The first stage in Jean Piaget's *cognitive development theory* is

    (a)   the preoperational stage.
    (b)   the preconventional stage.
    (c)   the concrete operations stage.
    (d)   the sensorimotor stage.

11. According to *Jean Piaget*, which of the following best describes the *preoperational stage* of cognitive development?

    (a)   the level of human development in which the world is experienced only through sensory contact

    (b)   the level of human development characterized by the use of logic to understand objects and events

    (c)   the level of human development in which language and other symbols are first used

    (d)   the level of human development characterized by highly abstract thought

12. For a person operating at the *conventional stage* of Lawrence Kohberg's moral development theory

    (a)   "rightness" amounts to "what feels good to me".

    (b)   an attempt is made to assess the intention in reaching moral judgements instead of simply observing what others do.

    (c)   abstract ethical principles are applied, instead of just using her or his culture's norms to make moral judgements.

    (d)   moral decisions are based on avoidance of punishment.

13. According to research by Carol Gilligan, *males* use a _____ perspective concerning moral reasoning.

    (a)   justice

    (b)   independent

    (c)   visual

    (d)   mechanical

14. *George Herbert Mead's* perspective has often been described as

    (a)   psychological pragmatism.

    (b)   behaviorism.

    (c)   social behaviorism.

    (d)   psychoanalysis.

    (e)   naturalism.

15. The concept of the *looking-glass self* refers to

    (a)   Freud's argument that through psychoanalysis a person can uncover the unconscious.

    (b)   Piaget's view that through biological maturation and social experience individuals become able to logically hypothesize about thoughts without relying on concrete reality.

    (c)   Watson's behaviorist notion that one can see through to a person's mind only by observing the person's behavior.

    (d)   Cooley's idea that the self-image we have is based on how we suppose others perceive us.

16. George Herbert Mead said that by taking the role of the other, we become *self-aware*. He called the active (subjective) side of the self the *I* and the social (objective) side of the self the

    (a) me.
    (b) us.
    (c) we.
    (d) they.

17. George Herbert Mead used the term _____ to describe the widespread cultural norms and values shared by us and others that we use as a point of reference in evaluating ourselves.

    (a) looking-glass self
    (b) socialization
    (c) significant other
    (d) generalized other

18. According to Erik H. Erikson, what is the challenge of *middle adulthood*?

    (a) integration versus despair
    (b) initiative versus guilt
    (c) industry versus inferiority
    (d) making a difference versus self-absorption

19. The process of social learning directed toward assuming a desired status and role in the future is called

    (a) resocialization.
    (b) socialization.
    (c) looking-glass self.
    (d) anticipatory socialization.

20. Which of the following is *not* one of the three distinctive characteristics of a *total institution*?

    (a) staff members supervise all spheres of daily life
    (b) staff members encourage the maintenance of individuality, and encourage creativity
    (c) food, sleeping quarters and activities are standardized
    (d) formal rules dictate how virtually every moment is spent

Matching

1. ___ A person's fairly consistent patterns of acting, thinking, and feeling.
2. ___ A theory developed by John Watson that holds that behavior patterns are not instinctive but learned.
3. ___ According to Sigmund Freud, the presence of culture within the individual.
4. ___ In Piaget's theory, the level of development at which individuals perceive causal connections in their surroundings.
5. ___ The self-image we have based on how we suppose others perceive us.
6. ___ According to George Herbert Mead, the subjective side of the self.
7. ___ A group whose members have interests, social position, and age in common.
8. ___ Impersonal communications directed to a vast audience.
9. ___ A category of people with a common characteristic, usually their age.
10. ___ Deliberate socialization intended to radically alter the individual's personality.

a.	looking-glass self	f.	cohort
b.	behaviorism	g.	peer group
c.	mass media	h.	personality
d.	concrete operational stage	i.	superego
e.	resocialization	j.	I

Fill-In

1. The approach called _____ developed by *John Watson* in the early twentieth century provided a perspective that stressed learning rather than instincts as the key to personality development.
2. *Sigmund Freud* termed society's controlling influence on the drives of each individual as _____, whereas he called the process of transforming fundamentally selfish drives into more socially acceptable objectives _____.
3. According to Jean Piaget's theory of *cognitive development*, the level of human development at which individuals think abstractly and critically is known as the _____ _____ *stage*.
4. *Lawrence Kohlberg* identifies three stages in moral development, these include the _____, the _____, and the _____.
5. Carol Gilligan suggests that boys tend to use a *justice perspective* in moral reasoning, relying on formal rules in reaching a judgement about right and wrong. On the other hand, says Gilligan, girls tend to use a _____ and _____ *perspective* in moral reasoning, which leads them to judge a situation with an eye toward personal relationships.
6. *George Herbert Mead* explained that infants with limited social experience respond to others only in terms of _____.
7. According to Erik H. Erikson's developmental theory, the *challenge of adolescence* involves gaining _____ versus _____.
8. The process of social learning directed toward gaining a desired position is called _____ *socialization*.

9.	Elisabeth Kubler-Ross has described *death* as an orderly transition, involving five distinct responses. These include, in order of occurrence: _____, _____, _____, _____, and _____.

10.	Prisons and mental hospitals are examples of _____ _____.

Discussion

1.	How did the work of *Charles Darwin* influence the understanding of personality development in the last nineteenth century? What was *John Watson's* view concerning personality development?

2.	Review the research by *Harry* and *Margaret Harlow* on social isolation. What were the important discoveries they made?

3.	Discuss the cases of *childhood isolation* presented in the text. What are the important conclusions being drawn from these cases?

4.	What are the four stages of cognitive development according to *Jean Piaget*? Briefly describe the qualities of each stage. What is one major criticism of his theory?

5.	What are the stages of personality development according to Erik H. Erikson? In what two important ways does his theory differ from Sigmund Freud's?

6.	Define the concept *looking-glass self*. Provide an illustration from your own personal experience.

7.	Define and differentiate between the terms *generalized other* and *significant other*. What are the four important *agents of socialization*? Provide an illustration of how each is involved in the socialization process.

8.	What are the stages of *adulthood* and the qualities of each?

9.	What is a *total institution*? What are the typical experiences of a person who is living within a total institution? How do these experiences affect personality development?

10.	Based on the sociological research cited in this chapter, to what extent can it be argued that humans are like "puppets?" What conclusions are being made by the author concerning the *life course*?

PART VI: ANSWERS TO STUDY QUESTIONS

Key Concepts

1.	Socialization (p. 115)
2.	personality (p. 115)
3.	id (p. 119)
4.	ego (p. 119)
5.	superego (p. 119)
6.	sensorimotor stage (p. 119)
7.	preoperational stage (p. 119)
8.	concrete operations stage (p. 120)
9.	formal operations (p. 120)
10.	self (p. 122)
11.	looking-glass self (p. 122)
12.	generalized other (p. 123)
13.	peer group (p. 126)
14.	Anticipatory socialization (p. 126)

15. mass media (p. 126)
16. cohort (p. 133)
17. total institution (p. 133)
18. Resocialization (p. 134)

True-False

1.	F	(p. 116)	6.	F	(p. 122)
2.	F	(p. 117)	7.	F	(p. 122)
3.	F	(p. 118)	8.	T	(pp. 122-123)
4.	T	(p. 117)	9.	F	(p. 123)
5.	F	(p. 118)	10.	F	(p. 133)

Multiple Choice

1.	b	(p. 116)	11.	c	(p. 119)
2.	b	(p. 117)	12.	b	(p. 120)
3.	c	(p. 117)	13.	a	(p. 121)
4.	b	(p. 119)	14.	c	(p. 122)
5.	e	(p. 119)	15.	d	(p. 122)
6.	c	(p. 119)	16.	a	(p. 123)
7.	e	(p. 119)	17.	d	(p. 123)
8.	b	(p. 119)	18	d	(p. 124)
9.	c	(p. 119)	19.	d	(p. 126)
10.	d	(p. 119)	20.	b	(pp. 133-135)

Matching

1.	h	(p. 115)	6.	j	(pp. 122-123)
2.	b	(p. 116)	7.	g	(p. 126)
3.	i	(p. 119)	8.	c	(p. 126)
4.	d	(p. 120)	9.	f	(p. 133)
5.	a	(p. 122)	10.	e	(p. 134)

Fill-In

1. behaviorism (p. 116)
2. repression, sublimation (p. 119)
3. formal (p. 120)
4. preconventional, conventional, postconventional (p. 120)
5. care, responsibility (p. 121)
6. imitation (p. 123)
7. gaining identity, confusion (p. 124)
8. anticipatory (p. 126)

9. denial, anger, negotiation, resignation, acceptance (p. 133)
10. total institution (p. 137)

PART VII: IN FOCUS: IMPORTANT POINTS

- Social Experience: The Key To Our Humanity

According to Charles Darwin, what role does *nature* play in human personality development?

Review the conclusions being made by social scientists concerning the role of *nurture* in human personality development, focusing on each of the following.

Studies of nonhuman primates

Studies of isolated children

- Understanding Socialization

Briefly review the major points being made by the following theorists concerning personality development. Identify and describe/define the stages of development for each theory discussed.

Sigmund Freud

Jean Piaget

Lawrence Kohlberg

Carol Gilligan

George Herbert Mead

Erik H. Erikson

- Agents of Socialization

  Briefly describe the significance for each of the following major agents of socialization on personality development.

     the family

     the school

     peer groups

     the mass media

- Socialization and the Life Course

  Identify two major points being made in the text concerning each of the following stages of the human life course.

     childhood

     adolescence

     adulthood

     old age

     dying

- Resocialization: Total Institutions

    What are the three major qualities of a *total institution*?

    What does the author mean by saying that *resocialization* is a two-part process?

Chapter 6 | Social Interaction In Everyday Life

PART I: CHAPTER OUTLINE

I. Social Structure: A Guide to Everyday Living
II. Status
    A.   Status Set
    B.   Ascribed Status and Achieved Status
    C.   Master Status
III. Role
    A.   Role Set
    B.   Role Conflict and Role Strain
    C.   Role Exit
IV. The Social Construction of Reality
    A.   "Street Smarts"
    B.   The Thomas Theorem
    C.   Ethnomethodology
    D.   Reality Building: Class and Culture
V. Dramaturgical Analysis: "The Presentation of Self"
    A.   Performances
        1.   An Application: The Doctor's Office
    B.   Nonverbal Communication
        1.   Body Language and Deception
    C.   Gender and Personal Performances
        1.   Demeanor
        2.   Use of Space
        3.   Staring, Smiling, and Touching
    D.   Idealization
    E.   Embarrassment and Tact
VI. Interaction in Everyday Life: Two Applications
    A.   Language: The Gender Issue
        1.   Language and Power
        2.   Language and Value
        3.   Language and Attention
    B.   Humor: Playing with Reality
        1.   The Foundation of Humor
        2.   The Dynamics of Humor: "Getting It"

PART II: LEARNING OBJECTIVES

- To be able to identify the characteristics of social structure.
- To be able to discuss the relationship between social structure and individuality.
- To be able to distinguish between the different types of statuses and roles.
- To be able to describe and illustrate the social construction of reality.
- To see how the technological capacity of a society influences the social construction of reality.
- To be able to describe and illustrate the approach known as ethnomethodology.
- To see the importance of performance, nonverbal communication, idealization, and embarrassment to the "presentation of the self".
- To be able to describe and illustrate dramaturgical analysis.
- To be able to use gender and humor to illustrate how people construct meaning in everyday life.

PART III: KEY CONCEPTS

In the blank spaces below write in the appropriate concept.

1. _____ _____ refers to the process by which people act and react in relation to others.
2. A _____ is a social position that a person occupies.
3. A _____ _____ refers to all the statuses a person holds at a given time.
4. An _____ _____ is a social position a person receives at birth or assumes involuntarily later in life.
5. An _____ _____ is a social position a person assumes voluntarily that reflects personal ability and effort.
6. A _____ _____ is a status that has special importance for social identity, often shaping a person's entire life.
7. A _____ refers to behavior expected of someone who holds a particular status.
8. A _____ _____ is a number of roles attached to a single status.
9. _____ _____ refers to conflict between roles corresponding to two or more statuses.
10. _____ _____ refers to conflict between roles connected to a single status.
11. The _____ _____ ____ _____ refers to the process by which people creativity shape reality through social interaction.
12. The _____ _____ refers to W.I. Thomas's assertion that situations that are defined as to be real are real in their consequences.

71

13. _____Harold Garkinkel's term for the study of the way people make sense of their everyday surroundings.

14. _____ _____ is Goffman's term for the study of social interaction in terms of theatrical performance.

15. The _____ ____ _____ refers to Goffman's term for an individual's efforts to create specific impressions in the minds of others.

16. _____ _____ refers to communication using body movements, gestures, and facial expressions rather than speech.

17. _____ _____ refers to the surrounding area over which a person makes some claim to privacy.

PART IV: IMPORTANT RESEARCHERS

Identified below are some of the more important sociologists and other social and behavioral scientists discussed in this chapter. In the space provided under each name write two or three sentences to help you remember their important contributions to sociology.

Robert Merton   Harold Garfinkel

Erving Goffman   Paul Ekman

PART V: STUDY QUESTIONS

True-False

1.	T	F	A *status* refers to a pattern of expected behavior for individual members of society.
2	T	F	Both *statuses* and *roles* vary by culture.
3	T	F	Being an honors student, being a spouse, and being a computer programmer are examples of *ascribed statuses*.
4	T	F	*Role strain* refers to the incompatibility among roles corresponding to a single status.
5	T	F	The phrase *the social construction of reality* relates to the sociologist's view that statuses and roles structure our lives along narrowly delineated paths.
6.	T	F	According to *Erving Goffman*, *performances* are very rigidly scripted, leaving virtually no room for individual adaptation.
7.	T	F	According to research on gender and personal performances, men use significantly more space than women.
8.	T	F	*Erving Goffman's* research, suggests that *tact* is relatively uncommon in our society.
9.	T	F	An important foundation of *humor* lies in the contrast between two incongruous realities--the *conventional* and *unconventional*.
10.	T	F	One trait of humorous material which appears to be universal is *controversy*.

1.   What is the term for a recognized social position that an individual occupies?

        (a)   prestige
        (b)   status
        (c)   social power
        (d)   role
        (e)   dramaturgy

2.   *Ralph Linton* described _____ as the dynamic expression of a status.

        (a)   master status
        (b)   nonverbal communication
        (c)   performance
        (d)   dramaturgy
        (e)   role

3.   What is the term for a status that has exceptional importance for social identity, often shaping a person's entire life?

        (a)   role
        (b)   ascribed status
        (c)   achieved status
        (d)   master status
        (e)   role set

4.   What is the term for patterns of expected behavior attached to a particular status?

        (a)   role
        (b)   master status
        (c)   achieved status
        (d)   ascribed status
        (e)   performance

5.   A number of roles attached to a single status refers to

        (a)   a role set.
        (b)   a status set.
        (c)   a master status.
        (d)   role conflict.
        (e)   role platform.

6.   The incompatibility among the roles corresponding to two or more statuses refers to

      (a)   role conflict.
      (b)   role strain.
      (c)   status overload.
      (d)   status inconsistency.
      (e)   role set.

7.   Methods of reducing *role strain* include which of the following?

      (a)   discarding one or more roles
      (b)   compartmentalizing roles
      (c)   emphasizing some roles more than others
      (d)   all of the above
      (e)   none of the above

8.   The *Thomas theorem* states

      (a)   roles are only as important as the statuses to which they are attached.
      (b)   statuses are only as important as the roles on which they are dependent.
      (c)   the basis of humanity is built upon the dual existence of creativity and conformity.
      (d)   common sense is only as good as the social structure within which it is embedded.
      (e)   situations defined as real become real in their consequences.

9.   What is the term for the study of the way people make sense of their everyday lives?

      (a)   naturalism
      (b)   phenomenology
      (c)   ethnomethodology
      (d)   social psychology

10.   The approach used by *ethnomethodologists* to study everyday interaction involves

      (a)   conducting surveys.
      (b)   unobtrusive observation.
      (c)   secondary analysis.
      (d)   breaking rules.
      (e)   laboratory experiment.

11.   The investigation of social interaction in terms of *theatrical performance* is referred to as

      (a)   ethnomethodology.
      (b)   dramaturgical analysis.
      (c)   theatrical analysis.
      (d)   phenomenology.

12. The process of the *presentation of the self* is also known as

    (a) ethnomethodology.
    (b) achieved status.
    (c) status consistency.
    (d) ascribed status.
    (e) impression management.

13. *Mr. Preedy*, the fictional character introduced in the text, provides an example of

    (a) role conflict.
    (b) role strain.
    (c) nonverbal communication.
    (d) status inconsistency.

14. According Paul Ekman, there are several *universal emotions*. Which of the following is *not* one he has identified?

    (a) hope
    (b) fear
    (c) sadness
    (d) happiness

15. What is *demeanor*?

    (a) general conduct and deportment
    (b) a non-felony crime
    (c) a form of mental illness
    (d) gender-specific activity

16. Trying to convince others (and perhaps ourselves) that what we do reflects ideal cultural standards rather than selfish motives refers to

    (a) backstaging.
    (b) idealization
    (c) ethnomethodology
    (d) tact

17. Helping a person to "save face," or avoid embarrassment, is called

    (a) diplomacy.
    (b) generosity.
    (c) altruism.
    (d) tact.

18.   Which of the following is *not* an example provided in the text to illustrate how *language* functions to define the sexes?

    (a)   the attention function
    (b)   the power function
    (c)   the value function
    (d)   the affective function

19.   Research by Deborah Tannen concerning communication problems between women and men focuses on the issue of

    (a)   power.
    (b)   humor.
    (c)   language.
    (d)   tact.
    (e)   personal space.

20.   Which of the following is *not* a *function of humor*?

    (a)   Humor can be used to ease tension in uncomfortable situations.
    (b)   Humor limits racism and sexism.
    (c)   Humor can be a safety valve.
    (d)   Humor can be used to express feelings without being serious.

Matching

1.   ____   The process by which people act and react in relation to others.
2.   ____   A recognized social position that an individual occupies.
3.   ____   A social position a person receives at birth or assumes involuntarily later in life.
4.   ____   Expected behavior of someone who holds a particular status.
5.   ____   Incompatibility among roles corresponding to a single status.
6.   ____   Incompatibility among roles corresponding to two or more statuses.
7.   ____   Situations defined as real become real in their consequences.
8.   ____   The study of the way people make sense of their everyday lives.
9.   ____   The investigation of social interaction in terms of theatrical performance.
10.   ____   General conduct or deportment.

    a.   ascribed status   f.   role
    b.   ethnomethodology   g.   demeanor
    c.   Thomas theorem   h.   status
    d.   role strain   i.   dramaturgical analysis
    e.   social interaction   j.   role conflict

<u>Fill-In</u>

1. _____ _____ refers to the process by which people act and react in relation to others.
2. _____ refers to a recognized social position that an individual occupies in society, while _____ refers to patterns of expected behaviors attached to a particular status.
3. _____ refers to the incompatibility among the roles corresponding to two or more statuses.
4. The _____ _____ suggests that situations that are defined as real are real in their consequences.
5. The study of everyday, common-sense understandings that people within a culture have of the world around them is known as _____.
6. Props in a doctor's office, like books and framed diplomas, are examples of the _____*region* of the setting.
7. According to Paul Ekman there are four *elements of a performance* that can be used to detect deception. These include: _____, _____, _____ _____, and _____ _____.
8. When people try to convince others that what they are doing reflects ideal cultural standards rather than less virtuous motives, *Erving Goffman* said they are involved in _____.
9. Language defines men and women differently in at least three ways--in terms of _____, _____, and _____.
10. According to *Deborah Tannen*, women and men use language differently. The problems couples face in communicating is that what one partner _____ by a comment is not always what the other _____.

<u>Discussion</u>

1. Review the story of the physician's office and *performances* in the text. Using this account as an example, select a social situation you have been involved in and do a dramaturgical analysis to describe its context.
2. Provide an illustration of *nonverbal communication* using the story of *Mr. Preedy* as a model.
3. Identify the types of information provided by a *performer* through nonverbal communication which can be used to determine whether or not a person is telling the truth? Provide illustrations.
4. Referring to *Figure 6-1* (p. 143) and using it as a model, diagram your own status and role sets. Identify points of *role conflict* and *role strain*.
5. What are three ways in which language functions to define the sexes differently? Provide an illustration for each of these.
6. What is *ethnomethodology*? Provide an illustration using your own example.
7. Define the concept *idealization*. Provide an illustration using the doctor's office account as a model.
8. Provide an example of the *Thomas theorem* using your own experiences either at home or in school.
9. What are the basic characteristics of *humor*? Write out a joke and analyze how it manifests the characteristics discussed in the text.
10. Create a two person dialogue between a woman and a man that illustrates Deborah Tannen's points concerning the different languages of males and females.

PART VI: ANSWERS TO STUDY QUESTIONS

Key Concepts

1. Social interaction (p. 139)
2. status (p. 140)
3. status set (p. 140)
4. ascribed status (pp. 140-141)
5. achieved (p. 141)
6. master status (p. 141)
7. role (p. 141)
8. role set (p. 141)
9. Role conflict (p. 143)
10. Role strain (p. 143)
11. social construction of reality (p. 144)
12. Thomas theorem (p. 145)
13. Ethnomethodology (p. 146)
14. Dramaturgical analysis (p. 147)
15. presentation of self (p. 147)
16. Nonverbal communication (p. 149)
17. Personal space (p. 152)

True-False

1.	F	(p. 140)	6.	F	(p. 147)
2.	T	(pp. 140-141)	7.	T	(p. 152)
3.	F	(pp. 140-141)	8.	F	(p. 153)
4.	T	(p. 143)	9.	T	(p. 155)
5.	F	(p. 144)	10.	T	(p. 157)

Multiple Choice

1.	b	(p. 140)	11.	b	(p. 147)
2.	e	(pp.141)	12.	e	(p. 147)
3.	d	(p. 141)	13.	c	(p. 148)
4.	a	(p. 141)	14.	a	(p. 148)
5.	a	(p. 142)	15.	a	(p. 151)
6.	a	(p. 143)	16.	b	(p. 152)
7.	d	(p. 143)	17.	d	(p. 153)
8.	e	(p. 145)	18.	d	(pp. 153-155)
9.	c	(p. 146)	19.	c	(p. 154)
10.	d	(p. 146)	20.	b	(p. 156)

Matching

1.	e	(p. 140)	6.	j	(p. 143)
2.	h	(p. 140)	7.	c	(p. 145)
3.	a	(p. 140)	8.	b	(p. 146)
4.	f	(p. 141)	9.	i	(p. 147)
5.	d	(p. 143)	10.	g	(p. 152)

Fill-In

1. social interaction (p. 140)
2. status, role (p. 140)
3. role conflict (p. 143)
4. Thomas theorem (p. 145)
5. ethnomethodology (p. 146)
6. back (p. 147)
7. words, voice, body language, facial expressions (p. 151)
8. idealization (p. 152)
9. power, value, attention (pp. 153-155)
10. intends, hears (p. 154)

PART VII: IN FOCUS—IMPORTANT ISSUES

- Social Structure: A Guide To Everyday Living

  Provide an illustration to support the point being made by the author that members of every society rely on social structure to make sense out of everyday situations.

- Status

  Outline your current *status set*.

  Outline your *status set* as you believe it will look ten years from now.

- Role

  Provide an example for each of the following from your own life.

  > role strain

  > role conflict

  > role exit

- The Social Construction of Reality

  Provide an illustration (from your own experience) of the *Thomas theorem*.

Using the illustration given in the text, make up an example of how *ethnomethodology* can be used to explore the process of how people make sense of social encounters.

- Dramaturgical Analysis: "The Presentation of Self"

Define and illustrate each of the following.

performance

nonverbal communication

gender and personal performances (demeanor, use of space, staring, smiling, and touching)

idealization

embarrassment and tact

- Interaction In Everyday Life: Two Applications

Language defines men and women differently. Illustrate how for each of the following ways this is true.

      power

      value

      attention

Identify three *foundations of humor.*

Identify and illustrate three major *topics of humor.*

Identify and illustrate three major *functions of humor.*

What is the relationship between *humor and conflict?* Provide two illustrations.

Chapter 7

Groups and Organizations

PART I: CHAPTER OUTLINE

I. Social Groups
    A. Primary and Secondary Groups
    B. Group Leadership
        1. Two Leadership Roles
        2. Three Leadership Styles
    C. Group Conformity
        1. Asch's Research
        2. Milgram's Research
        3. Janis's Research
    D. Reference Groups
        1. Stouffer's Research
    E. Ingroups and Outgroups
    F. Group Size
        1. The Dyad
        2. The Triad
    G. Social Diversity: Race, Class, and Gender
    H. Networks
II. Formal Organizations
    A. Types of Formal Organizations
        1. Utilitarian Organizations
        2. Normative Organizations
        3. Coercive Organizations
    B. Origins of Bureaucracy
    C. Characteristics of Bureaucracy
    D. Organizational Environment
    E. The Informal Side of Bureaucracy
    F. Problems of Bureaucracy
        1. Bureaucratic Alienation
        2. Bureaucratic Inefficiency and Ritualism
        3. Bureaucratic Inertia
    G. Oligarchy

PART II: LEARNING OBJECTIVES

- To be able to identify the differences between primary groups, secondary groups, aggregates, and categories.
- To be able to identify the various types of leaders associated with social groups.
- To be able to compare the research of several different social scientists on group conformity.
- To be able to recognize the importance of reference groups to group dynamics.
- To be able to distinguish between ingroups and outgroups.
- To understand the relevance of group size to the dynamics of social groups.
- To be able to identify the types of formal organizations.
- To be able to identify and describe the basic characteristics of bureaucracy.
- To become aware of both the limitations and informal side of bureaucracy.
- To be able to identify and discuss three important challenges of the scientific management organizational model.
- To consider the issue of the McDonaldization of society.
- To become aware of ways in which today's organizations differ from those of a century ago.
- To analyze the two opposing trends concerning the future of organizations.

PART III: KEY CONCEPTS

Fill in the following blank spaces with the appropriate concepts.

1. A _____ _____ refers to two or more people who identify and interact with one another.
2. A small social group whose members share personal and enduring relationships is known as a _____ _____.
3. A large and impersonal group whose members pursue a specific goal or activity is known as a _____ _____.
4. _____ _____ refers to group leadership that emphasizes the completion of tasks.

5. _____ _____ refers to group leadership that focuses on collective well-being.

6. _____ refers to the tendency of group members to conform, resulting in a narrow view of some issue.

7. A _____ _____ is a social group that serves as a point of reference in making evaluations and decisions.

8. An _____ is a social group commanding a member's esteem and loyalty.

9. A social group toward which one feels competition or opposition is known as an _____.

10. A _____ is a social group with two members.

11. A _____ is a social group with three members.

12. A web of social ties is known as a _____.

13. A _____ _____ is a large secondary group organized to achieve its goals efficiently.

14. A _____ is an organizational model rationally designed to perform tasks efficiently.

15. The _____ _____ refers to factors outside an organization that affects its operations.

16. _____ _____ refers to a preoccupation with rules and regulations to the point of thwarting an organization's goals.

17. _____ _____ refers to the tendency of bureaucratic organizations to perpetuate themselves.

18. An _____ refers to the rule of the many by the few.

19. _____ _____ refers to Frederick Taylor's term for the application of scientific principles to the operation of a business or other large organization.

PART IV: IMPORTANT RESEARCHERS

In the space provided below each of the following researchers, write two or three sentences to help you remember his or her respective contributions to sociology.

Max Weber

Georg Simmel

Charles Horton Cooley

Amitai Etzioni

Stanley Milgram   Solomon Asch

Irving Janis   Samuel Stouffer

Rosabeth Moss Kanter   Robert Michels

William Ouchi   Deborah Tannen

Sally Helgesen   George Ritzer

Frederick Winslow Taylor

PART V: STUDY QUESTIONS

<u>True-False</u>

1. T   F   Any collection of individuals can be called a *group*.
2. T   F   *Secondary groups* tend to be smaller than *primary groups*.
3. T   F   *Expressive leadership* emphasizes the completion of tasks.
4. T   F   *Networks* tend to be more enduring and provide a greater sense of identity than most other types of social groups.

5.	T	F	*Normative organizations* are defined as those which impose restrictions on people who have been labeled as deviant.
6.	T	F	The *organizational environment* includes economic and political trends.
7.	T	F	*Bureaucratic inertia* refers to a preoccupation with rules and regulations to the point of thwarting an organization's goals.
8.	T	F	According to research by Deborah Tannen, a "female advantage" for organizations is that women have a greater *information focus* than men.
9.	T	F	According to research by William Ouchi, formal organizations in Japan tend to be characterized by greater *holistic involvement* than formal organizations in the United States.
10.	T	F	A basic organizational principle involved in the *McDonaldization of society* is efficiency.

Multiple Choice

1. People who have some status in common, such as teachers, exemplify a

    (a) social group.
    (b) category.
    (c) crowd.
    (d) status set.

2. A social group characterized by long-term personal relationships usually involving many activities is a

    (a) primary group.
    (b) secondary group.
    (c) category.
    (d) aggregate.
    (e) normative organization.

3. Temporary, loosely formed collections of anonymous people are referred to as

    (a) crowds.
    (b) groups.
    (c) categories.
    (d) populations.
    (e) social organizations.

4. Which of the following is *not* true of *primary groups*?

    (a) They provide security for their members.
    (b) They are focused around specific activities.
    (c) They are valued in and of themselves.
    (d) They are viewed as ends in themselves.

5. Which of the following is *not* a characteristic of a *secondary group*?

    (a) large size
    (b) weak emotional ties
    (c) personal orientation
    (d) variable, often short duration

6. Members of *secondary groups* display what type of orientation?

    (a) personal
    (b) residual
    (c) natural
    (d) closed
    (e) goal

7. What is the term for a *group leadership* that emphasizes the completion of tasks?

    (a) task group leadership
    (b) secondary group leadership
    (c) expressive leadership
    (d) instrumental leadership
    (e) laissez-faire leadership

8. Which of the following is *not* identified in the text as a *leadership style*?

    (a) laissez-faire
    (b) democratic
    (c) authoritarian
    (d) utilitarian

9. Solomn Asch's classic investigation of group dynamics revealed the dramatic effects of

    (a) leadership styles.
    (b) leadership types.
    (c) triads.
    (d) group conformity.
    (e) networking.

10. Which researcher concluded that people are not likely to question authority figures even though common sense dictates that they should?

    (a) Solomon Asch
    (b) David Klein
    (c) Stanley Milgram
    (d) Charles Horton Cooley

11. What is the sociological term for a limited understanding of some issue due to group conformity?

   (a) conformist cognizance
   (b) groupthink
   (c) doublethink
   (d) red tape

12. A social group commanding a member's esteem and loyalty is a(n)

   (a) ingroup.
   (b) outgroup.
   (c) reference group.
   (d) subculture.
   (e) residual group.

13. Large secondary groups that are organized to achieve their goals efficiently are referred to as

   (a) social organizations.
   (b) bureaucracies.
   (c) formal organizations.
   (d) businesses.
   (e) aggregates.

14. What types of *formal organizations* bestow material benefits on their members?

   (a) normative organizations
   (b) coercive organizations
   (c) social organizations
   (d) utilitarian organizations

15. What term refers to an *organizational model* rationally designed to perform complex tasks efficiently?

   (a) bureaucracy
   (b) complex organization
   (c) humanized organization
   (d) social organization

16. Which of the following is not part of the *organizational environment*?

   (a) economic trends
   (b) political trends
   (c) population patterns
   (d) other organizations
   (e) company employees

17.   *Bureaucratic ritualism* refers to

(a)   the process of promoting people to their level of incompetence.
(b)   the tendency of bureaucratic organizations to persist over time.
(c)   the rule of the many by the few.
(d)   a preoccupation with rules and regulations to the point of thwarting an organizations goals.
(e)   the tendency for formal organizations to become more humanized as membership becomes more diversified.

18.   Research by Deborah Tannen on gender and management styles has found that *men* tend to have a(n)

(a)   image focus.
(b)   information focus.
(c)   flexibility focus.
(d)   developmental focus.
(e)   historical focus.

19.   Which of the following is *not* identified by *Sally Helgesen* as a gender-linked issue in organizations?

(a)   attentiveness to interconnections
(b)   flexibility
(c)   worker productivity
(d)   communication skills

20.   According to *William Ouchi* which of the following lists of qualities highlight the distinctions between formal organizations in Japan and the United States?

(a)   hiring and advancement, lifetime security, holistic involvement, nonspecialized training, and collective decision making
(b)   predictability, calculability, control through automation, and efficiency
(c)   oligarchy, ritualism, privacy, and alienation
(d)   competence, tasks, inertia, and networks
(e)   productivity, developmental focus, physical plant characteristics

Matching

1. ___ Two or more people who identify and interact with one another.
2. ___ People who share a status in common.
3. ___ A small social group in which relationships are personal and enduring.
4. ___ Large and impersonal groups based on a specific interest or activity.
5. ___ Group leaders who emphasize the completion of tasks.
6. ___ The tendency of group members to conform by adopting a narrow view of some issue.
7. ___ A social group that serves as a point of reference in making evaluations or decisions.
8. ___ A social group with two members.
9. ___ Large, secondary groups that are organized to achieve their goals efficiently.
10. ___ An organizational model rationally designed to perform complex tasks efficiently.

a. secondary group   f. reference group
b. formal organization   g. dyad
c. groupthink   h. bureaucracy
d. instrumental leadership   i. primary group
e. social group   j. category

Fill-In

1. A _____ _____ is defined as two or more people who identify and interact with one another.
2. While *primary* relationships have a _____ orientation, *secondary* relationships have a _____ orientation.
3. _____ *leadership* refers to group leadership that emphasizes the completion of tasks.
4. _____ *leaders* focus on instrumental concerns, make decisions on their own, and demand strict compliance from subordinates.
5. Peter Blau points out four ways in which the *diversity of social groups* affects intergroup association, including: Large groups turn _____, heterogeneous groups turn _____, social _____ promotes contact, and physical boundaries create _____ boundaries.
6. Amitai Etzioni has identified three *types of formal organizations*, distinguished by why people participate in them. Ones that pay their members are called _____ organizations. People become members of _____ organizations to pursue goals they consider morally worthwhile. Finally, _____ organizations are distinguished by involuntary membership.
7. The *problems of bureaucracy,* especially the alienation it produces and its tendency toward oligarchy, stem from two organizational traits: _____ and _____.
8. *Deborah Tannen's* research on management styles suggests that women have a greater _____ *focus* and men have greater _____ focus.
9. Several ways in which today's *organizations* differ from those of a century ago are identified in the text, including: greater creative _____ for skilled workers, more use of _____ work teams, a _____ organizational structure, and greater _____.
10. The four characteristics of the *McDonaldization of society* include _____, _____, _____ and _____, and _____ *through automation.*

91

1. Differentiate between the qualities of *bureaucracies* and *small groups*. In what ways are they similar?
2. What are the three factors in decision-making processes in groups that lead to *groupthink*?
3. What are three major *limitations* of bureaucracy? Define and provide an illustration for each. What is meant by questioning "is rationality *irrational*"?
4. In what ways do bureaucratic organizations in *Japan* differ from those in the *U.S*? What are the consequences of these differences? Relate this comparison to the issue of *humanizing* organizations.
5. Differentiate between the concepts of *aggregate* and *category*.
6. Identify the basic *types of leadership* in groups and provide examples of the relative advantages and disadvantage for each type.
7. What are the general characteristics of the *McDonaldization* of society? Provide an illustration of this phenomenon in our society based on your own experience.
8. What are Peter Blau's major points concerning how the structure of social groups regulates intergroup association?
9. What are the three *types of organizations* identified by Amitai Etzioni? Describe and provide an illustration for each. From your own experience, illustrate two of the *characteristics of bureaucracy*—specifying which of Etzioni's type or types of organizations are being represented.
10. What are the three steps involved in *scientific management*? How might this approach work against employees?

PART VI: ANSWERS TO STUDY QUESTIONS

Key Concepts

1. social group (p. 163)
2. primary group (p. 164)
3. secondary group (p. 164)
4. instrumental leadership (p. 165)
5. expressive leadership (p. 165)
6. Groupthink (p. 167)
7.   reference group (p. 167)
8. ingroup (p. 167)
9. outgroup (p. 168)
10. dyad (p. 168)
11. triad (p. 169)
12. network (p. 170)
13. formal organization (P. 171)
14. bureaucracy (p. 174)
15. organizational environment (p. 175)
16. Bureaucratic ritualism (p. 177)
17. Bureaucratic inertia (p. 177)
18. oligarchy (p. 177)
19. Scientific management (p. 178)

True-False

1.	F	(p. 163)	6.	T	(p. 175)
2.	F	(p. 164)	7.	F	(p. 177)
3.	F	(p. 165)	8.	T	(p. 179)
4.	F	(p. 170)	9.	T	(p. 180)
5.	F	(p. 173)	10.	T	(p. 184)

Multiple Choice

1.	b	(p. 163)	11.	b	(p. 167)
2.	a	(p. 164)	12.	a	(p . 168)
3.	a	(p. 164)	13.	c	(p. 171)
4.	b	(pp. 164-165)	14.	d	(p. 173)
5.	c	(pp. 164-165)	15.	a	(p. 174)
6.	e	(p. 165)	16.	e	(p. 175)
7.	d	(p. 165)	17.	d	(p. 177)
8.	d	(pp. 165-166)	18.	a	(p. 179)
9.	d	(p. 166)	19.	c	(pp. 179-180)
10.	c	(pp. 166-167)	20.	a	(pp. 180-181)

Matching

1.	e	(p. 163)	6.	c	(p. 167)
2.	j	(p. 163)	7.	f	(p. 167)
3.	i	(p. 164)	8.	g	(p. 168)
4.	a	(p. 164)	9.	b	(p. 171)
5.	d	(p. 165)	10.	h	(p. 174)

Fill-In

1. social group (p. 163)
2. personal, goal (p. 165)
3. Instrumental (p. 165)
4. Authoritarian (pp. 165-166)
5. inward, outward, equality, social (pp. 169-170)
6. utilitarian, normative, coercive (p. 173) (p. 170)
7. hierarchy, rigidity (p. 178)
8. information, image (p. 179)
9. autonomy, competitive, flatter, flexibility (p. 182)
10. efficiency, calculability, uniformity, predictability, control (p. 184)

PART VII: IN FOCUS--IMPORTANT ISSUES

- Social Groups

Define and illustrate each of the following.

category

crowd

primary group

secondary group

Define and provide an example for each of the following *types of leadership*.

instrumental leadership

expressive leadership

Describe each of the following *leadership styles*.

authoritarian leadership

democratic leadership

laissez-faire leadership

Describe the research procedures and findings/conclusions for each of the following researcher's work on *group conformity*.

Asch's research

Milgram's research

Janis's research

Identify three *ingroups* of yours.

Identify three *outgroups* of yours.

What are the patterns you see in the above two lists?

According to Georg Simmel, how does *group size* affect group dynamics and group stability?

Identify and describe the four ways in which *social diversity* influences intergroup contact as outlined by Peter Blau.

What is a *network*? How do networks differ for men and women?

- Formal Organizations

What is a *formal organization*?

Define and illustrate each of the following *types* of formal organizations

    utilitarian

    normative

    coercive

What is meant by the term *bureaucracy?*

Max Weber identified six *key elements* of the ideal bureaucratic organization. Define and illustrate each of these elements.

    specialization

    hierarchy of offices

    rules and regulations

    technical competence

    impersonality

    formal, written communications

Identify three examples of the *informal side of bureaucracy.*

Identify and describe three major *problems of bureaucracy.*

- The Evolution of Formal Organizations

  What are the three steps involved in *scientific management?*

  Describe the nature of the *three challenges* facing formal organizations in our society today.

    race and gender

    Japanese organization

    the changing nature of work

  What are the major characteristics of the *McDonaldization of society?* Provide evidence for the existence of each in our society today.

- The Future of Organizations: Opposing Trends

  What are the two *opposing tendencies* identified by the author?

Chapter 8 — Deviance

PART I: CHAPTER OUTLINE

I. What is Deviance?
    A. Social Control
    B. The Biological Context
    C. Personality Factors
    D. The Social Foundations of Deviance

II. The Functions of Deviance: Structural-Functional Analysis
    A. Emile Durkheim: The Functions of Deviance
        1. An Illustration: The Puritans of Massachusetts Bay
    B. Merton's Strain Theory
    C. Deviant Subcultures

III. Labeling Deviance: Symbolic-Interaction Analysis
    A. Labeling Theory
        1. Primary and Secondary Deviance
        2. Stigma
        3. Retrospective and Projective Labeling
        4. Labeling and Mental Illness
    B. The Medicalization of Deviance
        1. The Difference Labels Make
    C. Sutherland's Differential Association Theory
    D. Hirschi's Control Theory

IV. Deviance and Inequality: Social Conflict Analysis
    A. Deviance and Power
    B. Deviance and Capitalism
    C. White-Collar Crime
    D. Corporate Crime
    E. Organized Crime

V. Deviance and Social Diversity
    A. Hate Crimes
    B. Deviance and Gender

VI. Crime
    A. Types of Crime
    B. Criminal Statistics

PART II: LEARNING OBJECTIVES

- To be able to explain how deviance is interpreted as a product of society.
- To be able to identify and evaluate the biological explanation of deviance.
- To be able to identify and evaluate the psychological explanation of deviance.
- To be able to identify and evaluate the sociological explanations of deviance.
- To be able to compare and contrast different theories representative of the three major sociological paradigms.
- To be able to evaluate empirical evidence used to support these different sociological theories of deviance.
- To be able to distinguish among the types of crime.
- To become more aware of the demographic patterns of crime in our society.
- To evaluate deviance in global context.
- To be able to identify and describe the elements of our criminal justice system.

PART III: KEY CONCEPTS

Fill in the blank spaces below with the appropriate concepts.

1. _____ refers to the recognized violation of cultural norms.
2. _____ refers to the violation of a society's formally enacted criminal law.
3. Attempts by society to regulate people's thought and behavior is known as _____ _____.
4. The _____ _____ _____ refers to a formal response by police, courts, and prison officials to alleged violations of the law.

5. _____ _____ is the assertion that deviance and conformity result not so much from what people do as from how others respond to those actions.

6. A powerfully negative label that greatly changes a person's self-concept and social identity is called a _____.

7. The _____ _____ _____ refers to the transformation of moral and legal deviance into a medical condition.

8. _____ _____ refers to crime committed by people of high social position in the course of their occupations.

9. The illegal actions of a corporation or people acting on its behalf is known as _____ _____.

10. _____ _____ refers to a business supplying illegal goods or services.

PART IV: IMPORTANT RESEARCHERS

In the space provided below each of the following researchers, write two or three sentences to help you remember his or her respective contributions to the field of sociology.

Caesare Lombroso   William Sheldon

Steven Spitzer   Richard Cloward and Lloyd Ohlin

Charles Goring   Albert Cohen and Walter Miller

Walter Reckless and Simon Dintz   Edwin Sutherland

Thomas Szasz   Emile Durkheim

Robert Merton   Travis Hirschi

Howard Becker   Erving Goffman

PART V: STUDY QUESTIONS

True-False

1.   T   F   Scientific research clearly concludes that there is absolutely no relationship between *biology* and crime.

2.   T   F   *Containment theory* focuses our attention on how certain behaviors are linked to, or contained by, our genes.

3.   T   F   One of the *social foundations of deviance* is that deviance exists only in relation to cultural norms.

4.   T   F   Walter Miller's *subcultural theory* of deviance points out that deviant subcultures have *no focal concerns*, and therefore have no social norms to guide the behavior of their members.

5.   T   F   Edwin Sutherland's *differential association theory* suggests that certain individuals are incapable of learning from experience and therefore are more likely to become deviant.

6.   T   F   The *social-conflict* perspective links deviance to social inequality and power in society.

7.   T   F   While *civil law* regulates business dealings between private parties, *criminal law* defines the individual's moral responsibilities to society.

8.   T   F   Almost every society in the world applies more stringent normative controls on *men* than to *women*.

9.   T   F   Using *index crimes*, the crime rate in the United States is relatively high compared to European societies.

10.   T   F   *Plea bargaining* accounts for about forty percent of criminal cases resolved by the courts.

Multiple Choice

1. _____ refers to the recognized violation of cultural norms.

    (a)   Crime
    (b)   Deviance
    (c)   Residual behavior
    (d)   Social control

2.	*Containment theory* is an example of a(n) _____ explanation of deviance.

	(a)	biological
	(b)	economic
	(c)	anthropological
	(d)	sociological
	(e)	psychological

3.	*Emile Durkheim* theorized that all but which of the following are *functions of deviance*?

	(a)	It clarifies moral boundaries.
	(b)	It affirms cultural values and norms.
	(c)	It encourages social stability.
	(d)	It promotes social unity.

4.	Kai Erikson's investigation of the early Puritans of Massachusetts Bay is a good illustration of whose *theory of deviance*?

	(a)	Durkheim's functional theory
	(b)	Merton's strain theory
	(c)	Sutherland's differential association theory
	(d)	Hirchi's control theory

5.	*Robert Merton's strain theory* is a component of which broad theoretical paradigm?

	(a)	social-conflict
	(b)	symbolic-interactionism
	(c)	social-exchange
	(d)	human ecology
	(e)	structural-functional

6.	According to Robert Merton's *strain theory*, one response to the inability to succeed is _____, or the rejection of both cultural goals and means--so one, in effect, "drops out."

	(a)	innovation
	(b)	retreatism
	(c)	inertia
	(d)	ritualism

7.   Which of the following is *not* an example of a *deviant subculture* identified in *Richard Cloward* and *Lloyd Olhin's* research on delinquents.

   (a)   criminal
   (b)   retreatist
   (c)   conflict
   (d)   residual

8.   Which of the following is *not* an appropriate criticism of *structural-functional theories* of deviance?

   (a)   The theories assume a diversity of cultural standards.
   (b)   The theories seem to imply that everyone who breaks the rules is labeled at deviant.
   (c)   The theories seem to focus on, and unfairly target, the lower-class.
   (d)   The theories cannot explain very well certain types of crime.

9.   Skipping school for the first time as an eighth grader is an example of

   (a)   recidivism.
   (b)   primary deviance.
   (c)   a degradation ceremony.
   (d)   secondary deviance.

10. What is Erving Goffman's term for a powerful negative social label that radically changes a person's self-concept and social identity?

   (a)   anomie
   (b)   secondary deviance
   (c)   medicalization of deviance
   (d)   retribution
   (e)   stigma

11. Sometimes an entire community formally stigmatizes an individual through what *Harold Garfinkel* called a

   (a)   hate crime.
   (b)   retrospective label
   (c)   recidivism process.
   (d)   degradation ceremony.
   (e)   conflict subculture.

12. Once people stigmatize an individual, they may engage in _____, or interpreting someone's past in light of some present deviance.

   (a)   retrospective labeling
   (b)   projective labeling
   (c)   residual labeling
   (d)   ad hoc labeling

13. What is the *medicalization of deviance*?

   (a)   the recognition of the true source of deviance
   (b)   the objective, clinical approach to deviant behavior
   (c)   the transformation of moral and legal issues into medical models
   (d)   the discovery of the links between biochemical properties and deviance

14. *Attachment, involvement, commitment,* and *belief* are all types of social control in

   (a)   Sutherland's differential association theory.
   (b)   Durkheim's functional theory.
   (c)   Goffman's labeling theory.
   (d)   Cohen's subcultural theory.
   (e)   Hirschi's control theory.

15. According to the *social-conflict paradigm*, who and what is labeled deviant is based primarily on

   (a)   the severity of the deviant act.
   (b)   psychological profile.
   (c)   the functions being served.
   (d)   relative power.
   (e)   the location of the deviant act.

16. _____ defines the individual's moral responsibility to society.

   (a)   Civil law
   (b)   Criminal law
   (c)   Medicalization
   (d)   Stigma
   (e)   Attachment

17.   The statements: "While what is deviant may vary, deviance itself is found in all societies"; Deviance and the social response it provokes serve to maintain the moral foundation of society"; "Deviance can direct social change". All help to summarize which sociological explanation of deviance?

(a)   structural-functional
(b)   social-conflict
(c)   symbolic-interaction
(d)   labeling
(e)   social exchange

18.   Which of the following are criticisms of *social-conflict theory*?

(a)   It is an oversimplification to imply that all the laws and other cultural norms are created directly by the rich and powerful.
(b)   It implies that criminality springs up only to the extent that a society treats its members unequally.
(c)   Both (a) and (b) are criticisms of social-conflict theory.
(d)   Neither (a) nor (b) are criticisms of social-conflict theory.

19.   Which contribution below is attributed to the *structural-functional theory* of deviance?

(a)   Nothing is inherently deviant.
(b)   Deviance is found in all societies.
(c)   The reactions of others to deviance are highly variable.
(d)   Laws and other norms reflect the interests of the powerful in society.

20.   Which of the following are included as part of the FBI *index crimes*?

(a)   white-collar crime and property crime
(b)   victimless crime and federal crime
(c)   crime against the state and civil crime
(d)   crimes against the person and crimes against property
(e)   violent crime and white-collar crime

Matching

1. _____ Attempts by society to regulate people's thought and behavior.
2. _____ Identified the key insight of the structural-functional paradigm as the recognition that deviance is a necessary part of social organization.
3. _____ Saw deviance as a result of the strain between our culture's emphasis on certain goals and the limited opportunity some people have to achieve these goals.
4. _____ A theory that suggests that a person's tendency toward conformity or deviance depends on the amount of contact with others who encourage or reject conventional behavior.
5. _____ The illegal actions of a corporation or people acting on its behalf.

6.   ____   A business supplying illegal goods or services.
7.   ____   A legal negotiation in which a prosecutor reduces a charge in exchange for a defendant's guilty plea.
8.   ____   The use of punishment to discourage criminality.
9.   ____   A program for reforming the offender to prevent subsequent offenses.
10.   ____   Subsequent offenses by people convicted of crimes.

a.	differential association theory	f.	plea bargaining
b.	rehabilitation	g.	organized crime
c.	criminal recidivism	h.	Emile Durkheim
d.	corporate crime	i.	Robert Merton
e.	social control	j.	deterrence

Fill-In

1. Activity that is initially defined as deviant is called _____ *deviance*. On the other hand, a person who accepts the label of deviant may then engage in _____ *deviance*, or behavior caused by the person's incorporating the deviant label into their self-concept.
2. Psychiatrist Thomas Szasz argues that *mental illness* is a _____.
3. Whether we define deviance as a *moral* or *medical* issue has three consequences. First, it affects who _____ to the deviance. Second, it affects _____ people will respond to deviance. And third, the two labels differ on the personal _____ of the deviant person.
4. Travis Hirschi links *conformity* to four types of social control, including _____, _____, _____, and _____.
5. _____ *crime* is defined as crimes committed by persons of high social position in the course of their occupations.
6. _____ *law* refers to general regulations involving business dealings between private parties.
7. Technically, all crime is composed of two elements: the _____ and the criminal _____.
8. The four basic *justifications for punishment* include: _____, _____, _____, and _____ _____.
9. Subsequent offenses by people previously convicted of crimes is termed *criminal* _____.
10. The United States and _____ are the only two high-income countries in which the government imposes the *death penalty*.

Discussion

1. According to *Travis Hirschi's control theory* there are four types of social controls. What are these? Provide an example of each.
2. According to *Robert Merton's strain theory*, what are the four deviant responses by individuals to dominant cultural patterns when there is a gap between *means* and *goals*? Provide an illustration of each.

3. What are the three consequences for the deviant person depending on whether a *moral model* or *medical model* is applied?

4. *Social-conflict* theorist *Steven Spitzer* argues that deviant labels are applied to people who impede the operation of *capitalism*. What are the four reasons he gives for this phenomenon?

5. How do researchers using *differential association theory* explain deviance?

6. What is meant by the term *medicalization of deviance*? Provide two illustrations.

7. According to *Elliott Currie*, what factors are responsible for the relatively high crime rates in the United States? Critique the official statistics of crime in the United States. What are the weaknesses of the measures used in the identification of *crime rates*?

8. Briefly review the demographic *profile* of the *street criminal*. What are the four *justifications* for the use of punishment against criminals? What evidence exists for their relative effectiveness?

9. *Richard Cloward* and *Lloyd Ohlin* investigated delinquent youth and explain deviance and conformity in terms of the *relative opportunity structure* young people face in their lives. Identify and define the three types of *subcultures* these researchers have identified as representing the criminal lifestyles of delinquent youth.

10. Describe *Thomas Szasz's* view of mental illness and deviance. What are your opinions of his arguments?

PART VI: ANSWERS TO STUDY QUESTIONS

Key Concepts

1. Deviance (p. 191)
2. Crime (p. 191)
3. social control (p. 192)
4. criminal justice system (p. 192)
5. Labeling theory (p. 197)
6. stigma (p. 198)
7. medicalization of deviance (p. 199)
8. White-collar crime (p. 202)
9. corporate crime (p. 203)
10. Organized crime (p. 203)

True-False

1.	F	(p. 192)	6.	T	(p. 201)
2.	F	(pp. 192-193)	7.	T	(p. 203)
3.	T	(p. 193)	8.	F	(p. 204)
4.	F	(p. 197)	9.	T	(p. 210)
5.	F	(p. 200)	10.	F	(p. 213)

Multiple Choice

1.	b	(p. 191)	11.	d	(p. 198)
2.	e	(pp. 192-193)	12.	a	(p. 198)
3.	c	(p. 194)	13.	c	(p. 199)
4.	a	(p. 195)	14.	e	(p. 200)
5.	e	(p. 195)	15.	d	(p. 201)
6.	b	(p. 195)	16.	b	(p. 203)
7.	d	(p. 196)	17.	a	(p. 204)
8.	a	(p. 197)	18.	c	(p. 204)
9.	b	(p. 197)	19.	b	(p. 204)
10.	e	(p. 198)	20.	d	(p. 206)

Matching

1.	e	(p. 192)	6.	g	(p. 203)
2.	h	(p. 194)	7.	f	(p. 213)
3.	i	(p. 195)	8.	j	(p. 214)
4.	a	(p. 200)	9.	b	(p. 214)
5.	d	(p. 203)	10.	c	(p. 215)

Fill-In

1. primary, secondary (p. 197)
2. myth (p. 199)
3. responds, how, competence (pp. 199-200)
4. attachment, commitment, involvement, belief (p. 200)
5. White-collar (p. 202)
6. Civil (p. 203)
7. act, intent (p. 206)
8. retribution, deterrence, rehabilitation, societal protection (pp. 213-214)
9. recidivism (p. 215)
10. Japan (p. 216)

PART VII: IN FOCUS--IMPORTANT ISSUES

- What is Deviance?

What role does *biology* play in helping us explain deviance?

Using *containment theory*, how did Walter Reckless and Simon Dinitz explain delinquency among young boys?

Illustrate each of the following *social foundations of deviance.*

Deviance varies according to cultural norms.

People become deviant as others define them that way.

Both rule-making and rule-breaking involve social power.

- Structural-Functional Analysis

According to Emile Durkheim, what are the four *functions of deviance*?

In Robert Merton's *strain theory,* four adaptations to conformity are identified. List, define, and illustrate each of these.

Define and illustrate each of the following types of *deviant subcultures* as identified by Richard Cloward and Lloyd Ohlin.

What are two *criticisms* of the structural-functional analysis of deviance?

- Symbolic-Interaction Analysis

How is deviance explained using *labeling theory*?

What is meant by the *medicalization of deviance*? Provide an illustration of this phenomenon.

How is deviance explained using Edwin Sutherland's *differential association theory*?

Using Travis Hirschi's *control theory*, four types of social control are identified. Illustrate each of these.

attachment

commitment

involvement

belief

- Social-Conflict Analysis

Social-conflict theory explains the relationship between *deviance and power* in three ways. Identify each of these ways.

Steven Spitzer suggests that deviant labels are applied to people who interfere with the operation of *capitalism*. Identify the four ways he says this is the case.

- Deviance and Social Diversity

Differentiate between the following *types of crime.*

    crimes against the person

    crimes against property

Using the following categories, describe the demographic patterns of *street crime* in our societies.

    age

    gender

    social class

    race and ethnicity

What are five explanations given by the text as to why African American males are overrepresented among those who are arrested in our society?

Describe how *crime rates* in the U.S. have changed over the last forty years. Make reference to specific types of violent and property crimes.

How does the crime rate in the U.S. compare to other *industrialized societies*? Why do you think these differences exist?

- The Criminal Justice System

Identify two important points being made by the author about each of the following *components of the criminal justice system.*

police

courts

punishment

Applying the sociological theories discussed in this chapter, identify and illustrate five reasons why *violent crime* rates have declined over the last decade in our society.

Chapter 9 — Sexuality

PART I: CHAPTER OUTLINE

I. Understanding Sexuality
   A. Sex: A Biological Issue
   B. Sex and the Body
      1. Hermaphrodites
      2. Transsexuals
   C. Sex: A Cultural Issue
      1. Cultural Variation
   D. The Incest Taboo
II. Sexual Attitudes in the United States
   A. The Sexual Revolution
   B. The Sexual Counterrevolution
   C. Premarital Sex
   D. Sex between Adults
   E. Extramarital Sex
III. Sexual Orientation
   A. What Gives Us A Sexual Orientation?
      1. Sexual Orientation: A Product of Society
      2. Sexual Orientation: A Product of Biology
   B. How Many Gay People?
   C. The Gay Rights Movement
IV. Sexual Controversies
   A. Teen Pregnancy
   B. Pornography
   C. Prostitution
      1. Types of Prostitution
      2. A Victimless Crime?
   D. Sexual Violence and Abuse
      1. Rape
      2. Date Rape
V. Theoretical Analysis of Sexuality
   A. Structural-Functional Analysis
      1. The Need to Regulate Sexuality
      2. Latent Functions: The Case of Prostitution
   B. Symbolic-Interaction Analysis
      1. The Social Construction of Sexuality
      2. Global Comparisons

C.   Social-Conflict Analysis
1.   Sexuality: Reflecting Social Inequality
2.   Sexuality: Creating Social Inequality
3.   Queer Theory
VI.   Summary
VII.   Key Concepts
VIII.   Critical-Thinking Questions
IX.   Applications and Exercises
X.   Sites to See

PART II: LEARNING OBJECTIVES

- To gain a sociological understanding of human sexuality focusing on both biological and cultural factors.
- To become more aware of the sexual attitudes found in the United States today.
- To be able to describe both the sexual revolution and sexual counter-revolution that occurred during the last half century in the United States.
- To be able to discuss human sexuality as it is experienced across different stages of the human life course.
- To be able to discuss issues relating to the biological and social causes of sexual orientation.
- To be able to describe the demographics of sexual orientation in our society, including the research methods used to obtain such information about our population.
- To gain a sociological perspective on several sexual controversies, including teen pregnancy, pornography, prostitution, and sexual violence and abuse.
- To be able to discuss issues relating to human sexuality from the viewpoints offered by structural-functional, symbolic-interactionist, and social-conflict analysis.

PART III: KEY CONCEPTS

Fill in the blank spaces below with the appropriate concepts.

1.   _____ refers to the biological distinction between females and males.
2.   The genitals—or organs used for reproduction refer to _____ _____ _____.
3.   _____ _____ _____ refer to bodily differences, apart from the genitals, that distinguishes biologically mature females and males.
4.   A _____ is a human being with some combination of female and male genitalia.
5.   _____ are people who feel they are one sex even though biologically they are the other.
6.   An _____ _____ is a norm forbidding sexual relations or marriage between certain relatives.
7.   _____ _____ refers to a person's romantic and emotional attraction to another person.
8.   _____ is a sexual orientation in which a person is sexually attracted to someone of the other sex.

9. _____ is a sexual orientation in which a person is sexually attracted to someone of the same sex.

10. _____ is a sexual orientation in which a person is sexually attracted to people of both sexes.

11. _____ is a sexual orientation in which a person is not sexually attracted to people of either sex.

12. The dread of close personal interaction with people thought to be gay, lesbian, or bisexual refers to _____.

13. _____ refers to sexually explicit material that causes sexual arousal.

14. The selling of sexual services is known as _____.

15. _____ _____ is a growing body of research findings that challenges the heterosexual bias in U.S. society.

16. _____ refers to a view stigmatizing anyone who is not heterosexual as "queer."

17. _____ refers to the deliberate termination of a pregnancy.

PART IV: IMPORTANT RESEARCHERS

In the space provided below each of the following researchers, write two or three sentences to help you remember his or her respective contributions to the field of sociology.

Alfred Kinsey   Helen Colton

Simon LeVay   Kingsley Davis

PART V: STUDY QUESTIONS

True-False

1.	T	F	In *fertilization*, the male contributes either an X or Y chromosome.
2.	T	F	*Primary sex characteristics* are those that develop during puberty.
3.	T	F	*Hermaphrodites* are people who feel they are one sex even though biologically they are of the other.
4.	T	F	One cultural universal—an element found in every society the world over—is the *incest taboo*.
5.	T	F	Research data suggests that married people have *sexual intercourse* more frequently than single people.
6.	T	F	*Sexual orientation* refers to the biological distinction of being female or male.
7.	T	F	Most research indicates that among *homosexuals*, lesbians outnumber gays by a ratio of about two-to-one.

8.	T	F	*Pornography* refers to sexually explicit material that causes sexual arousal.
9.	T	F	Among the types of *prostitutes*, call girls have the lowest status.
10.	T	F	According to national survey research, over one-third of adults in the U.S. think that a woman should be able to obtain a legal *abortion* for any reason if she wants to.

Multiple-Choice

1. _____ refers to the biological distinction between females and males.

   (a) Gender
   (b) Sex
   (c) Sexual orientation
   (d) Human sexuality

2. In reproduction, a female ovum and a male sperm, each containing_____ chromosomes, combine to form a fertilized embryo. One of these chromosome pairs determines the child's sex.

   (a) 12
   (b) 7
   (c) 23
   (d) 31

3. _____ are people who feel they are one sex even though biologically they are of the other sex.

   (a) Hermaphrodites
   (b) Transvestites
   (c) Homophobics
   (d) Transsexuals

4. If an Islamic woman is disturbed by another person while she is bathing, what body part is she most likely to cover?

   (a) her feet
   (b) her breasts
   (c) her navel
   (d) her genitals
   (e) her face

5. During the last century, people witnessed profound changes in sexual attitudes and practices. The first indications of this change occurred in the

   (a) 1920s.
   (b) 1940s.
   (c) 1960s.
   (d) 1970s.

117

6. According to the _____, society allows (and even encourages) men to be sexually active, while expecting women to remain chaste before marriage and faithful to their husbands afterwards.

   (a) sexual counterrevolution
   (b) sexual revolution
   (c) double-standard
   (d) permissiveness index

7. Approximately ____ *percent* of U.S. adults say that premarital sexual intercourse is "always wrong",

   (a) 20
   (b) 35
   (c) 15
   (d) 60
   (e) 8

8. _____ refers to a person's romantic and emotional attraction to another person.

   (a) Sexual orientation
   (b) Sex
   (c) Gender
   (d) Sexual response

9. One question asked in the text is: what gives us a sexual orientation? Which of the following statements is *inaccurate* based on the findings of social scientists?

   (a) Homosexuality and heterosexuality are not mutually exclusive categories, but rather exist on a continuum.
   (b) Anthropological studies show that various kinds of homosexuality exist in different societies.
   (c) There was no distinct category of people called "homosexual" until a century ago.
   (d) There is mounting evidence that sexual orientation is rooted in biology.
   (e) Only about one-third of adults in the United States have the attitude that homosexuality is "always" or "almost always" wrong.

10. Approximately _____ percent of men and _____ percent of women in the U.S. define themselves as partly or entirely *homosexual*.

   (a) 10.4/12.4
   (b) 12.1/ 8.7
   (c) 6.5/ 7.0
   (d) 11.3/ 2.6
   (e) 2.8/ 1.4

11.   Which of the following are accurate concerning *teen pregnancy* in the United States?

    (a)   Approximately one million teens become pregnant each year.
    (b)   Most teens who get pregnant did not intend to.
    (c)   Teens who become pregnant are at great risk of poverty.
    (d)   The U.S. has a higher rate of teen pregnancy than that found in other industrial societies.
    (e)   All of the above are accurate.

12.   Which of the following statements reflects the current position of the Supreme Court of the United States regarding *pornography*?

    (a)   The Court has never made a ruling concerning pornography.
    (b)   The Court has established federal guidelines regarding what material is to be considered pornographic.
    (c)   The Court's ruling has given local communities the power to decide for themselves what violates "community standards" of decency and lacks any redeeming social value.
    (d)   The Court has ruled the First Amendment to the United States Constitution forbids any legal definitions for pornography.

13.   Which of the following is *inaccurate* about *prostitution*?

    (a)   Most prostitutes are women.
    (b)   Most prostitutes offer heterosexual services.
    (c)   Call girls are the lowest prestige type of prostitution.
    (d)   Prostitution is greatest in poor countries where patriarchy is strong and traditional cultural norms limit women's ability to earn a living.

14.   *Prostitution* is classified as being what type of crime?

    (a)   property
    (b)   victimless
    (c)   white-collar
    (d)   violent

15.   Which of the following is/are evidence of a societal need to *regulate* sex?

    (a)   Most societies condemn married people for having sex with someone other than their spouse.
    (b)   Every society has some form of incest taboo.
    (c)   Historically, the social control of sexuality was strong, mostly because sex commonly led to childbirth.
    (d)   all of the above

16. Which of the following is *inaccurate* concerning the perspective offered by the *structural-functionalist paradigm*?

   (a) It helps us to appreciate how sexuality plays an important part in how society is organized.
   (b) It focuses attention on how societies, through the incest taboo and other cultural norms have always paid attention to who has sex with who, especially who reproduces with whom.
   (c) This approach pays considerable attention to the great diversity of sexual ideas and practices found around the world.
   (d) All of the above are accurate.

17. Which of the following is a criticism of the *symbolic-interactionist paradigm*?

   (a) It fails to take into account how social patterns regarding sexuality are socially constructed.
   (b) It fails to help us appreciate the variety of sexual practices found over the course of history and around the world.
   (c) It fails to identify the broader social structures that establish certain patterns of sexual behaviors cross-culturally.
   (d) None of the above are criticisms of symbolic-interactionism.

18. *Queer theory* is most likely accepted by proponents of which of the following paradigms?

   (a) structural-functionalists
   (b) symbolic-interactionsists
   (c) social-conflict theorists
   (d) none of the above

19. _____ refers to a view stigmatizing anyone who is not heterosexual as "queer".

   (a) Asexuality
   (b) Heteterosexism
   (c) Bisexuality
   (d) Homophobia

20. Overall, there are approximately _____ *abortions* performed each year in the United States.

   (a) 2.5 million
   (b) 900,000
   (c) 500,000
   (d) 1.3 million

Matching

1. ____ The biological distinction between females and males.
2. ____ The genitals, organs used for reproduction.
3. ____ People who feel they are one sex even though biologically they are of the other.
4. ____ Sexual attraction to someone of the same sex.
5. ____ No sexual attraction to people of either sex.
6. ____ Sexual attraction to people of both sexes.
7. ____ Refers to sexually explicit material that causes sexual arousal.
8. ____ The selling of sexual services.
9. ____ A view stigmatizing anyone who is not heterosexual as "queer".
10. ____ Refers to a growing body of knowledge that challenges heterosexism.

a.	transsexuals	f.	prostitution
b.	queer theory	g.	bisexuality
c.	asexuality	h.	sex
d.	primary sex characteristics	i.	pornography
e.	heterosexism	j.	homosexuality

Fill-In

1. _____ refers to the biological distinction between females and males.
2. _____ *sex characteristics* refer to bodily differences, apart from the genitals, that distinguish biologically mature females and males.
3. Human beings with some combination of female and male genitalia are referred to as _____.
4. One cultural universal--an element found in every society the world over--is the _____ _____, a norm forbidding sexual relations or marriage between certain relatives.
5. Given current scientific research evidence, the best guess at present is that *sexual orientation* is derived from both _____ and _____.
6. Recent research suggests that about _____ percent of U.S. *males* and _____ percent of U.S. *females* aged between eighteen and fifty-nine reported *homosexual activity* at some time in their lives.
7. _____ describes the dread of close personal interaction with people thought to be gay, lesbian, or bisexual.
8. Traditionally, people have criticized *pornography* on _____ grounds. Today, however, pornography is seen as a _____ issue because it depicts women as the sexual playthings of men.
9. At the bottom of the *sex-worker hierarchy* are _____ _____.
10. *Prostitution* is against the law almost everywhere in the United States, but many people consider it a _____ *crime*.

Discussion

1. What are the important anatomical differences between *males* and *females*? In what ways are these differences important in term of the relatives statuses and roles of women and men in social institutions such as the family and the economy?
2. What evidence was used by Alfred Kinsey to suggest considerable *cultural variation* exists in terms of sexual practices? What does Alfred Kinsey mean by the *sexual orientation continuum*? What is the data he uses to argue for its existence?
3. What are the functions served by the *incest taboo* for both individuals and society as a whole?
4. What does the author mean by saying that sexual attitudes in the United States are both *restrictive* and *permissive*? When was the *sexual revolution*? What social and cultural factors influenced this revolution? What was the *sexual counterrevolution*? What social and cultural factors helped bring it about? How would you summarize our society's attitudes concerning *premarital sex*?
5. What is the evidence that sexual orientation is a *product of society*? What is the evidence that it is a *product of biology*?
6. Why do you think *teen pregnancy* rates are higher in the United States than in other modern industrial societies? What are your opinions regarding *sex education* in the schools? What is the evidence for its effectiveness?
7. To what extent would you agree that *pornography* today is less a moral issue than it is an issue concerning power? Why?
8. Is *prostitution* really a victimless crime? Why? What are the *functions* of prostitution for society?
9. What evidence do symbolic-interactionists use to suggest sexuality is *socially constructed*? Social-conflict theorists argue that sexuality is at the root of *inequality* between women and men. How is this so? Further, using each of these paradigms, discuss the problem of *sexual violence* in our society. Why is sexual violence so prevalent in our society?
10. What do national survey tell us about attitudes in our society regarding the *abortion issue*? Differentiate between the specific arguments being made by "pro-choice" and pro-life" advocates.

PART VI: ANSWERS TO STUDY QUESTIONS

Key Concepts

1. Sex (p. 222)
2. primary sex characteristics (p. 223)
3. Secondary sex characteristics (p. 223)
4. hermaphrodite (p. 223)
5. Transsexuals (p. 223)
6. incest taboo (p. 224)
7. Sexual orientation (p 228).
8. Heterosexuality (p. 228)
9. Homosexuality (p. 228)
10. Bisexuality (p. 228)
11. Asexuality (p. 228)
12. homophobia (p. 231)

13. Pornography (p. 232)
14. prostitution (p. 232)
15. Queer theory (p. 239)
16. Heterosexism (p. 239)
17. Abortion (p. 239)

True-False

1.	T	(p. 222)	6.	F	(p. 228)
2.	F	(p. 223)	7.	F	(p. 230)
3.	F	(p. 223)	8.	T	(p. 232)
4.	T	(p. 224)	9.	F	(p. 234)
5.	T	(p. 228)	10.	T	(p. 240)

Multiple-Choice

1.	b	(p. 222)	11.	e	(pp. 231-232)
2.	c	(p. 222)	12.	c	(p. 232)
3.	d	(p. 223)	13.	c	(pp. 232-234)
4.	e	(p. 224)	14.	b	(p. 235)
5.	a	(p. 225)	15.	d	(pp. 235-236)
6.	c	(p. 225)	16.	c	(p. 237)
7.	b	(p. 226)	17.	c	(p. 238)
8.	a	(p. 228)	18.	c	(p. 239)
9.	e	(p. 230)	19.	b	(p. 239)
10.	e	(p. 230)	20.	d	(p. 240)

Matching

1.	h	(p. 222)	6.	g	(p. 228)
2.	d	(p. 222)	7.	i	(p. 232)
3.	a	(p. 223)	8.	f	(p. 232)
4.	j	(p. 228)	9.	e	(p. 239)
5.	c	(p. 228)	10.	b	(p. 239)

Fill-In

1. Sex (p. 222)
2. Secondary (p. 222)
3. hermaphrodite (p. 223)
4. incest taboo (p. 224)
5. society, biology (p. 229)
6. 9, 4 (p. 230)
7. Homophobia (p. 231)
8. moral, power (p. 232)
9. street walkers (p. 235)
10. victimless (p. 235)

PART VII: IN FOCUS--IMPORTANT ISSUES

- Understanding Sexuality

  Differentiate between sex as a *biological issues* and as a *cultural issue*.

  What evidence exists to support the theory that there is considerable variation in *sexual practices* around the world?

- Sexual Attitudes In the United States

  What does the author mean by saying that our cultural orientation toward sexuality has always been *inconsistent*?

  How strong do you believe the *sexual double standard* is in our society today? What is you evidence?

What does the research suggest about behavioral patterns for each of the following?

premarital sex

sex among adults

extramarital sex

- Sexual Orientation

What is the evidence concerning each of the following in terms of giving us our *sexual orientation?*

biology

society

How have attitudes toward *homosexuality* changed in our society over the last fifty years? What factors have influenced our society's altitudes toward homosexuality?

- Sexual Controversies

  Identify two major points made in the text concerning each of the following four controversial issues:

    teen pregnancy

    pornography

    prostitution

    sexual violence

- Theoretical Analysis of Sexuality

  According to *structural-functionalists*, why is it important for society to regulate sexuality?

  What are three *latent functions* of prostitution?

  Can you think of two latent functions of *pornography*? What are they?

  Provide an illustration of how global comparisons can be used to illustrate the symbolic-interactionists view that sexuality is *socially constructed*.

  According to social-conflict theorists, how is sexuality involved in the creation and maintenance of *social inequality*?

Chapter 10

Social Stratification

PART I: CHAPTER OUTLINE

I. What is Social Stratification?

II. Caste and Class Systems
    A. The Caste System
        1. Two Illustrations: India and South Africa
        2. Caste and Agrarian Life
    B. The Class System
        1. Meritocracy
        2. Status Consistency
    C. Birth and Achievement: The United Kingdom
        1. The Estate System
        2. The United Kingdom Today
    D. Another Example: Japan
        1. Feudal Japan
        2. Japan Today
    E. The Former Soviet Union
        1. A Classless Society?
        2. The Second Russian Revolution
    F. Ideology: The Power Behind Stratification
        1. Plato and Marx on Ideology
        2. Historical Patterns of Ideology

III. The Functions of Social Stratification
    A. The Davis-Moore Thesis

IV. Stratification and Conflict
    A. Karl Marx: Class and Conflict
    B. Why No Marxist Revolution?
        1. A Counterpoint
    C. Max Weber: Class, Status, and Power
        1. The Socioeconomic Status Hierarchy
        2. Inequality in History

V. Stratification and Technology in Global Perspective
    A. Hunting and Gathering Societies
    B. Horticultural, Pastoral, and Agrarian Societies
    C. Industrial Societies
    D. The Kuznets Curve

PART II: LEARNING OBJECTIVES

- To understand the four basic principles of social stratification.
- To be able to differentiate between the caste and class system of stratification.
- To begin to understand the relationship between ideology and stratification.
- To be able to describe and differentiate between the structural-functional and social-conflict perspectives of stratification.
- To be able to describe the views of Max Weber concerning the dimensions of social class.
- To be able to describe the approach to understanding social stratification as presented by theLenskis.

PART III: KEY CONCEPTS

Fill in the blank spaces below with the appropriate concepts.

1. _____ _____ refers to a system by which a society ranks categories of people in a hierarchy.

2. Change in one's position in the social hierarchy is called _____ _____.

3. A _____ _____ refers to social stratification based on ascription, or birth.

4. A _____ _____ refers to social stratification based on both birth and individual achievement.

5. Social stratification based on personal merit is known as a _____.

6. _____ _____ refers to the degree of consistency in a person's social standing across various dimensions of social inequality.

7. _____ _____ _____ refers to a shift in the social position of large numbers of people due more to changes in society itself than to individual efforts.

8. _____ refers to cultural beliefs that justify social stratification.

9. The _____ _____ refers to the assertion that social stratification is a universal pattern because it benefits the operation of society.

10. _____ _____ refer to lower-prestige work that involves mostly manual labor.

11. _____ _____ refer to higher-prestige work that involves mostly mental activity.

12. _____ _____ (SES) refers to a composite ranking based on various dimensions of social inequality.

PART IV: IMPORTANT RESEARCHERS

In the space provided below each of the following researchers, write two or three sentences to help you remember his or her respective contributions to the field of sociology.

Karl Marx

Max Weber

Gerhard and Jean Lenski

Herbert Spencer

Kurt Vonnegut

Plato

Ralph Dahrendorf

Melvin Turin

PART V: STUDY QUESTIONS

True-False

1.	T	F	Social stratification is *universal*--found in all societies.
2.	T	F	*Ascription* is fundamental to social-stratification systems based on *castes*.
3.	T	F	*Social mobility* is defined as the system by which a society ranks categories of people in a hierarchy.
4.	T	F	A *meritocracy* is a social stratification system based on birth and other ascribed statuses.
5.	T	F	The *working class* is the largest segment of the population in *Great Britain*.
6.	T	F	Greater *income inequality* exists in the U.S. than in any other society in the world.
7.	T	F	*Ideology* refers to cultural beliefs that serve to justify social stratification.
8.	T	F	*Karl Marx's* social conflict theory of social stratification identified two basic relationships to the means of production--those who own productive property, and those who labor for others.
9.	T	F	Sociologist *Max Weber* developed a unidimensional model of social stratification which was dominant in the early part of the twentieth century.
10.	T	F	The *Kuznets curve* projects greater social inequality as industrial societies continue to advance technologically into postindustrial societies.

Multiple Choice

1. A system by which a society ranks categories of people in a hierarchy is called

    (a)   social inequality.
    (b)   meritocracy.
    (c)   social stratification.
    (d)   social mobility.

2. Which of the following principles is *not* a basic factor in explaining the existence of social stratification?

    (a)   Although universal, social stratification also varies in form.
    (b)   Social stratification persists over generations.
    (c)   Social stratification rests on widely held beliefs.
    (d)   Social stratification is a characteristic of society, not simply a function of individual differences.
    (e)   All are factors in explaining social stratification.

3. A change in one's position in a social hierarchy refers to

    (a)   ideology.
    (b)   social mobility.
    (c)   meritocracy.
    (d)   social inequality.
    (e)   endogamy.

4. What is a *caste system*?

    (a)   social stratification based on ascription
    (b)   social stratification based on meritocracy
    (c)   social stratification based on achievement
    (d)   any system in which there is social inequality

5. Which of the following is *not* one of the four *castes* in India's traditional caste system?

    (a)   Vaishya
    (b)   Jaishra
    (c)   Shudra
    (d)   Brahmin
    (e)   Kshatriya

6.   *Apartheid* became law in South Africa in

    (a)   1916.
    (b)   1971.
    (c)   1948.
    (d)   1876.

7.   What is the term for a system of social stratification based entirely on *personal merit*?

    (a)   classlessness
    (b)   meritocracy
    (c)   primogeniture
    (d)   egalitarianism

8.   Which of the characteristics that follow is/are most accurate in terms of *class systems*?

    (a)   They are more clearly defined than castes.
    (b)   They have variable status consistency.
    (c)   They have occupations based on ascription.
    (d)   all of the above
    (e)   none of the above

9.   What is the term for the degree of consistency in a person's social standing across various dimensions of social inequality?

    (a)   status consonance
    (b)   status congruity
    (c)   status balance
    (d)   status consistency

10.   In the Middle Ages, social stratification in England was a system of three

    (a)   open classes.
    (b)   absolute castes.
    (c)   meritocracies.
    (d)   closed classes.
    (e)   caste-like estates.

11.   The *United Kingdom* today is identified as a(n)

    (a)   neomonarchy.
    (b)   caste system.
    (c)   estate system.
    (d)   open estate system.
    (e)   class society.

12. In *feudal Japan*, the warrior caste was known as the

   (a)   samurai.
   (b)   shoguns.
   (c)   burakumin.
   (d)   gurukula.

13. What do sociologists call a shift in the social position of large numbers of people due more to changes in society itself than to individual efforts?

   (a)   perestroika
   (b)   bureaucratization
   (c)   linear social stratification
   (d)   structural social mobility

14. What is *ideology*?

   (a)   a system in which entire categories of people are ranked in a hierarchy
   (b)   ideas that are generated through scientific investigation
   (c)   views and opinions that are based on the principle of cultural relativism
   (d)   ideas that limit the amount of inequality of a society
   (e)   cultural beliefs that serve to justify social stratification

15. The *Davis-Moore thesis* asserts that

   (a)   social stratification has beneficial consequences for the operation of society.
   (b)   industrialization produces greater, and more harmful social stratification than previous forms of subsistence.
   (c)   social stratification based on meritocracy has dysfunctional consequences for society and its individual members.
   (d)   ideology undermines social stratification.
   (e)   industrial capitalism is moving toward a classless social order.

16. In Karl Marx's analysis of social stratification, another name for the working class is the

   (a)   primogeniture.
   (b)   perestroika.
   (c)   apparatchiks.
   (d)   proletariat.
   (e)   bourgeoisie.

17. Which of the following is *not* one of the dimensions of social stratification according to Max Weber?

    (a)   class
    (b)   education
    (c)   power
    (d)   status

18. According to the model of *sociocultural evolution* developed by *Gerhard* and *Jean Lenski,* social stratification is at its peak in

    (a)   hunting and gathering societies.
    (b)   postindustrial societies.
    (c)   large-scale agrarian societies.
    (d)   industrial societies.

19. The *Kuznets curve* suggests

    (a)   industrialization and social stratification are unrelated.
    (b)   industrial societies are represented by greater social inequality than agrarian societies.
    (c)   the emergence of postindustrial society may signal greater social inequality.
    (d)   greater technological sophistication is generally accompanied by greater social equality.

20. The novel by Kurt Vonnegut, Jr., about an imaginary account of a future United States concerned

    (a)   a society in which social inequality was abolished and was not as appealing as one might expect.
    (b)   a caste-like society in which extreme inequality has emerged from capitalist roots.
    (c)   a technocratic society in which human productive labor is no longer required.
    (d)   a return to an agrarian way of life in which social stratification was based on family lineage and land ownership.

Matching

1.   ____ Social stratification based on *ascription.*
2.   ____ Social stratification based on personal merit.
3.   ____ The degree of consistency in a person's social standing across various dimensions of social inequality
4.   ____ An economic program, meaning *restructuring,* developed by Mikhail Gorbachev.
5.   ____ Cultural beliefs that justify social stratification.
6.   ____ The assertion that social stratification is universal because it has beneficial consequences for the operation of society.
7.   ____ According to Karl Marx, the people who own and operate factories and other productive businesses in pursuit of profit.

8.   ___   According to Karl Marx, the people who sell their productive labor for wages.
9.   ___   Developed a multidimensional model of social class which included the variables of *class, status,* and *power*.
10.   ___   Reveals that greater *technological* sophistication is generally accompanied by more pronounced *social-stratification,* to a point.

a.	proletariat	f.	the Davis-Moore thesis
b.	perestroika	g.	Max Weber
c.	Kuznets curve	h.	status consistency
d.	capitalists	i.	meritocracy
e.	caste	j.	ideology

Fill-In

1. Social stratification is a matter of four *basic principles*: it is a characteristic of _____, not simply a reflection of individual differences; it _____ over generations; it is _____ but variable; and, it involves not just inequality but _____.
2. Caste systems mandate that people marry others of the same ranking. Sociologists call this pattern _____ *marriage*.
3. In feudal past of the United Kingdom, the *law of* _____ mandated that only the eldest son inherited property of parents.
4. In feudal Japan, the *warrior caste* was known as _____.
5. _____ *social mobility* refers to a shift in the social position of large numbers of people due more to changes in society itself than to individual efforts.
6. _____ refers to cultural beliefs that justify social stratification.
7. Four reasons listed in the text as to why there has been *no Marxist revolution*, these include the _____ of the capitalist class, a _____ standard of living, more extensive worker _____, and more extensive legal _____.
8. Advocates of *social-conflict analysis* believe that Karl Marx's analysis of capitalism is still largely valid. They offer the following reasons: wealth remains largely _____, _____ work offers little to workers, many benefits enjoyed by today's workers came about through the _____ Marx described, and the _____ still favors the private property of the rich.
9. The *Kuznets curve* shows that greater _____ sophistication is generally accompanied by more pronounced social stratification.
10. The authors of the _____ *Curve* argue that there is something called "general intelligence", that much of it is related to genetics, that it is important for the type of work required in the period of the Information Revolution, and that it is related to social class.

Discussion

1. What are the four *fundamental principles* of social stratification?
2. Briefly describe the social-stratification system of the *United Kingdom*.
3. What are the four reasons given in the text for why the *Marxist Revolution* has not occurred?
4. What are the basic qualities of a *caste system*?

5. List and discuss the components of *Max Weber's* multidimensional model of social stratification?
6. What are three criteria of the *Davis-Moore thesis*? What is your opinion of this thesis and its relevance for helping us understand our social stratification? What evidence exists in support of this thesis? What evidence exists that contradicts it?
7. Define *Karl Marx's* concepts of *proletariat* and *capitalists*. What value does Marx's perspective offer to the understanding of modern social stratification?
8. Review the basic points being made by *Gerhard* and *Jean Lenski* concerning global inequality in historical perspective.
9. Describe the *second Russian Revolution*.
10. Provide an illustration of *structural social mobility* in our society.

PART VI: ANSWERS TO STUDY QUESTIONS

Key Concepts

1. Social stratification (p. 247)
2. social mobility (p. 248)
3. caste system (p. 248)
4. class system (p. 250)
5. meritocracy (p. 250)
6. Status consistency (p. 251)
7. Structural social mobility (p. 255)
8. Ideology (p. 256)
9. Davis-Moore thesis (p. 257)
10. Blue-collar occupations (p. 260)
11. White-collar occupation (p. 260)
12. Socioeconomic status (SES) (p. 261)

True-False

1.	T	(p. 248)	6.	F	(p. 255)
2.	T	(p. 248)	7.	T	(p. 256)
3.	F	(p. 248)	8.	T	(p. 259)
4.	F	(p. 250)	9.	F	(p. 261)
5.	T	(p. 252)	10.	T	(p. 263)

Multiple Choice

1.	c	(p. 247)	11.	e	(p. 252)
2.	e	(p. 248)	12.	a	(p. 253)
3.	b	(p. 248)	13.	d	(p. 255)
4.	a	(p. 248)	14.	e	(p. 256)
5.	b	(pp. 248-249)	15.	a	(p. 257)
6.	c	(p. 250)	16.	d	(p. 259)
7.	b	(p. 250)	17.	b	(p. 261)
8.	b	(p. 250-251)	18.	c	(p. 262)
9.	d	(p. 251)	19.	c	(p. 263)
10.	e	(p. 252)	20.	a	(p. 265)

Matching

1.	e	(p. 248)	6.	f	(p. 257)
2.	i	(p. 250)	7.	d	(p. 259)
3.	h	(p. 251)	8.	a	(p. 259)
4.	b	(p. 254)	9.	g	(p. 261)
5.	j	(p. 256)	10.	c	(p. 263)

Fill-In

1. society, persists, universal, beliefs (p. 248)
2. endogamous (p. 249)
3. primogeniture (p. 252)
4. samurai (p. 253)
5. Structural (p. 255)
6. Ideology (p. 256)
7. fragmentation, higher, organizations, protections (p. 260)
8. concentrated, white-collar, social conflict, law (p. 261)
9. technological (p. 263)
10. Bell (pp. 266-267)

PART VII: IN FOCUS--IMPORTANT ISSUES

• What is Social Stratification?

What are the four basic *principles of social stratification*?

1.
2.
3.
4.

- Caste and Class Systems

  Identify three major characteristics of a *caste system.*

  Identify three major characteristics of a *class system.*

  What are the Functions of Social Stratification?

  What is the *Davis-Moore thesis?*

  What is the evidence that this thesis is valid?

  What are three major criticisms of this thesis?

- Stratification and Conflict

  What was Karl Marx's argument about *class and conflict?*

  What is the evidence that Marx's view is still relevant today?

  What are four reasons why a *Marxist Revolution* has not occurred in capitalist societies?

Define each of the three *dimensions of social stratification* as identified by Max Weber.

class

status

power

- Stratification and Technology: A Global Perspective

According to the *Kuznets curve*, describe the relationship between technology and social stratification throughout history:

hunting and gathering societies

horticultural, pastoral, and agrarian

industrial societies

postindustrial societies

- Social Stratification: Facts and Values

What are the major questions being raised by the novel by Kurt Vonnegut, Jr. cited in the text concerning social stratification?

Chapter 11 | Social Class in the United States

PART I: CHAPTER OUTLINE

I.   Dimensions of Social Inequality
    A.   Income
    B.   Wealth
    C.   Power
    D.   Occupational Prestige
    E.   Schooling

II. Social Stratification and Birth
    A.   Ancestry
    B.   Gender
    C.   Race and Ethnicity
    D.   Religion

III. Social Classes in the United States
    A.   The Upper Class
        1.   Upper-Uppers
        2.   Lower-Uppers
    B.   The Middle Class
        1.   Upper-Middles
        2.   Average-Middles
    C.   The Working Class
    D.   The Lower Class

IV. The Difference Class Makes
    A.   Health
    B.   Values
    C.   Politics
    D.   Family and Gender

V.   Social Mobility
    A.   Myth Versus Reality
        1.   Mobility by Income Level
        2.   Mobility: Race, Ethnicity, and Gender
    B.   The American Dream: Still A Reality?

VI. The Global Economy and the U.S. Class Structure

VII. Poverty in the United States
    A.   The Extent of U.S. Poverty

PART II: LEARNING OBJECTIVES

- To have a clear sense of the extent of social inequality in the United States.
- To critically consider the meaning of the concept of socioeconomic status, and to be aware of its dimensions.
- To recognize the role of economic resources, power, occupational prestige, and schooling in the class system of the United States.
- To be able to identify and trace the significance of various ascribed statuses for the construction and maintenance of social stratification in the United States.
- To see the significance of the global economy and its impact on our economic system.
- To be able to generally describe the various social classes in our social stratification system.
- To become aware of how health, values, family life, and gender are related to our social-class system.
- To begin to develop a sociological sense about the nature of social mobility in the United States.
- To develop a general understanding of the demographics of poverty in the United States.
- To become aware and critical of different explanations of poverty.
- To develop an awareness of the problem of homelessness in the United States.
- To appreciate some of the dilemmas involved in public assistance and welfare reform.

PART III: KEY CONCEPTS

Fill in the following blank spaces with the appropriate concepts.

1. _____ refers to wages or salary from work and earnings from investments.
2. _____ refers to the total value of money and other assets, minus outstanding debts.
3. _____ _____ _____ refers to a change in social position occurring during a person's lifetime.

4. _____ _____ _____ refers to upward or downward social mobility of children in relation to their parents.

5. The deprivation of some people in relation to those who have more is known as _____ _____.

6. A deprivation of resources that is life threatening is referred to as _____ _____. The _____ ___ _____ refers to the trend by which women represent an increasing proportion of the poor.

PART IV: IMPORTANT RESEARCHERS

In the space provided below each of the following researchers, write two or three sentences to help you remember his or her respective contributions to sociology.

William Julius Wilson   Edward Banfield

Oscar Lewis   Max Weber

Elizabeth Bott

PART V: STUDY QUESTIONS

<u>True-False</u>

1.	T	F	*Wealth* in the United States is distributed more equally than income.
2.	T	F	Recent government calculations place the wealth of the average U.S. family at about $50,100.
3.	T	F	When financial assets are balanced against debits, the lowest--ranking 40 percent of families in the U.S. have virtually no wealth at all.
4.	T	F	The *working class* is the largest social class in the United States.
5.	T	F	Cultural values vary by social class. *Affluent* people with greater education and financial security are more tolerant of controversial behavior such as homosexuality.
6.	T	F	Parents in *working-class* families are characterized by an emphasis on *conformity* to conventional beliefs and practices, more so than are middle- class families.
7.	T	F	*Intragenerational social mobility* refers to a change in social position occurring during a person's lifetime.
8.	T	F	The *middle-class slide* is an example of downward structural mobility.
9.	T	F	The concept *culture of poverty* is a term relating poverty to a lower-class subculture that inhibits personal achievement and foster resignation.
10.	T	F	People in the U.S. are more likely to blame *social injustice* rather than *personal laziness* for poverty compared to people in other industrialized societies.

Multiple Choice

1. People in the United States tend to *underestimate* the amount of inequality that exists in our society. Which of the following is *not* a reason for this phenomenon?

    (a)   We embrace the legal principle of equality.
    (b)   We are an affluent society.
    (c)   We emphasize statuses conferred at birth.
    (d)   Our culture celebrates individual autonomy and achievement.
    (e)   In principle, the law gives equal standing to all.

2. Census Bureau data show that *income* and *wealth* are unequally distributed in the United States. Which of the following statements is most accurate?

    (a)   The median household income in the United States in 2000 was $68,036.
    (b)   The top five percent of households (by income) receive sixty-five percent of the income earned in the United States.
    (c)   The poorest twenty percent of households only receive ten percent of the income earned in the United States
    (d)   Wealth is distributed more unequally in the United States than is income.

3. Recent government calculations put the *wealth* of the average U.S. household at about

    (a) $10,000.
    (b) $25,000.
    (c) $38,000.
    (d) $50,000.
    (e) $71,600.

4. *Education* is distributed unequally in the U.S. as evidenced by the fact that

    (a)   about twenty-five percent of the adult population on has a college education.
    (b)   only about fifty-five percent of the adult population has a high school education.
    (c)   thirty percent of adults have not completed high school.
    (d)   all of the above

5. In 2000, African American families earned _____ percent of that earned by white families.

    (a)   90
    (b)   84
    (c)   73
    (d)   64
    (e)   55

6.   The *median* wealth for minority families, including African Americans, Hispanics, and Asians (about $16,400), is just _____ percent of the median for white households.

      (a)   fifty
      (b)   eight
      (c)   sixty-five
      (d)   seventeen

7.   The *middle class* includes approximately what percentage of the U.S. population?

      (a)   20-25
      (b)   40-45
      (c)   30-35
      (d)   55-60

8.   Which of the following is inaccurate about the *Social Register*?

      (a)   It lists families, not individuals.
      (b)   It lists addresses and phone numbers.
      (c)   It lists occupations.
      (d)   It lists schools attended by a family's children.

9.   In 2000, the federal government officially classified _____ percent of the U.S. population as being *poor*.

      (a)   8.2
      (b)   11.3
      (c)   18.5
      (d)   22.7

10.   The term *conspicuous consumption* refers to

      (a)   the practice of buying things to get noticed.
      (b)   purchasing food and other necessities.
      (c)   items purchased by the poor using public assistance funds.
      (d)   buying items on credit.

11.   Which of the following statements is/are accurate regarding general patterns in our society?

      (a)   Working-class parents tend to encourage children to conform to conventional norms and obey and respect authority.
      (b)   Middle-class parents tend to teach children to express their individuality.
      (c)   Most working-class couples divide their responsibilities according to gender.
      (d)   Middle-class couples tend to be more egalitarian than working-class couples.
      (e)   all of the above

12. Regarding *politics*, which of the following is most accurate?

   (a) Wealthier people tend to support the Democratic Party.
   (b) Higher income people are less likely to vote than poorer people.
   (c) On social issues, wealthier and more highly educated people tend to be more liberal than people of lower social standing.
   (d) People of lower social standing are more conservative on economic issues than wealthier people.

13. What does research reveal about *social mobility* in the United States?

   (a) Social mobility, at least among men, has been relatively low.
   (b) The long-term trend in social mobility has been downward.
   (c) Within a single generation, social mobility is usually dramatic, not incremental.
   (d) The short-term trend has been stagnation, with some income polarization.

14. A change in social position of children relative to that of their parents is called

   (a) horizontal social mobility.
   (b) structural social mobility.
   (c) intergenerational social mobility.
   (d) intragenerational social mobility.

15. What evidence exists to suggest that there is *income stagnation* in our society in recent years?

   (a) For many workers, earnings have stalled.
   (b) Multiple-job holding is up.
   (c) More jobs offer little income.
   (d) More young people are remaining at home.
   (e) all of the above

16. Which of the following statements is/are accurate?

   (a) Most young people aged eighteen to twenty-four are now living with their parents.
   (b) Over the last twenty years the earnings gap between women and men has been narrowing.
   (c) In 2000, women in the U.S. earned approximately seventy-four percent of what men earned.
   (d) The percentage of workers who the government classifies as "low-income workers" has increased since 1979.
   (e) All of the above are accurate statements.

17. For a family of four, the 2000 poverty line was set at

   (a) 17,603.
   (b) 9,453.
   (c) 26,068.
   (d) 12,892.

18. Poverty statistics in the United States reveal that

(a) the elderly are more likely than any other age group to be poor.
(b) almost 70 percent of all African Americans are poor.
(c) urban and suburban poverty rates are considerably higher than rural poverty rates.
(d) about 61 percent of poor people over the age eighteen are female.

19. The *culture of poverty* view concerning the causes of poverty

(a) holds that the poor are primarily responsible for their own poverty.
(b) blames poverty on economic stagnation relating to the globalization of the U.S. economy.
(c) sees lack of ambition on the part of the poor as a consequence, not a cause for poverty.
(d) views the conservative economic policies of the last two decades in the U.S. as the primary reason for relatively high poverty rates.

20. What does sociologist William Julius Wilson see as a solution to the problem of *inner-city poverty*?

(a) busing children to better schools
(b) improving welfare programs
(c) creating jobs
(d) enforcing the law

Matching

1. ___ The total value of money and other assets, minus outstanding debts.
2. ___ Encompasses 40 to 45 percent of the U.S. population and exerts a tremendous influence on U.S. culture.
3. ___ Accounts for about one-third of the U.S. population.
4. ___ A change in social position occurring within a person's lifetime.
5. ___ Upward or downward social mobility of children in relation to their parents.
6. ___ A form of downward structural social mobility.
7. ___ The deprivation of some people in relation to those who have more.
8. ___ Describes the trend by which women represent an increasing proportion of the poor.
9. ___ Developed the concept of the *culture of poverty*, or a lower-class subculture that inhibits personal achievement and fosters resignation to one's plight.
10. ___ Argued that *society* is primarily responsible for poverty and that any lack of ambition on the part of the poor is a *consequence* of insufficient opportunity.

a. William Julius Wilson
b. intergenerational social mobility
c. feminization of poverty
d. wealth
e. intragenerational social mobility

f. the working-class
g. Oscar Lewis
h. the middle-class
i. the middle-class slide
j. relative poverty

<u>Fill-In</u>

1. We underestimate the extent of stratification in the United States for several reasons, including: In principle, the law gives _____ standing to all, our culture celebrates individual _____ and _____, we tend to _____ with people like ourselves, and the United States is an _____ society.

2. When financial assets are balanced against debits, the lowest-ranking _____ percent of U.S. families have virtually no *wealth* at all.

3. Much of the disparity in income between whites and African Americans is due to the larger share of single-parent families among African Americans. Comparing only families headed by *married couples*, African-Americans earn _____ percent as much as whites.

4. While the relationship between social class and politics is complex, generally, members of high social standing tend to have _____ *views on economic issues* and _____ *views on social issues*.

5. Evidence of "income stagnation" in the United States today includes: for many workers, earnings have _____, _____ job-holding is up, more jobs offer little _____, and young people are remaining _____.

6. In the United States in 2000, the poverty rate in *urban* areas (inner-cites and suburbs) was _____ percent and in *rural* areas was _____ percent.

7. _____ percent of poor families *own their homes.*

8. *Conservatives* see a clear connection between being poor and being _____.

9. Compared to other industrial societies, more of the U.S. population attributes poverty to _____ and personal _____ rather than societal _____.

10. Welfare reform has included replacing the federal AFDC program with TANF or _____ _____ _____ _____ _____, a program with funding for new state-run programs.

<u>Definition and Short-Answer</u>

1. What are some of the reasons why people in the United States might tend to underestimate the extent of social inequality in our society?

2. What are the basic components of *socioeconomic status*? How are they measured? How do these components differ from Max Weber's components of social class?

3. To what extent do *ascribed statuses* affect a person's place in our social-stratification system? Provide examples using the variables of race, ethnicity, and gender.

4. Using the factors of health, values, and politics, discuss the difference social class makes in the lives of people within our society.

5. Identify six significant *demographic characteristics* of the poor in our society today.

6. What is meant by the term *culture of poverty*? What policies and programs do you think could be instituted to counteract this phenomenon?

7. What is meant by the term *femininization of poverty*? What can be done to reverse this trend in our society?

8. Review the basic points being made by *Gerhard* and *Jean Lenski* concerning global inequality in historical perspective.

9. What are the four general conclusions being made about *social mobility* in the United States today?

10. What is the evidence that the *American Dream* is waning in our society?

PART VI: ANSWERS TO STUDY QUESTIONS

Key Concepts

1. Income (p. 272)
2. Wealth (pp. 272-273)
3. Intragenerational social mobility (p. 282)
4. Intergenerational social mobility (p. 282)
5. relative poverty (p. 285)
6. absolute poverty (p. 285)
7. feminization of poverty (p. 287)

True-False

1.	F	(p. 272)	6.	T	(p. 281)
2.	F	(p. 273)	7.	T	(p. 282)
3.	T	(p. 273)	8.	T	(p. 285)
4.	F	(pp. 278-279)	9.	T	(p. 290)
5.	T	(p. 281)	10.	F	(p. 295)

Multiple Choice

1.	c	(p. 271)	11.	e	(pp. 281-282)
2.	d	(p. 273)	12.	c	(p. 281)
3.	e	(p. 273)	13.	d	(pp. 282-283)
4.	a	(p. 274)	14.	c	(p. 282)
5.	d	(p. 275)	15.	e	(pp. 284)
6.	d	(p. 275)	16.	e	(pp. 283-284)
7.	b	(p. 278)	17.	a	(p. 286)
8.	c	(p. 279)	18.	d	(p. 287)
9.	b	(p. 280)	19.	a	(p. 290)
10.	a	(p. 281)	20.	c	(p. 291)

Matching

1.	d	(pp. 272-273)	6.	i	(p. 285)
2.	h	(p. 278)	7.	j	(p. 286)
3.	f	(p. 279)	8.	c	(p. 287)
4.	e	(p. 282)	9.	g	(p. 290)
5.	b	(p. 282)	10.	a	(p. 290)

Fill-In

1. equal, autonomy, achievement, interact, affluent (p. 271)
2. 40 (p. 273)
3. 85 (p. 275)
4. conservative, liberal (p. 281)

5.   stalled, multiple, income, home (p. 284)
6.   10.8, 13.4 (p. 289)
7.   41 (p. 289)
8.   unmarried (p. 294)
9.   laziness, failure, injustice (p.295)
10   Temporary Assistance for Needy Families (p. 295)

PART VII: IN FOCUS--IMPORTANT ISSUES

- Dimensions of Social Inequality

    Our author suggests that U.S. society is *highly stratified*. What are two pieces of evidence that support this view?

    Identify the five variables discussed in the text which are used to determine the *socioeconomic status* of a household.

    Briefly describe how each of these variables is distributed in the United States today.

- Social Stratification and Birth

    In what five ways does the ascribed status of *birth* affect a person's status in our social class system? Provide evidence for two of these as influencing one's social class status.

- Social Classes In the United States

  Briefly describe each of the following *social classes* in the United States.

    the upper class

      upper-uppers

      lower-uppers

    the middle class

      upper-middles

      middle-middles

    the working class

    the lower class

- The Difference Class Makes

  Social stratification affects many dimensions of our lives. How are each of the following connected to social class?

    health

    values

    politics

    family and gender

- Social Mobility

  What are the four *general conclusions* being made in the text concerning social mobility in the United States?

  1.

  2.

  3.

  4.

  What are the four pieces of evidence identified in the text suggesting that upward social mobility in the United states is becoming harder to achieve, particularly for middle-class families?

  1.

  2.

  3.

  4.

- Poverty in the United States

  Describe the *demographics of poverty* using the following variables.

  age

  race and ethnicity

  gender and family patterns

  urban and rural poverty

Briefly summarize the following two *explanations of poverty*.

blame the poor

blame society

Research suggest that there are more *homeless* people in our society than ever before. Identify two examples for each of the following explanations for this increase.

personal traits

societal factors

<table>
<tr><td>Chapter</td><td rowspan="2"></td><td rowspan="2"># Global
Stratification</td></tr>
<tr><td>**12**</td></tr>
</table>

Chapter 12 — Global Stratification

PART I: CHAPTER OUTLINE

I.   Global Stratification: An Overview
   A.   A Word About Terminology
   B.   High-Income Countries
   C.   Middle-Income Countries
   D.   Low-Income Countries
II.   Global Wealth and Poverty
   A.   The Severity of Poverty
       1.   Relative Versus Absolute Poverty
   B.   The Extent of Poverty
   C.   Poverty and Children
   D.   Poverty and Women
   E.   Slavery
   F.   Correlates of Global Poverty
III.   Global Stratification: Theoretical Analysis
   A.   Modernization Theory
       1.   Historical Perspective
       2.   The Importance of Culture
       3.   Rostow's Stages of Modernization
       4.   The Role of Rich Nations
   B.   Dependency Theory
       1.   Historical Perspective
       2.   The Importance of Colonialism
       3.   Wallerstein's Capitalist World Economy
       4.   The Role of Rich Nations
IV.   Global Stratification: Looking Ahead
V.   Summary
VI.   Key Concepts
VII.   Critical-Thinking Questions
VIII.   Applications and Exercises
IX.   Sites to See

PART II: LEARNING OBJECTIVES

- To be able to define and describe the demographics of the three "economic development" categories used to classify nations of the world.
- To begin to understand both the severity and extensiveness of poverty in the low-income nations of the world.
- To recognize the extent to which women are overrepresented among the poor of the world and the factors leading to this condition.
- To be able to identify and define the different types of human slavery that still exists around the globe.
- To be able to identify and discuss the correlates of global poverty.
- To be able to identify and discuss the two major theories used to explain global inequality.
- To be able to identify and describe the stages of modernization.
- To be able to recognize the problems facing women as a result of modernization in the low-income nations of the world.
- To be able to identify the keys to combating global inequality over the next century.

PART III: KEY CONCEPTS

Fill in the blank spaces below with the appropriate concepts..

1. _____ refers to the process by which some nations enrich themselves through political and economic control of other nations.
2. _____ is a new form of global power relationships that involves not direct political control but economic exploitation by multinational corporations.
3. A large business that operates in many countries is known as a _____ _____.
4. _____ _____ is a model of economic and social development that explains global inequality in terms of technological and cultural differences between societies.
5. _____ _____ is a model of economic and social development that explains global inequality in terms of the historical exploitation of poor societies by rich ones.

PART IV: IMPORTANT RESEARCHERS

In the space provided below each of the following researchers, write two or three sentences to help you remember his respective contributions to sociology.

Immanuel Wallerstein   W. W. Rostow

PART V: STUDY QUESTIONS

<u>True-False</u>

1. T   F   Global income is so concentrated, even people in the United States with incomes *below the government's poverty line* live far better than the majority of the earth's people.
2. T   F   The richest twenty percent of the global population receive about fifty percent of all the *income*.
3. T   F   *High-income countries*, representing about eighteen percent of humanity, control over one-half of the world's income.
4. T   F   Approximately fifty percent of the world's population live in *low-income countries*.
5. T   F   The United States has the highest *quality of life score* in the world.
6. T   F   *Modernization theory* suggests the greatest barrier to economic development is *tradition*.
7. T   F   *Immanuel Wallerstein's* capitalist world economy model is used to illustrate and support *dependency theory*.
8. T   F   According to *dependency theory*, global inequality must be seen in terms of the distribution of wealth, as opposed to highlighting the productivity of wealth.
9. T   F   Empirical evidence indicates that most countries of the world are now providing living standards that are better than the living standards of two or three decades ago.
10. T   F   As low-income countries increase the standard of living for their citizens, *stress* on the *physical environment* is expected to be reduced.

<u>Multiple Choice</u>

1. The poorest twenty percent of the world's nations controls _____ percent of the *global income*.

    (a)   12
    (b)   10
    (c)   15
    (d)   1
    (e)   5

2. The *high-income countries*, representing 18 percent of the world's population, control over _____ percent of the world's income.

    (a)   25
    (b)   35
    (c)   50
    (d)   80

3.   Which of the following statements concerning the *high-income countries* is/are accurate?

(a)   Taken together, countries with the most developed economies cover roughly twenty-five percent of the earth's land area.
(b)   About three-fourths of the people in high-income countries live in or near cities.
(c)   Significant cultural differences exist among high-income countries.
(d)   Production in rich nations is capital-intensive.
(e)   All of the above are accurate statements.

4.   Which of the following is an *inaccurate* statement concerning *middle-income countries*?

(a)   In middle-income countries, per capita income ranges between $2,500 and $10,000.
(b)   About one-third of the people in middle-income countries still live in rural areas.
(c)   One cluster of middle-income countries includes the former Soviet Union and the nations of Eastern Europe.
(d)   Taken together, middle-income countries span roughly sixty-five percent of the earth's land area.

5.   *Middle-income countries* cover _____ percent of the earth's land area and contain slightly more than _____ percent of humanity.

(a)   47/50
(b)   30/80
(c)   25/15
(d)   10/25
(e)   65/30

6.   What percentage of the world's population lives in the *low-income countries* of the world?

(a)   52
(b)   28
(c)   77
(d)   85
(e)   95

7.   The nickname of the *Manila dump* is

(a)   Rohooven Heights.
(b)   Svendoven Mire.
(c)   Swollen Hollow.
(d)   Smokey Mountain.

8. The *per-capita GDP* in the United States in 1999 was

    (a) $10,033.
    (b) $51,300.
    (c) $15,400.
    (d) $31,872.

9. Half of all deaths in *low-income countries* occur among

    (a)   elderly people beyond the age of 65.
    (b)   children under the age of 10.
    (c)   adults between the age of 40 and 59.
    (d)   young adults aged 18-35.

10. Which of the following is *inaccurate*?

    (a)   Families in poor societies typically do not depend on women's incomes.
    (b)   In high-income countries, the median age at death is over 65 years of age.
    (c)   The United Nations estimates that in poor countries men own 90 percent of the land.
    (d)   About 70 percent of the world's 1 billion people living near absolute poverty are women.

11. Which of the following is *not* a type of *slavery* identified in the text?

    (a)   chattel
    (b)   child
    (c)   colonial
    (d)   servile forms of marriage
    (e)   debt bondage

12. Which of the following is *not* discussed as a correlate of *global poverty*?

    (a)   gender inequality
    (b)   population growth
    (c)   technology
    (d)   social stratification
    (e)   all are discussed

13. *Neocolonialism* is

    (a)   primarily an overt political force.
    (b)   a form of economic exploitation that does not involve formal political control.
    (c)   the economic power of the low-income countries being used to control the consumption patterns in the high-income countries.
    (d)   the exploitation of the high-income countries by the low-income countries.
    (e)   none of the above

14. A model of economic and social development that explains global inequality in terms of technological and cultural differences among societies is _____ theory.

    (a) colonial
    (b) dependency
    (c) modernization
    (d) ecological

15. *Modernization theory* identifies _____ as the greatest barrier to economic development.

    (a) technology
    (b) social equality
    (c) social power
    (d) tradition

16. Which of the following is *not* a stage in *Rostow's model of modernization*?

    (a) colonialism
    (b) traditional
    (c) take-off
    (d) drive to technological maturity
    (e) high mass consumption

17. According to *W. W. Rostow's* modernization model, which stage is Thailand currently in?

    (a) traditional
    (b) take-off
    (c) drive to technological maturity
    (d) residual-dependency

18. Which of the following is *not* a criticism of modernization theory?

    (a) It tends to minimize the connection between rich and poor societies.
    (b) It tends to blame the low-income countries for their own poverty.
    (c) It ignores historical facts that thwart development in poor countries.
    (d) It has held up the world's most developed countries are the standard for judging the rest of humanity.
    (e) All are criticisms of this theory.

19. _____ *theory* is a model of economic and social development that explains global inequality in terms of the historical exploitation of poor societies by rich ones.

    (a)   Modernization
    (b)   Colonial
    (c)   Dependency
    (d)   Evolutionary
    (e)   Ecological

20. Which of the following is an *inaccurate* statement regarding *global stratification*?

    (a)   According to the United Nations, one-third of the world's countries are living better than they were in the past.

    (b)   One insight, offered by modernization theory, is that poverty is partly a problem of technology.

    (c)   One insight, derived from dependency theory, is that global inequality is also a political issue.

    (d)   While economic development increases living standards, it also establishes a context for less strain being placed on the environment.

Matching

1. ____ Percentage of the world's income controlled by the poorest fifth of the world's population.
2. ____ Two high-income countries.
3. ____ Two middle-income countries.
4. ____ The percentage of people in low-income countries who live in cities.
5. ____ The percentage of the world's population living in low-income countries.
6. ____ The percentage of births attended by trained health personnel in Brazil.
7. ____ The process by which some nations enrich themselves through political and economic control of other nations.
8. ____ Huge businesses that operate in many countries.
9. ____ A model of economic and social development that explains global inequality in terms of technological and cultural differences among societies.
10. ____ A model of economic and social development that explains global inequality in terms of the historical exploitation of poor societies by rich ones.

a.	Chile and Malaysia	f.	28
b.	modernization theory	g.	Canada and Singapore
c.	multinational corporations	h.	88
d.	colonialism	i.	dependency theory
e.	1	j.	31

158

1. According to the author, compared to the older "three worlds" model, the new classification system used in the text has two main advantages, including a focus on the single most important dimension that underlies social life--_____ _____.

2. According to our author, poverty in *low-income countries* is more _____ and more _____ than it is in the United States.

3. The *correlates of global poverty* include: _____, population _____, _____ patterns, social _____, _____ inequality, and global _____ relationships.

4. _____ is a new form of economic exploitation that does not involve formal political control.

5. *W. W. Rostow's* stages of modernization include: the _____, _____, drive to _____ maturity, and high mass _____.

6. _____ *theory* maintains that global poverty historically stems from the exploitation of poor societies by rich societies.

7. Immanuel Wallerstein calls the *rich nations* the _____ of the world economy, while he says the *low-income countries* represent the _____ of the world economy.

8. *Modernization theory* maintains that rich societies _____ through capital investment and technological innovation.

9. *Dependency theory* claims that the world economy makes poor nations dependent on rich ones. This dependency involves three factors: narrow, _____ *economies*, lack of _____ *capacity*, and _____ *debt*.

10. Two keys to combating global inequality during this century will be seeing it partly as a problem of _____ and that it is also a _____ issue.

1. Define the terms *high-income, middle-income,* and *low-income countries*. Identify the key characteristics of each category. Does this resolve the "terminology" problem?

2. How do the economies in each of the three *levels* or *categories* of countries differ from one another? Make specific reference to *Figures 11-1* and *11-2* in your answer.

3. What factors create the condition of *women* being overrepresented in poverty around the world?

4. What are the *correlates* of global poverty? Describe each.

5. What is *neocolonialism*? Provide an illustration.

6. What are the four stages of *modernization* in Rostow's model of societal change and development?

7. What are the *problems* faced by women in poor countries as a result of modernization?

8. According to *modernization* theorists, in what respects are rich nations part of the solution to global poverty?

9. Differentiate between how *modernization theory* and *dependency theory* view the primary causes of global inequality. Critique each of these theories, identifying the strengths and weaknesses of each in terms of explaining global poverty. How do each differ in terms of recommendations to improve the conditions in low-income countries?

10. Write an essay about *poverty in low-income countries*. What are the statistics of *global poverty*?

PART VI: ANSWERS TO STUDY QUESTIONS

Key Concepts

1. Colonialism (p. 309)
2. Neocolonialism (p. 309)
3. multinational corporation (p. 309)
4. Modernization theory (p. 310)
5. Dependency theory (p. 315)

True-False

1.	T	(p. 299)	6.	T	(p. 311)
2.	F	(pp. 300-301)	7.	T	(p. 315)
3.	T	(pp. 300-301)	8.	T	(p. 316)
4.	F	(p. 302)	9.	F	(pp. 319-320)
5.	F	(p. 304)	10.	F	(p. 320)

Multiple Choice

1.	d	(p. 300)	11.	c	(pp. 307-308)
2.	c	(pp. 300-301)	12.	e	(p. 308)
3.	e	(pp. 300-301)	13.	b	(p. 309)
4.	d	(p. 302)	14.	c	(p. 310)
5.	a	(p. 302)	15.	d	(p. 311)
6.	b	(p. 302)	16.	a	(p. 312)
7.	d	(p. 303)	17.	b	(p. 312)
8.	d	(p. 304)	18.	e	(p. 314)
9.	b	(p. 306)	19.	c	(p. 315)
10.	a	(pp. 305-307)	20.	d	(p. 320)

Matching

1.	e	(p. 300)	6.	h	(p. 308)
2.	g	(p. 300)	7.	d	(p. 309)
3.	a	(p. 301)	8.	c	(p. 309)
4.	j	(p. 302)	9.	b	(p. 310)
5.	f	(p. 302)	10.	i	(p. 315)

Fill-In

1. economic development (p. 300)
2. severe, extensive (pp. 303 and 305)
3. technology, growth, cultural, stratification, gender, power (pp. 308-309)

4.   Neocolonialism (p. 309)
5.   traditional, take-off, technological, consumption (p. 312)
6.   Dependency (p. 315)
7.   core, periphery (p. 316)
8.   produce wealth (p. 316)
9.   export-oriented, industrial, foreign (p. 316)
10.   technology, political (p. 320)

PART VII: IN FOCUS—IMPORTANT ISSUES

- Global Stratification

  Describe the general characteristics for each of the following categories of countries.

  high-income countries

  middle-income countries

  low-income-countries

- Global Wealth and Poverty

  What is the evidence that poverty in poor countries is *more severe* and *more extensive* than in the rich nations?

  Identify and illustrate the four types of *slavery* found around the world.

Describe how each of the following are *correlates of poverty*.

technology

population growth

cultural patterns

social stratification

gender inequality

global power relationships

- Global Stratification: Theoretical Analysis

What are the major tenets of *modernization theory*?

Outline and describe *Rostow's stages of modernization*.

According to modernization theory, what is the *role of rich nations* in terms of global stratification?

What are the five basic *criticisms* of modernization theory?

162

What are the basic tenets of *dependency theory*?

According to Immanuel Wallerstein, what are the three factors involved in the dependency of poor nations on rich nations?

What are the five basic *criticisms* of dependency theory?

- Global Stratification: Looking Ahead

What is the evidence that global stratification is both an issue of *technology* and *politics*?

What do you suggest can be done to reduce the polarization of high-income and low-income countries?

Chapter 13 Gender Stratification

PART I: CHAPTER OUTLINE

I.   Gender and Inequality
    A.   Male-Female Differences
    B.   Gender In Global Perspective
        1.   The Israeli Kibbutzim
        2.   Margaret Mead's Research
        3.   George Murdock's Research
        4.   In Sum: Gender and Culture
    C.   Patriarchy and Sexism
        1.   The Cost of Sexism
        2.   Is Patriarchy Inevitable?
III. Gender and Socialization
    A.   Gender and the Family
    B.   Gender and the Peer Group
    C.   Gender and Schooling
    D.   Gender and the Mass Media
IV.   Gender and Social Stratification
    A.   Working Women and Men
        1.   Gender and Occupations
    B.   Housework
    C.   Gender, Income, and Wealth
    D.   Gender and Education
    E.   Gender and Politics
    F.   Gender and the Military
    G.   Are Women A Minority?
    H.   Minority Women
    I.   Violence Against Women
        1.   Sexual Harassment
        2.   Pornography

PART II: LEARNING OBJECTIVES

- To know the distinction between male-female differences and gender stratification.
- To become aware of the various types of social organizations found globally based upon the relationship between females and males.
- To be able to describe the link between patriarchy and sexism, and to see how the nature of each is changing in modern society.
- To be able to describe the role that gender plays in socialization in the family, the peer group, schooling, the mass media, and adult interaction.
- To see how gender stratification occurs in the work world, education, and politics.
- To consider key arguments in the debate over whether women constitute a minority.
- To consider how the structural-functional and social-conflict paradigms help explain the origins and persistence of gender inequality.
- To begin to recognize the extent to which women are victims of violence, and to begin to understand what we can do to change this problem.
- To consider the central ideas of feminism, the variations of feminism, and resistance to feminism.

PART III: KEY CONCEPTS

1.   _____ refers to the personal traits and social positions that members of a society attach to being female and male.
2.   _____ _____ refers to the unequal distribution of wealth, power, and privilege between men and women.
3.   _____ is a form of social organization in which males dominate females.
4.   _____ is a form of social organization in which females dominate males.
5.   _____ refers to the belief that one sex is innately superior to the other.

6. Attitudes and activities that a society links to each sex refers to _____ _____.
7. A _____ refers to any category of people, distinguished by physical or cultural difference, that a society sets apart and subordinates.
8. _____ _____ refers to comments, gestures, or physical contact of a sexual nature that are deliberate, repeated, and unwelcome.
9. _____ refers to the advocacy of social equality for men and women, in opposition to patriarchy and sexism.

PART IV: IMPORTANT RESEARCHERS

Margaret Mead   George Murdock

Talcott Parsons   Janet Lever

Jesse Bernard   Carol Gilligan

Friedrich Engels   Felice Schwartz

PART V: STUDY QUESTIONS

True-False

1.   T   F   *Gender* refers to the biological distinction between females and males.
2.   T   F   The experience of the *Israeli Kibbutzim* suggests that cultures have considerable latitude in defining what is masculine and feminine.
3.   T   F   The conclusions made by *Margaret Mead* in her research on three New Guinea societies is consistent with the sociobiological argument that "persistent biological distinctions may undermine gender equality."
4.   T   F   *George Murdock's* cross-cultural research has shown some general patterns in terms of which type of activities are classified as *masculine* or *feminine;* however, beyond this general pattern, significant variation exists.
5.   T   F   Carol Gilligan's research on patterns of moral reasoning suggests that boys learn to reason according to abstract principles more so than girls. For boys, say Gilligan, "rightness" amounts to "playing by the rules".
6.   T   F   According to Naomi Wolf, the *beauty myth* arises, first, because society teaches women to measure themselves in terms of physical appearance, with standards that are unattainable.
7.   T   F   Women with children under the age of six years have only about half the proportion of their number working in the labor force as do married women with older children.
8.   T   F   Approximately two-thirds of the *pay gap* between men and women is the result of two factors--types of work and family responsibilities.
9.   T   F   According to the definition given in the text, *sexual harassment* always involves physical contact.
10.   T   F   For structural-functionalist Talcott Parsons, gender, at least in the traditional sense, forms a *complementary* set of roles that links men and women together.

Multiple Choice

1. The personal traits and social positions that members of a society attach to being female and male refers to

   (a)   gender.
   (b)   sex.
   (c)   sexual orientation.
   (d)   gender stratification.

2. The unequal distribution of wealth, power, and privilege between men and women refers to

   (a)   secondary sex characteristics.
   (b)   gender division.
   (c)   gender stratification.
   (d)   gender discrimination.

3.   Investigations of the *Israeli Kibbutzim* have indicated

    (a)   they are collective settlements.
    (b)   their members historically have embraced social equality.
    (c)   they support evidence of wide cultural latitude in defining what is feminine and masculine.
    (d)   men and women living there share both work and decision making.
    (e)   all of the above

4.   Which of the following studies illustrate a connection between *culture* and *gender*?

    (a)   Murdock's cross-culture research
    (b)   Mead's research in New Guinea
    (c)   The Israeli Kibbutz research
    (d)   All of the above
    (e)   None of the above

5.   Margaret Mead's research on gender in three societies in New Guinea illustrates that

    (a)   diffusion tends to standardize gender role assignments for women and men.
    (b)   gender is primarily biologically determined.
    (c)   gender is treated virtually the same across societies.
    (d)   gender is a variable creation of culture.
    (e)   while gender roles vary cross-culturally for men, they are very consistent for women.

6.   Among the *Mundugumor*, Margaret Mead found

    (a)   both females and males to be very passive.
    (b)   females to be very aggressive and males to be passive.
    (c)   both males and females to be aggressive and hostile.
    (d)   sex roles to be very similar to what they are in the U.S.

7.   A form of social organization in which females are dominated by males is termed

    (a)   matriarchal.
    (b)   oligarchal.
    (c)   patriarchy.
    (d)   egalitarian.

8.   The belief that one sex is innately superior to the other refers to

    (a)   homophobia.
    (b)   heterosexism.
    (c)   sexism.
    (d)   sexual individualism.

9. _____ are attitudes and activities that a society links to each sex.

    (a)   Gender roles
    (b)   Sexual orientation
    (c)   Gender stratification
    (d)   Gender identity

10. Which sociologist suggests that, soon after birth, family members introduce infants to either a *pink* or a *blue* world, depending on whether the infant is a she or a he?

    (a)   Karl Marx
    (b)   Jessie Bernard
    (c)   George Peter Murdock
    (d)   Talcott Parsons

11. Research by Carol Gilligan and Janet Lever demonstrates the influence of _____ on gender roles.

    (a)   the peer group
    (b)   biology
    (c)   religion
    (d)   personality

12. What percentage of *married couples* in the U.S. today depend on two incomes?

    (a)   25
    (b)   62
    (c)   87
    (d)   36

13. On average, what percentage of a male's income does a female earn?

    (a)   39
    (b)   48
    (c)   57
    (d)   73
    (e)   89

14. Two-thirds of the *earnings disparity* between men and women is explained by the two variables

    (a)   age and geography.
    (b)   marital status and education.
    (c)   type of work and family responsibilities.
    (d)   father's occupation and health.

15. As a woman, where are you most likely to suffer *physical violence*?

   (a) at work
   (b) at home
   (c) among friends
   (d) on the streets

16. Many feminists want our society to use a(n) _____ standard when measuring for *sexual harassment*.

   (a) effect
   (b) intention
   (c) quid pro quo
   (d) quid pro quid

17. *Talcott Parsons* argued that there exist two *complementary role sets* which exist to link males and females together with social institutions. He called these

   (a) rational and irrational.
   (b) effective and affective.
   (c) fundamental and secondary.
   (d) residual and basic.
   (e) instrumental and expressive.

18. Which theorist suggested that the male dominance over women was linked to technological advances which led to surpluses of valued resources?

   (a) Talcott Parsons
   (b) Erving Goffman
   (c) Friedrich Engels
   (d) Janet Lever

19. Which of the following is *not* a variation with *feminism*?

   (a) liberal
   (b) socialist
   (c) radical
   (d) expressive

20. The highest rate of *contraception use* by women of childbearing age is found in

   (a) Norway.
   (b) the United Kingdom.
   (c) the United States.
   (d) Ireland.

Matching

1. ____ The personal traits and social positions that members of a society attach to being female and male.
2. ____ The unequal distribution of wealth, power, and privilege between men and women.
3. ____ Did groundbreaking research on gender in New Guinea.
4. ____ A form of social organization in which females dominate males.
5. ____ The belief that one sex is innately superior to the other.
6. ____ Attitudes and activities that a society links to each sex.
7. ____ After spending a year watching children at play, concluded that boys favor team sports with complex rules and clear objectives.
8. ____ Any category of people, distinguished by physical or cultural difference, that is socially disadvantaged.
9. ____ A structural-functionalist, differentiated between instrumental and expressive roles.
10. ____ The advocacy of social equality for the men and women in opposition to patriarchy and sexism.

a. matriarchy
b. feminism
c. sexism
d. Janet Lever
e. gender stratification

f. gender
g. Margaret Mead
h. a minority
i. gender roles
j. Talcott Parsons

Fill-In

1. According to research cited in the text, adolescent males exhibit greater _____ ability, while adolescent females excel in _____ skills.
2. Today in the United States, _____ percent of *married women with children under the age of six* are in the labor force.
3. In 2000, women were _____ percent of the *labor force* in the United States.
4. With women's entry into the labor force, the amount of *housework* performed by women has declined, but the _____ women do has stayed about the same.
5. Two factors--type of _____ and _____ responsibilities--account for about two-thirds of the earnings disparities between women and men.
6. A _____ is any category of people, distinguished by physical or cultural difference, that is socially disadvantaged.
7. Traditionally in our society, *pornography* has been viewed as a _____ issue. But, pornography also plays a role in gender stratification and so must also be understood as a _____ issue.
8. Talcott Parsons identified two *complementary roles* that link men and women. These include the _____ and _____.
9. _____ refers to the advocacy of social equality for men and women, in opposition to patriarchy and sexism.
10. Basic *feminist ideas* include the importance of _____, expanding human _____, eliminating gender _____, ending sexual _____, and promoting sexual _____.

Discussion

1. Briefly review the significant events in the history of the *Women's Movement* during the nineteenth century.

2. Compare the research by *Margaret Mead* in New Guinea with the research done at the Israeli *Kibbutzim* in terms of the cultural variability of gender roles. What generalizations about the linkage between *sex* and *gender* can be made based on the cross-cultural research of *George Murdock*?

3. According to the author, is *patriarchy* inevitable? Why? What roles have technological advances and industrialization played in the changes in the relative statuses of women and men in society?

4. *Table 13-1* presents lists of traits linked to the traditional gender identities of *femininity* and *masculinity*. Develop a questionnaire using the traits identified in this table to survey females and males to determine to what extent these traits differentiate the sexes.

5. Identify five important points about *gender stratification* within the occupational domain of our society.
   What evidence can you provide from your own experience and observations concerning the argument being made by *Jessie Bernard* about the *pink* and *blue* worlds? Do you think her points help you understand how the socialization process creates a context for social inequality between the sexes?

6. What are the explanations as to why males dominate *politics*? To what extent are the roles of women changing in this sphere of social life? What factors are influencing these changes?

7. Review the issue of *violence against women* in our society. What are the types of violence discussed? What are the demographics of violence?

8. Are women a *minority group*? What are the arguments for and against this idea? What is the evidence being presented in the Controversy and Debate box at the end of the chapter to suggest men may be a minority group?

9. Compare the analyses of gender stratification as provided through the *structural-functional* and *social-conflict* paradigms. What are three general criticisms of the conclusions being made by *social-conflict* theorists and *structural-functionalists* concerning gender stratification?

10. What are the five *basic principles* of *feminism*? Discuss the specific examples for each. What are the three types of *feminism*? Briefly differentiate between them in terms of the basic arguments being made about gender roles in society.

PART VI: ANSWERS TO STUDY QUESTIONS

Key Concepts

1. Gender (p. 325)
2. Gender stratification (p. 325)
3. Patriarchy (328)
4. Matriarchy (p. 328)
5. Sexism (p. 328)
6. gender roles (p. 330)
7. minority (p. 339)
8. Sexual harassment (p. 340)
9. Feminism (p. 345)

True-False

1.	F	(p. 325)		6.	T	(p. 332)
2.	T	(p. 327)		7.	F	(p. 333)
3.	F	(p. 327)		8.	T	(p. 336)
4.	T	(p. 327)		9.	F	(p. 340)
5.	T	(p. 331)		10.	T	(p. 344)

Multiple-Choice

1.	a	(p. 325)		11.	a	(p. 331)
2.	c	(p. 325)		12.	b	(p. 333)
3.	e	(p. 326)		13.	d	(p. 336)
4.	d	(p. 327)		14.	c	(p. 337)
5.	d	(p. 327)		15.	b	(p. 340)
6.	c	(p. 327)		16.	a	(p. 341)
7.	c	(p. 328)		17.	e	(p. 344)
8.	c	(p. 328)		18.	c	(p. 345)
9.	a	(p. 330)		19.	d	(p. 347)
10.	b	(p. 330)		20.	b	(pp. 346-347)

Matching

1.	f	(p. 325)		6.	i	(p. 330)
2.	e	(p. 325)		7.	d	(p. 331)
3.	g	(pp. 326-327)		8.	h	(p. 339)
4.	a	(p. 328)		9.	j	(p. 344)
5.	c	(p. 328)		10.	b	(p. 345)

Fill-In

1. mathematical, verbal (p. 326)
2. 62 (p. 333)
3. 47 (p. 334)
4. share (p. 336)
5. work, family (p. 337)
6. minority (p. 339)
7. moral, power (p. 343)
8. instrumental, expressive (p. 344)
9. Feminism (p. 345)
10. change, choice, stratification, violence, freedom (pp. 345-346)

PART VII: IN FOCUS--IMPORTANT ISSUES

- Gender and Inequality

  What does *Figure 13-1* indicate about the biological differences between females and males?

  What are the significant biological differences between females and males?

  What conclusions do you make when weighing the evidence presented by Margaret Mead and George Murdock concerning cross-cultural patterns of *gender roles*?

  What are three *costs of sexism*?

- Gender and Socialization

  Provide one illustration from the text concerning each of the following influences on *gender role socialization*.

    the family

    the peer group

schooling

the mass media

- Gender and Social Stratification

  Identify the percentages of employed people for each of the following categories.

  > males (sixteen and older): _____
  > females (sixteen and older): _____
  > married women with children under the age of six: _____
  > married women with children between the ages of six and seventeen: _____
  > divorced women with children: _____

  What does *Figure 13-2* tell us? Why do you think these changes in labor force participation rates have occurred?

  How does employment status affect women's *housework* labor? How about marital status? Presence of children? What about for men?

  What are the two factors that most influence the differences in pay for women and men?

  What do you think should be done about these differences?

How has women's participation in the *military* changed since the Revolutionary War?

Are women a *minority group*? Why?

How is *sexual harassment* defined?

How is *pornography* defined?

In what ways do sexual harassment and pornography represent *violence against women*?

- Theoretical Analysis of Gender

  Briefly discuss how each of the following theoretical paradigms views the issue of gender in society:

  structural-functionalism

  social-conflict

- Feminism

  What are the four basic *feminist ideas* identified in the text?

  Describe each of the following *types of feminism.*

  liberal

  socialist

  radical

  Why is there *opposition to feminism*?

- Looking Ahead: Gender In the Twenty-First Century

  What is the vision offered by the author concerning the role of gender in society over the next century?

Chapter 14

Race and Ethnicity

PART I: CHAPTER OUTLINE

I. The Social Meaning of Race and Ethnicity
    A. Race
        1. Racial Types
        2. A Trend toward Mixture
    B. Ethnicity
    C. Minorities
II. Prejudice
    A. Stereotypes
    B. Racism
    C. Theories of Prejudice
        1. Scapegoat Theory
        2. Authoritarian Personality Theory
        3. Culture Theory
        4. Conflict Theory
III. Discrimination
    A. Institutional Prejudice and Discrimination
    B. Prejudice and Discrimination: The Vicious Cycle
IV. Majority and Minority: Patterns of Interaction
    A. Pluralism
    B. Assimilation
    C. Segregation
    D. Genocide
V. Race and Ethnicity in the United States
    A. Native Americans
    B. White Anglo-Saxon Protestants
    C. African Americans
    D. Asian Americans
        1. Chinese Americans
        2. Japanese Americans
        3. Recent Asian Immigrants

PART II: LEARNING OBJECTIVES

- To develop an understanding about the biological basis for definitions of race.
- To be able to distinguish between the biological concept of race and the cultural concept of ethnicity.
- To be able to identify the characteristics of a minority group.
- To be able to identify and describe the two forms of prejudice.
- To be able to identify and describe the four theories of prejudice.
- Be able to distinguish between prejudice and discrimination.
- To be able to provide examples of institutional prejudice and discrimination.
- To be able to see how prejudice and discrimination combine to create a vicious cycle.
- To be able to describe the patterns of interaction between minorities and the majority.
- To be able to describe the histories and relative statuses of each of the racial and ethnic groups identified in the text.

PART III: KEY CONCEPTS

Fill in the spaces below with the appropriate concepts.

1. _____ refers to a socially constructed category composed of people who share biologically transmitted traits that members of a society consider important.
2. _____ is a shared cultural heritage.
3. A _____ is a category of people, distinguished by cultural or physical differences, that society sets apart and subordinates.
4. _____ refers to a rigid and irrational generalization about an entire category of people.
5. A _____ an exaggerated description applied to an entire category of people.
6. _____ is the belief that one racial category is innately superior or inferior to another.
7. A _____ is a person or category of people, typically with little power, who people unfairly blame for their own troubles.
8. _____ refers to any action that involves treating various categories of people unequally.
9. _____ _____ _____ _____ refers to bias inherent in the operation of society's institutions.

10. A state in which racial and ethnic groups are distinct but have social parity is known as
     _____.

11. _____ refers to the process by which minorities gradually adopt patterns of the dominant culture.

12. _____ refers to the biological reproduction by partners of different racial categories.

13. _____ is the physical and social separation of categories of people.

14. _____ refers to the systematic annihilation of one category of people by another.

PART IV: IMPORTANT RESEARCHERS

In the blank space below each of the following researchers, write two of three sentences to help you remember his her respective contributions to sociology.

Robert Merton   Emory Bogardus

T. W. Adorno   Thomas Sowell

PART V: STUDY QUESTIONS

True-False

1. T   F   Although *racial categories* point to some biological elements, *race* is a socially constructed concept.

2. T   F   According to the author of our text, for sociological purposes the concepts of *race* and *ethnicity* can be used interchangeably.

3. T   F   A racial or ethnic *minority* is a category of people, distinguished by physical or cultural traits, who are socially disadvantaged.

4. T   F   The *scapegoat theory* links prejudice to frustration and suggests that prejudice is likely to be pronounced among people who themselves are disadvantaged.

5. T   F   In *Robert Merton's* typology of patterns of prejudice and discrimination, an unprejudiced-nondiscriminator is labeled an "all-weather liberal."

6. T   F   The United States Supreme Court decisions such as the *1954 Brown case* have reduced the presence of *de jure segregation* in the United States.

7. T   F   *Native Americans* were not granted citizenship in the United States until 1924.

8. T   F   The *Dred Scott* Supreme Court decision declared that blacks were to have full rights and privileges as citizens of the United States.

9. T   F   More than one-half of *Hispanics* in the United States are *Mexican Americans*.

10. T   F   The highest rates of *immigration* to the United States occurred during the 1920s and 1930s.

Multiple Choice

1. Linda Brown was not permitted to enroll in the second grade at an elementary school near her home in Topeka, Kansas because she was

    (a)   Jewish.
    (b)   African American.
    (c)   blind.
    (d)   HIV positive.

2. A socially constructed category composed of people who share biologically transmitted traits that members of a society deem socially significant is the definition for

    (a)   race.
    (b)   minority group.
    (c)   ethnicity.
    (d)   assimilation.

3. A shared cultural heritage is the definition for

    (a)   a minority group.
    (b)   race.
    (c)   assimilation.
    (d)   pluralism.
    (e)   ethnicity.

4. Members of an *ethnic category* share

    (a)   common ancestors, language, and religion.
    (b)   only biological distinctions.
    (c)   residential location.
    (d)   social class ranking.

5. Among people of *European descent,* the largest number of people in the U.S. trace their ancestry back to

    (a)   Italy.
    (b)   Ireland.
    (c)   England.
    (d)   Germany.

6. *Minority groups* have two major characteristics

    (a)   race and ethnicity.
    (b)   religion and ethnicity.
    (c)   physical traits and political orientation.
    (d)   sexual orientation and race.
    (e)   distinctive identity and subordination.

7. What is the term for a category of people, set apart by physical or cultural traits, that is socially disadvantaged?

    (a)   minority group
    (b)   stereotype
    (c)   ethnicity
    (d)   race

8. What is the term for a rigid and irrational generalization about an entire category of people?

    (a)   racism
    (b)   discrimination
    (c)   stereotype
    (d)   prejudice

9. What is the term for an exaggerated description applied to every person in some category?

    (a)   racism
    (b)   stereotype
    (c)   discrimination
    (d)   prejudice

10. A *form of prejudice* referring to the belief that one racial category is innately superior or inferior to another is called

    (a)   stereotyping.
    (b)   discrimination.
    (c)   racism.
    (d)   scapegoating.

11. One explanation of the origin of prejudice is found in the concept of the *authoritarian personality*. Such a personality exhibits

    (a)   an attitude of authority over others believed to be inferior.
    (b)   frustration over personal troubles directed toward someone less powerful.
    (c)   rigid conformity to conventional cultural norms and values.
    (d)   social distance from others deemed inferior.

12. Treating various categories of people unequally refers to

   (a) prejudice.
   (b) stereotyping.
   (c) miscegenation.
   (d) discrimination.

13. *Robert Merton's* study of the relationship between prejudice and discrimination revealed one behavioral type that discriminates against persons even though he or she is not prejudiced. This person would be called a(n)

   (a) active bigot.
   (b) all-weather liberal.
   (c) timid bigot.
   (d) fair-weather liberal.

14. According to the work of W. I. Thomas, a *vicious cycle* is formed by which variables?

   (a) miscegenation and authoritarianism
   (b) race and ethnicity
   (c) pluralism and assimilation
   (d) segregation and integration
   (e) prejudice and discrimination

15. A state in which racial and ethnic minorities are distinct but have social parity is termed

   (a) segregation.
   (b) pluralism.
   (c) integration.
   (d) assimilation.

16. The process by which minorities gradually adopt patterns of the dominant culture is known as

   (a) pluralism.
   (b) amalgamation.
   (c) assimilation.
   (d) miscegnation.

17. *Miscegenation* is

   (a) the biological reproduction by partners of different racial categories.
   (b) the process by which minorities gradually adopt patterns of the dominant culture.
   (c) a state in which all categories of people are distinct but have social parity.
   (d) a condition of prejudice leading to discrimination.

18. Which of the following statements is/are accurate concerning *white Anglo Saxon Protestants (WASPs)?*

    (a)   They represent about twenty percent of our nation's population.
    (b)   Historically, WASP immigrants were highly skilled and motivated to achieve by what we now call the Protestant work ethic.
    (c)   WASPs were never one single social group.
    (d)   The majority of people in the upper-class in the United States are still WASPs.
    (e)   All of the above are accurate statements about WASPs.

19. In 1865, the _____ to the Constitution *outlawed slavery.*

    (a)   Thirteenth Amendment
    (b)   Civil Rights Act
    (c)   Equal Rights Amendment
    (d)   Twenty-sixth Amendment

20. *Jim Crow Laws*

    (a)   protected freed slaves prior to the Civil War.
    (b)   gave Native Americans residency rights west of the Mississippi.
    (c)   integrated schools.
    (d)   are examples of institutional discrimination.

Matching

1. ____ A socially constructed category composed of people who share biologically transmitted traits that members of a society consider important.
2. ____ A shared cultural heritage.
3. ____ A category of people, distinguished by physical or cultural traits, that is socially disadvantaged.
4. ____ A person or category of people, typically with little power, whom people unfairly blame for their troubles.
5. ____ A theory holding that prejudice springs from frustration among people who are themselves disadvantaged.
6. ____ An approach contending that while extreme prejudice may characterize some people, some prejudice is found in everyone.
7. ____ A state in which racial and ethnic minorities are distinct but have social parity.
8. ____ The process by which minorities gradually adopt patterns of the dominant culture.
9. ____ Non-WASPs whose ancestors lived in Ireland, Poland, Germany, Italy, or other European countries.
10. ____ Hostility toward foreigners.

a.	xenophobia	f.	white ethnic Americans
b.	assimilation	g.	cultural theory
c.	minority	h.	pluralism
d.	scapegoat	i.	race
e.	ethnicity	j.	scapegoat theory

Fill-In

1. The term _____ refers to a socially constructed category composed of people who share biologically transmitted traits that members of society consider important.
2. While *race* is a _____ concept, *ethnicity* is a _____ concept.
3. Two major characteristics of *minorities* are that they have a _____ identity and are _____ by the social-stratification system.
4. A _____ refers to an exaggerated description applied to every person in some category.
5. _____ *theory* holds that prejudice springs from frustration.
6. Thomas Sowell has demonstrated that most of the documented racial difference in intelligence are not due to _____ but to people's _____.
7. _____ prejudice and discrimination refers to bias in attitudes or actions inherent in the operation of any of society's institutions.
8. In the _____ *case* of 1857, the U.S. Supreme Court addressed the question, "Are blacks citizens?" by writing "We think they are not....".
9. In 1865, the _____ _____ to the Constitution outlawed slavery.
10. *Gunnar Myrdal* said that the denial of basic rights and freedoms to entire categories of Americans was the _____.

Discussion

1. Identify and describe the four *explanations* of why prejudice exists.
2. Differentiate between the concepts *prejudice* and *discrimination*. What are the four types of people identified by *Robert Merton's* typology of patterns of prejudice and discrimination? Provide illustrations
3. What is *institutional prejudice and discrimination*? Provide two illustrations.
4. What are three criticisms of *affirmative action*? What are three reasons given by proponents of affirmative action to continue this social policy.
5. What are the four models representing the *patterns of interaction* between minority groups and the majority group? Define and discuss an illustration for each of these. In what three important ways did Japanese immigration and assimilation into U.S. society differ from the Chinese?
6. How do Native Americans, African Americans, Hispanic Americans, and Asian Americans compare to whites in terms of *educational achievement, family income,* and *poverty rates?*
7. What was the Court's ruling in *Brown vs. the Board of Education of Topeka case*?
8. What does the scientific evidence suggest about the relationship between *race* and *intelligence*?
9. How are the changing patterns in *immigration* likely to influence the future of the United States?
10. How you think the United States is becoming more color blind or less color blind? Why?

PART VI: ANSWERS TO STUDY QUESTIONS

1.   Race (p. 354)
2.   Ethnicity (p. 355)
3.   minority (p. 356)
4.   Prejudice (p. 357)
5.   stereotype (p. 358)
6.   Racism (p. 359)
7.   scapegoat (p. 359)
8.   Discrimination (p. 361)
9.   Institutional prejudice and discrimination (p. 362)
10.   pluralism (p. 363)
11.   Assimilation (p. 363)
12.   Miscegenation (p. 363)
13.   Segregation (p. 364)
14.   Genocide (p. 364)

True-False

1.	T	(p. 354)		6.	T	(p. 364)
2.	F	(p. 356)		7.	T	(p. 366)
3.	T	(p. 356)		8.	F	(p. 368)
4.	T	(p. 362)		9.	T	(p. 373)
5.	T	(p. 362)		10.	F	(p. 377)

Multiple Choice

1.	b	(p. 353)		11.	c	(p. 360)
2.	a	(p. 354)		12.	d	(p. 361)
3.	e	(p. 355)		13.	d	(p. 362)
4.	a	(p. 355)		14.	e	(pp. 362-363)
5.	d	(p. 356)		15.	b	(p. 363)
6.	e	(p. 356)		16..	c	(p. 363)
7.	a	(p. 356)		17.	a	(p. 363)
8.	d	(p. 357)		18.	e	(p. 367)
9.	b	(p. 358)		19.	a	(p. 369)
10.	c	(p. 359)		20.	d	(p. 369)

Matching

1.	i	(p. 354)		6.	g	(p. 360)
2.	e	(p. 355)		7.	h	(p. 363)
3.	c	(p. 356)		8.	b	(p. 363)
4.	d	(p. 359)		9.	f	(p. 376)
5.	j	(p. 359)		10.	a	(p. 377)

<u>Fill-In</u>

1. race (p. 364)
2. biological, cultural (p. 356)
3. distinctive, subordination (p. 356)
4. stereotype (p. 358)
5. Scapegoat (p. 359)
6. biology, environments (p. 360)
7. Institutional (p. 362)
8. Dred Scott (p. 368)
9. Thirteenth (p. 369)
10. American dilemma (p. 369)

PART VII: IN FOCUS--IMPORTANT ISSUES

- The Social Meaning of Race and Ethnicity

  Differentiate between the concepts of *race* and *ethnicity*.

  What does the author mean by saying that ethnicity involves more *variability* than race?

  What are the basic characteristics of a *minority group*?

- Prejudice

  Briefly describe each of the following *theories of prejudice*.

     scapegoat theory

     authoritarian personality theory

     cultural theory

     conflict theory

- Discrimination

  How does discrimination differ from prejudice?

  Provide two illustrations of *institutional discrimination*.

- Majority and Minority: Patterns of Interaction

  Define and illustrate each of the following *patterns of interaction* between racial and ethnic groups.

  pluralism

  assimilation

  segregation

  genocide

- Race and Ethnicity in the United States

Identify three important characteristics for the following racial and ethnic groups that differentially characterize them in our society's social stratification system.

Native Americans

White Anglo-Saxon Protestants

African Americans

Asian Americans

  Chinese Americans

  Japanese Americans

  recent Asian Immigrants

Hispanic Americans

    Mexican Americans

    Puerto Ricans

    Cuban Americans

    White Ethnic Americans

- Race and Ethnicity: Looking Ahead

What are the issues today that are different from the past concerning *immigration* to the United States?

What issues have not changed?

Chapter 15 — Aging and the Elderly

PART I: CHAPTER OUTLINE

I. The Graying of the United States
    A. The Birth Rate: Going Down
    B. Life Expectancy: Going Up
    C. An Aging Society: Cultural Change
    D. The "Young Old" and the "Old Old"

II. Growing Old: Biology and Culture
    A. Biological Changes
    B. Psychological Changes
    C. Aging and Culture
    D. Age Stratification: A Global Assessment
        1. Hunting and Gathering Societies
        2. Pastoral, Horticultural, and Agrarian Societies
        3. Industrial Societies
        4. Japan: An Exceptional Case

III. Transitions and Challenges of Aging
    A. Finding Meaning
    B. Social Isolation
    C. Retirement
    D. Aging and Poverty
    E. Caregiving
        1. Who are the Caregivers?
        2. Elder Abuse
    F. Ageism
    G. The Elderly: A Minority?

IV. Theoretical Analysis of Aging
    A. Structural-Functional Analysis: Aging and Disengagement
    B. Symbolic-Interaction Analysis: Aging and Activity
    C. Social-Conflict Analysis: Aging and Inequality

V. Death and Dying
    A. Historical Patterns of Death
    B. The Modern Separation of Life and Death
    C. Ethical Issues: Confronting Death
        1. When Does Death Occur?
        2. The Right-to-Die Debate
    D. Bereavement

VI. Looking Ahead: Aging In the Twenty-First Century

LEARNING OBJECTIVES

- To define and review the development of the graying of the United States.
- To be able to describe the interrelationship and respective roles of biology and culture in growing old.
- To be able to describe the role of the elderly in global and historical perspectives.
- To be able to describe the relationship between adjusting to old age and personality type.
- To be able to describe the problems and transitions involved in growing old.
- To become familiar with the viewpoints on old age which are being offered by three different sociological perspectives—structural-functional, symbolic-interactionism, and social-conflict.
- To consider the effects of ageism on society.
- To be able to cite the arguments in the debate over whether the elderly constitute a minority group.
- To be able to describe the changing character of death throughout history and into modern times.
- To be able to describe the process of bereavement in the United States.

PART III: KEY CONCEPTS

Fill-in the blank spaces below with the appropriate concepts.

1.   _____ is the study of aging and the elderly.
2.   _____ _____ refers to the unequal distribution of wealth, power, and privilege among people at different stages of the life course.
3.   A _____ is a form of social organization in which the elderly have the most wealth, power, and prestige.
4.   Informal and unpaid care provided to a dependent person by family members, other relatives, or friends is known as _____.
5.   _____ refers to prejudice and discrimination against the elderly.
6.   _____ _____ refers to the idea that society enhances its orderly operation but disengaging people from positions of responsibility as they reach old age.
7.   _____ _____ refers to the idea that a high level of activity enhances personal satisfaction in old age.
8.   Assisting in the death of a person suffering from an incurable disease is known as _____.

PART IV: IMPORTANT RESEARCHERS

In the space below the researcher's names, write two or three sentences to help you remember his or her contributions to sociology.

Bernice Neugarten   Betty Friedan

Gordon Streib

Elaine Cumming and William Henry

Steven Spitzer

Elisabeth Kübler-Ross

PART V: STUDY QUESTIONS

True-False

1. T F The elderly population in the U.S. is growing *twice as fast* as the general population.
2. T F The *old-age dependency ratio* refers to the number of ill or disabled elderly people for every one hundred healthy elderly people in a society.
3. T F The average *life span* in the world's poorest countries is less than twenty-five years.
4. T F A *gerontrocracy* is more likely to exist in hunting and gathering society than in a horticultural or agrarian society.
5. T F Most elderly people in the U.S. *live alone.*
6. T F Bernice Neugarten's research found that the most common personality type among the aged is referred to as *passive-dependent personalities.*
7. T F Children are more likely to be *poor* in the U.S. than are the aged.
8. T F *Symbolic-interactionists* readily accept *disengagement theory*, arguing that the elderly need to remove themselves from positions of responsibility in order to achieve a healthy lifestyle.
9. T F From a *structural-functionalist* point of view, a limitation of *activity theory* is the tendency to exaggerate the well-being and competence of the elderly.
10. T F *Euthanasia* refers to the unequal distribution of wealth, power, and privilege among people at different stages of the life course.

Multiple-Choice

1. In 1900, the United States was a young nation with half the population under the age of twenty-three; just _____ percent had reached the age of sixty-five.

    (a) one
    (b) four
    (c) ten
    (d) twenty

193

2. Currently, the aged represent about _____ *percent* of our population.

    (a) 6.1
    (b) 12.4
    (c) 18.7
    (d) 21.3

3. Between now and 2050 the *median age* in the U.S. will rise to almost _____ and the *percent* of our population over the age of 65 will be

    (a) 40/20.
    (b) 30/15.
    (c) 50/50.
    (d) 25/40.
    (e) 36/14.

4. The ratio of elderly people to working-age adults, termed the *old-age dependency ratio*, will rise by 2050-from twenty to _____ elderly people per one hundred people aged eighteen to sixty-four.

    (a) twenty-eight
    (b) thirty
    (c) thirty-seven
    (d) forty-six

5. _____ refers to the study of aging and the elderly.

    (a) Gerontocracy
    (b) Ageism
    (c) Elderology
    (d) Gerontology
    (e) Oldgrapphy

6. Most counties in the U.S. with a high percentage of older people are found in

    (a) the Sunbelt.
    (b) the Northeast.
    (c) the Midwest.
    (d) the West.

7. *Gerontocracy* is most likely to be a characteristic of what type of technologically developed society?

    (a) hunting and gathering
    (b) pastoral, horticultural, and agrarian
    (c) industrial
    (d) postindustrial
    (e) nomadic

8. The Abkhasian society exhibits exceptional *longevity* due to

   (a) a healthy diet.
   (b) regular exercise.
   (c) positive self-image of the elderly in society.
   (d) all of the above

9. Which of the following is *not* a personality type identified by Bernice Neugarten in her study of adjustment to old age?

   (a) disintegrated and disorganized
   (b) residual-active
   (c) passive-dependent
   (d) integrated
   (e) defended

10. Most elderly men

    (a) live alone.
    (b) live in nursing homes.
    (c) live with extended family members.
    (d) live with their spouse.

11. Approximately ___ percent of elderly women *live alone*.

    (a) 41
    (b) 23
    (c) 68
    (d) 16

12. Approximately what percentage of the aged population in the U.S. live in *poverty*?

    (a) less than 5
    (b) 18
    (c) 25
    (d) 33
    (e) 10

13. Which of the following statements concerning the elderly is *inaccurate*?

    (a) The poverty rate among elderly African Americans is over twice the rate for their white, non-Hispanic counterparts.
    (b) Women over the age of sixty-five who are working full-time earn about 63 percent of their male counterparts.
    (c) The poverty rate among the elderly is higher today than it was forty years ago.
    (d) The majority of elderly people have retired from the labor force.

14. Some sociologists argue that the elderly constitute a *minority group*, while others disagree. Which of the following reasons is an argument *against* the elderly being a minority group?

    (a)   The status of being elderly is an open status.
    (b)   The elderly think of themselves in terms of sex, race, and ethnicity.
    (c)   The social disadvantages of the elderly are not as great as for other categories of people.
    (d)   all of the above

15. According to _____ analysis, *disengagement* is a strategy to ensure the orderly operation of society by removing aging people from productive roles while they are still able to perform them.

    (a)   symbolic-interaction
    (b)   structural-functional
    (c)   social-conflict
    (d)   social-exchange

16. *Activity theory* is a sociological theory of aging based upon

    (a)   structural-functional analysis.
    (b)   social-conflict analysis.
    (c)   symbolic-interaction analysis.
    (d)   social-exchange analysis.

17. In modern U.S. society *death* has become

    (a)   more common to everyday experience.
    (b)   less of an ethical issue.
    (c)   easier to accept.
    (d)   an event that occurs often in the home of the dying person.
    (e)   defined as an unnatural event.

18. Which of the following statements is *inaccurate*?

    (a)   Less than two-thirds of deaths in the U.S. involve people over the age of fifty-five.
    (b)   In 1900, one-third of all deaths in the U.S. involved children under the age of five.
    (c)   Living wills are documents stating which medical procedures an individual wants and does not want under specific conditions.
    (d)   Euthanasia refers to assisting in the death of a person suffering from an incurable disease.

19. Which of the following is *not* a stage of *bereavement* according to the Elisabeth Kübler-Ross' stage model?

    (a)   integration
    (b)   anger
    (c)   acceptance
    (d)   resignation
    (e)   denial

20. The major purpose of the *hospice movement* is

   (a)   to lobby the federal government and state governments for support of "right-to-die" legislation.
   (b)   to help terminally ill patients find cures for their illnesses.
   (c)   to provide care and support for dying people.
   (d)   assist people who wish to end their own lives.

Matching

1. ___ The projected percentage of the U.S. population who will be over the age of sixty-five in the year 2050.
2. ___ The study of aging and the elderly.
3. ___ A form of social organization in which the elderly have the most wealth, power, and prestige.
4. ___ The percentage of aged women living with a spouse.
5. ___ Prejudice and discrimination against the elderly.
6. ___ A theory associated with symbolic-interaction analysis.
7. ___ A theory associated with the structural-functional paradigm.
8. ___ Assisting in the death of a person suffering from an incurable disease.
9. ___ A country with extremely liberal euthanasia laws.
10. ___ Found that people usually confront their own death in stages.

   a.   Elizabeth Kübler-Ross   f.   gerontology
   b.   the Netherlands   g.   ageism
   c.   gerontocracy   h   disengagement
   d.   activity   i.   euthanasia
   e.   42   j.   20

Fill-In

1. Typically, two factors combine to *drive up* the elderly population in a society. These include a low _____ _____ and increasing _____ .
2. The ratio of elderly people to working-age adults is termed the *old age* _____ _____ .
3. Today in the United States, _____ percent of people over the age of sixty-five characterize their overall health as "good" or "excellent."
4. Among full-time workers in 2000, *women* over the age of sixty-five had median earnings of $34,159 compared to $ _____ for *men*.
5. Our author believes the aged should not be identified as a minority group, but rather be considered a _____ *segment* of the U.S. population.
6. One criticism of *social-conflict theory* is that rather than blaming capitalism for the lower standard of living of the elderly, the real culprit is _____ .
7. _____ is the killing of infants and _____ is the killing of the elderly.

197

8.   Medical and legal experts in the United States now define *death* as an _____ state involving no response to stimulation, no movement or breathing, no reflexes, and no indication of brain activity.

9.   _____ refers to assisting in the death of a person suffering from an incurable disease.

10.   According to Elisabeth Kübler-Ross, like *death*, _____ involves four stages, including denial, anger, negotiation, and acceptance.

Discussion

1.   Define *gerontology*. Further, many different demographic facts concerning the aged in our society are presented on pages 392-394. Select the two which most interest you and discuss their significance for our society using your own opinions and experiences.

2.   Define and illustrate the concept of *age stratification*. How does it vary by a society's level of technological development?

3.   What are the four types of *personalities* identified by Bernice Neugarten? In what ways are they different in helping people adjust to old age? Are there people in your life whom you can identify with having any of these personality types?

4.   Differentiate between *activity theory* and *disengagement theory* in terms of how each helps us understand the changing status of the aged in society.

5.   Why is *elder abuse* so common in our society? What are some of the demographic facts concerning this critical social problem in our society?

6.   Discuss the relative economies of the aged in our society today.

7.   According to *social-conflict* theorists, why is the status of the aged diminished in capitalist societies? What do critics of this theory suggest?

8.   What are the arguments in the debate concerning whether the aged are a *minority group*?

9.   What are Daniel Callahan's points concerning how much old age the U.S. can afford?

10.   Review the points being made by Betty Friedan concerning the aged in our society. Do you agree with her viewpoint?

PART VI: ANSWERS TO STUDY QUESTIONS

Key Concepts

1.   Gerontology (p. 386)
2.   Age stratification (p. 389)
3.   gerontocracy (p. 390)
4.   caregiving (p. 395)
5.   Ageism (p. 396)
6.   Disengagement theory (p. 397)
7.   Activity theory (p. 397)
8.   euthanasia (p. 400)

True-False

1.	T	(p. 383)	6.	F	(p. 392)
2.	F	(p. 386)	7.	T	(p. 394)
3.	F	(p. 389)	8.	F	(p. 397)
4.	F	(p. 390)	9.	T	(p. 398)
5.	F	(p. 392)	10.	F	(p. 400)

Multiple-Choice

1.	b	(p. 383)	11.	a	(p. 392)
2.	b	(pp. 383-384)	12.	e	(p. 394)
3.	a	(p. 384)	13.	c	(p. 394)
4.	a	(p. 386)	14.	a	(p. 396)
5.	d	(p. 386)	15.	b	(p. 397)
6.	c	(p. 387)	16.	c	(p. 397)
7.	b	(p. 390)	17.	e	(p. 399)
8.	d	(p. 391)	18.	a	(pp. 399-400)
9.	b	(p. 392)	19.	a	(p. 401)
10.	d	(p. 392)	20.	c	(p. 401)

Matching

1.	j	(p. 384)	6.	d	(p. 397)
2.	f	(p. 386)	7.	h	(p. 397)
3.	c	(p. 390)	8.	i	(p. 400)
4.	e	(p. 392)	9.	b	(p. 400)
5.	g	(p. 395)	10.	a	(p. 401)

Fill-In

1. birth rate, longevity (p. 383)
2. dependency ratio (p. 386)
3. 73 (p. 387)
4. 45,985 (p. 394)
5. distinctive (p. 396)
6. industrialization (p. 398)
7. Infanticide, geronticide (p. 398)
8. irreversible (p. 399)
9. Euthanasia (p. 400)
10. bereavement (p. 401)

PART VII: IN FOCUS--IMPORTANT ISSUES

- The Graying of the United States

  What are the two major factors identified in the text that are contributing to the *graying* of the United States population? What evidence is being presented concerning each of these?

  What is meant by the *old-age dependency ratio*? How is it changing? Why should we be concerned about this change?

- Growing Old: Biology and Culture

  Review the major changes for the aged in each of the following domains.

      biological

      psychological

  Provide three examples of how aging is related to *culture*.

What is *age stratification*?

How is age stratification related to a society's level of *technological development*?

- Transitions and Challenges of Aging

  Summarize the key points being made in the text concerning each of the following transitions and challenges of aging.

  finding meaning

  social isolation

  retirement

  aging and poverty

  caregiving

Are the elderly a *minority group*? Provide one point to argue for this idea and one to argue against it.

- Theoretical Analysis of Aging

Review the major arguments concerning the aged in society according to structural-functionalists who use *disengagement theory*.

What are two major criticisms of this perspective?

Review the major arguments concerning the aged in society according to symbolic-interactionists who use *activity theory*.

What are two major criticisms of this perspective?

How do *conflict theorists* understand the relationship between industrial society and the social stratification of the aged?

- Death and Dying

  How has the place of death in society changed since medieval times?

  What are two arguments being made on each side of the *right-to-die* debate?

- Looking Ahead: Aging In the Twenty-First Century

  What are three major issues that will be confronting our society over the next fifty to sixty years given the growing number of aged people in the United States?

Chapter 16 — The Economy and Work

PART I: CHAPTER OUTLINE

I. The Economy: Historical Overview
   A. The Agricultural Revolution
   B. The Industrial Revolution
   C. The Information Revolution and the Postindustrial Society
   D. Sectors of the Economy
   E. The Global Economy
II. Economic Systems: Paths to Justice
   A. Capitalism
   B. Socialism
      1. Social and Communism
   C. Welfare Capitalism and State Capitalism
   D. Relative Advantages of Capitalism and Socialism
      1. Economic Productivity
      2. Economic Equality
      3. Personal Freedom
   E. Changes in Socialist Countries
III. Work in the Postindustrial Economy
   A. The Decline of Agricultural Work
   B. From Factory Work to Service Work
   C. The Dual Labor Market
   D. Labor Unions
   E. Professions
   F. Self-Employment
   G. Unemployment and Underemployment
   H. The Underground Economy
   I. Social Diversity in the Workplace
   J. New Information Technology and Work
IV. Corporations
   A. Economic Concentration
   B. Conglomerates and Corporate Linkages
   C. Corporations: Are They Competitive?
   D. Corporations and the Global Economy

204

PART II: LEARNING OBJECTIVES

- To be able to identify the elements of the economy.
- To be able to review the history and development of economic activity from the Agricultural Revolution through to the Postindustrial Revolution.
- To be able to identify and describe the three sectors of the economy.
- To be able to compare the economic systems of capitalism, state capitalism, socialism, and democratic socialism.
- To be able to explain the difference between socialism and communism.
- To be able to describe the general characteristics and trends of work in the U.S. postindustrial society.
- To begin to see the impact of multinational corporations on the world economy.

PART III: KEY CONCEPTS

Fill in the blank spaces below with the appropriate concept.

1. The _____ is the social institution that organizes a society's production, distribution, and consumption of goods and services.
2. The _____ _____ refers to a productive system based on service work and high technology.
3. The _____ _____ is the part of the economy that draws raw materials from the natural environment.
4. The _____ _____ is the part of the economy that transforms raw materials into manufactured goods.
5. The _____ _____ is the part of the economy involving services rather than goods.
6. The _____ _____ refers to the expanding economic activity with little regard for national borders.
7. _____ is an economic system in which natural resources and the means of producing goods and services are privately owned.
8. _____ is an economic system in which in which natural resources and the means of producing goods and services are collectively owned.
9. _____ refers to a hypothetical economic and political system in which all members of a society are socially equal.
10. _____ _____ is an economic and political system that combines a mostly market-based economy with extensive social welfare programs.
11. _____ _____ refers to an economic and political system in which companies are privately owned but cooperate closely with the government.

205

12. The _____ _____ _____ refers to jobs that provide extensive benefits to workers.

13. The _____ _____ _____ refers to jobs that provide minimal benefits to workers.

14. _____ _____ are organizations of workers that seek to improve wages and working conditions through various strategies, including negotiations and strikes.

15. A _____ is a prestigious white-collar occupation that requires extensive formal education.

16. The _____ _____ refers to economic activity involving income unreported to the government as required by law.

17. A _____ is an organization with a legal existence, including rights and liabilities, apart from those of its members.

18. A _____ is a giant corporation composed of many smaller corporations.

19. A _____ refers to the domination of a market by a single producer.

20. A _____ refers to the domination of a market by a few producers.

PART IV: IMPORTANT RESEARCHERS

In the space below the following researcher's name, write two or three sentences to help you remember his contributions to sociology.

Karl Marx

PART V: STUDY QUESTIONS

True-False

1. T F The *economy* includes the production, distribution, and consumption of both goods and services.

2. T F *Agriculture*, as a subsistence strategy, first emerged some five thousand years ago.

3. T F Most workers in the New England textile factories in the early nineteenth century were *women*.

4. T F The *primary sector* of the economy is the part of the economy that generates raw material directly from the natural environment.

5. T F The largest economic sector of *middle-income countries* is the secondary sector.

6. T F *Socialism* is being defined as both a political and economic system.

7. T F The *income ratio*, as a measure of the distribution of income in a society, tended to be higher in socialist systems as compared to capitalist systems during the 1970s and 1980s.

8. T F More than two-thirds of the labor force in the U.S. hold *service jobs*.

9. T F The *primary labor market* includes jobs providing minimal benefits to workers.
10. T F According to the text, the Information Revolution is changing the kind of work people do and where they do it. Part of the consequence of this process is that computers are *deskilling labor*.

Multiple Choice

1. A productive system based on service work and high technology refers to

    (a) the postindustrial economy.
    (b) the primary sector.
    (c) the secondary sector.
    (d) a cottage industry.

2. The *sector* of the economy that transforms raw materials into manufactured goods is termed the

    (a) primary sector.
    (b) competitive sector.
    (c) secondary sector.
    (d) basic sector.
    (e) manifest sector.

3. Your occupation is teaching. In what production *sector* of the economy do you work?

    (a) primary
    (b) secondary
    (c) tertiary
    (d) manifest

4. You mine gold for a living. In what production *sector* of the economy do you work?

    (a) tertiary
    (b) manifest
    (c) secondary
    (d) auxiliary
    (e) primary

5. Today, about _____ percent of the U.S. labor force is in *service work*, including secretarial and clerical work and positions in food service, sales, law, advertising, and teaching.

    (a) 72
    (b) 88
    (c) 61
    (d) 93
    (e) 52

6.   Which of the following is/are accurate statements concerning *capitalism*?

(a)   Justice, in a capitalist context, amounts to freedom of the marketplace where one can produce, invest, and buy according to individual self-interest.
(b)   A purely capitalist economy is a free-market system with no government interference, sometimes called a laissez-faire economy.
(c)   Consumers regulate a free-market economy.
(d)   All are accurate statements concerning capitalism.

7.   Which of the following is/are accurate concerning *socialism*?

(a)   Socialism is characterized by collective ownership of property.
(b)   Socialism rejects the laissez-faire approach.
(c)   Justice, in a socialist context, is not freedom to compete and accumulate wealth but, rather, meeting everyone's basic needs in a more or less equal manner.
(d)   All of the above are accurate statements concerning socialism.

8.   _____ is a hypothetical economic and political system in which all members of a society are socially equal.

(a)   Socialism
(b)   Communism
(c)   Welfare capitalism
(d)   State capitalism

9.   Sweden and Italy represent what type of economic and political system?

(a)   capitalism
(b)   socialism
(c)   communism
(d)   welfare capitalism

10.   An economic and political system that combines a mostly market-based economy with extensive social welfare programs.

(a)   socialism.
(b)   market socialism.
(c)   market communism.
(d)   an oligarchy.
(e)   welfare capitalism.

11.	During the 1970s and 1980s, *socialist economies* had about _____ as much *income inequality* as was found in capitalist economies during the same time period.

	(a)	one-tenth
	(b)	twice
	(c)	three times
	(d)	one-half
	(e)	four times

12.	By 2000, _____ percent of *new jobs* were in the *service sector*.

	(a)	50
	(b)	60
	(c)	70
	(d)	80
	(e)	90

13.	Today in the United States, two percent of the labor force works in farming. In 1900 the figure was

	(a)	10 percent.
	(b)	25 percent.
	(c)	40 percent.
	(d)	55 percent.

14.	Today, _____ percent of the U.S. nonfarm labor force was *unionized*.

	(a)	less than 5
	(b)	14
	(c)	25
	(d)	36
	(e)	over 50

15.	A _____ is a prestigious, white-collar occupation that requires extensive formal education.

	(a)	profession
	(b)	career
	(c)	technical occupation
	(d)	primary sector work

16.	Which of the following categories of people has the *lowest* unemployment rate in our society today?

	(a)	white women
	(b)	white men
	(c)	black women
	(d)	black men

17.   What is the term for giant corporations composed of many smaller corporations?

    (a)   megacorporations
    (b)   monopolies
    (c)   multinational corporations
    (d)   conglomerates
    (e)   oligarchies

18.   Which U.S. corporation leads the nation in sales and assets?

    (a)   IBM
    (b)   General Motors
    (c)   Exxon
    (d)   Ford Motor Company

19.   What is the term for a social network made up of people who simultaneously serve on the board of directors of many corporations?

    (a)   conglomerate
    (b)   corporate oligopolies
    (c)   interlocking directorate
    (d)   oligopoly
    (e)   onopoly

20.   In 1999, the average *hourly wage* for a U.S. worker in manufacturing was $15.23. At $19.62 per hour, which country had the highest average wage for working in the manufacturing sector?

    (a)   Germany
    (b)   Russia
    (c)   Canada
    (d)   France
    (e)   South Korea

Matching

1.   ___   The social institution that organizes a society's production, distribution, and consumption of goods and services.
2.   ___   A production system based on service work and high technology.
3.   ___   The part of the economy that transforms raw materials into manufactured goods.
4.   ___   The part of the economy involving services rather than goods.
5.   ___   Economic activity spanning many nations of the world with little regard for national borders.
6.   ___   An economic system in which natural resources and the means of producing goods and services are collectively owned.

7. ___ An economic and political system in which companies are privately owned although they cooperate closely with the government.
8. ___ Jobs that provide minimal benefits to workers.
9. ___ An organization with a legal existence, including rights and liabilities, apart from those of its members.
10. ___ Giant corporations composed of many smaller corporations.

a.	socialism	f.	state capitalism
b.	conglomerates	g.	economy
c.	secondary sector	h.	postindustrial economy
d.	tertiary sector	i.	global economy
e.	secondary labor market	j	corporation

Fill-In

1. _____ range from necessities like food to luxuries like swimming pools, while _____ include various activities that benefit others.

2. *Industrialization* introduced five fundamental changes in the economies of Western societies, including: new forms of _____, the centralization of work in _____, manufacturing and _____ _____, _____, and _____ _____.

3. A _____ *economy* is a productive system based on service work and high technology.

4. The Information Revolution unleashed three key changes, including: From tangible products to _____, from mechanical skills to _____ skills, and the movement of work from factories to _____.

5. Four major consequences of a *global economy* include: a global _____ ___ _____, an increasing number of products passing through more than one _____, _____ _____ no longer control the economic activity that takes place within their borders, and a _____ number of businesses, operating internationally, control a vast share of the world's economic activity.

6. A *capitalist system* has three distinctive features, including: _____ ownership of property, pursuit of personal _____, and free _____ and consumer sovereignty.

7. A *socialist system* has three distinctive features, including: _____ ownership of property, pursuit of _____ goals, and _____ control of the economy.

8. Sociologists divide the jobs in today's economy into two categories: the _____ *labor market* that includes occupations that provide extensive benefits to workers, and the _____ *labor market*, that includes jobs that provide minimal benefits to workers.

9. People describe their occupations as *professions* to the extent that they demonstrate the following four characteristics: _____ knowledge, _____ practice, _____ over clients, and _____ orientation rather than to self-interest.

10. The *Information Revolution* is changing the kind of work people do as well as where they do it. Computers are altering the character of work in four additional ways: they are _____ labor, making work more _____, _____ workplace interaction, and enhancing employer's _____ of workers.

Discussion

1. What were the five revolutionary changes brought about by the *Industrial Revolution*? Describe and illustrate each of these.
2. Define the concept *postindustrial society*, and identify three key changes unleashed by the *Information Revolution*.
3. What are the three basic characteristics of *capitalism*? What are the three basic characteristics of *socialism*? What is *democratic socialism*? What are the relative advantages and disadvantages of each for members of a society?
4. Comparing productivity and economic equality measures for *capitalist* and *socialist* economic systems, what are the relative advantages and disadvantages of each? Make comparisons in terms of *productivity, economic inequality,* and *civil liberties.*
5. What are the three main consequences of the development of a *global economy*?
6. What are the three major *sectors* of the economy? Define and illustrate each of these.
7. Identify and discuss the major characteristics of a *postindustrial economy*.
8. Refer to the 2000 *Statistical Abstract of the United States* and find four pieces of evidence to identify the existence of a large *secondary labor market* in our society.
9. What are the basic characteristics of a *profession*?
10. What are your interpretations of the data being presented in *Figure 16-2*?

PART VI: ANSWERS TO STUDY QUESTIONS

Key Terms

1. economy (p. 409)
2. postindustrial economy (p. 411)
3. primary sector (p. (412)
4. secondary sector (p. 412)
5. tertiary sector (p. 412)
6. global economy (p. 412)
7. Capitalism (p. 415)
8. Socialism (p. 417)
9. Communism (p. 417)
10. Welfare capitalism (p. 417)
11. State capitalism (p. 418)
12. primary labor market (p. 420)
13. secondary labor market (p. 420)
14. Labor unions (pp. 420-421)
15. profession (p. 421)
16. underground economy (p. 423)

17. corporation (p. 425)
18. conglomerate (p. 426)
19. monopoly (p. 427)
20. oligopoly (p. 427)

True-False

1.	T	(p. 409)	6.	F	(p. 416)
2.	T	(p. 409)	7.	F	(p. 418)
3.	T	(p. 411)	8.	T	(p. 419)
4.	T	(p. 412)	9.	F	(p. 420)
5.	F	(p. 412)	10.	T	(p. 423)

Multiple Choice

1.	a	(p. 411)	11.	d	(p. 418)
2.	c	(p. 412)	12.	e	(p. 420)
3.	c	(p. 412)	13.	c	(p. 420)
4.	e	(p. 412)	14.	b	(p. 421)
5.	a	(p. 412)	15.	a	(p. 421)
6.	d	(p. 416)	16.	b	(p. 423)
7.	d	(pp. 416-417)	17.	d	(p. 426)
8.	b	(p. 417)	18.	b	(p. 426)
9.	d	(p. 417)	19.	c	(p. 427)
10.	e	(p. 417)	20.	a	(p. 427)

Matching

1.	g	(p. 409)	6.	a.	(p. 416)
2.	h	(p. 411)	7.	f	(p. 418)
3.	c	(p. 412)	8.	e	(p. 420)
4.	d	(p. 412)	9.	j	(p. 425)
5.	i	(p. 412)	10.	b	(p. 426)

Fill-In

1. goods, services (p. 409)
2. energy, factories, mass production, specialization, wage labor (p. 410)
3. postindustrial (p. 411)
4. ideas, literacy, almost anywhere (p. 412)
5. division of labor, nation, national governments, small (pp. 413-414)
6. private, profit, competition (p. 415)
7. collective, collective, government (p. 416)
8. primary, secondary (p. 420)

9.   theoretical, self-regulating, authority, community (p. 421)
10.   deskilling, abstract, limiting, control (p. 425)

PART VII: IN FOCUS--IMORTANT ISSUES

- The Economy: Historical Overview

  Identify and describe the five fundamental ways in with *industrialization* changed the economy.

  In what ways is *postindustiral society* different from industrial society?

  What are the four major consequences of the *global economy*?

- Economic Systems: Paths to Justice

  What are the three distinctive features of *capitalism?*

      1.

      2.

      3.

How is *justice* understood in a capitalist context?

What are the three distinctive features of *socialism*?

    1.

    2.

    3.

How is *justice* understood in a socialist context?

What are the relative advantages of capitalism and socialism in each of the following domains?

    economic productivity

    economic equality

    personal freedom

- Work In the Postindustrial Economy

Differentiate between the major qualities of *industrial society* and *postindustrial society*.

What are the four characteristics of a *profession*?

1.
2.
3.
4.

The *unemployment rate* in the U.S. today is about four percent. What is *underemployment*? Why is it perhaps a bigger problem in our society than unemployment today?

What are the four ways in which *computers* are changing the character of work in the United States? Provide an illustration for each of these.

	change	illustration
1.		
2.		
3.		
4.		

- Corporations

What is the evidence that there is *economic concentration* in the United States?

What are four important consequences of a *global economy*?

- Looking Ahead: The Economy of the Twenty-First Century

What are three major patterns that are expected to continue to occur in terms of the our economy?

1.

2.

3.

216

Chapter 17 Politics And Government

PART I: CHAPTER OUTLINE

I.   Power and Authority
    A.   Traditional Authority
    B.   Rational-Legal Authority
    C.   Charismatic Authority

II.   Politics in Global Perspective
    A.   Monarchy
    B.   Democracy
        1.   Democracy and Freedom: Capitalist and Socialist Approaches
    C.   Authoritarianism
    D.   Totalitarianism
    E.   A Global Political System?

III. Politics in the United States
    A.   U.S. Culture and the Rise of the Welfare State
    B.   The Political Spectrum
        1.   Economic Issues
        2.   Social Issues
        3.   Mixed Positions
        4.   Party Identification
    C.   Special-Interest Groups
    D.   Voter Apathy

IV.   Theoretical Analysis of Power in Society
    A.   The Pluralist Model: The People Rule
    B.   The Power-Elite Model: A Few People Rule
    C.   The Marxist Model: Bias in the System Itself
        1.   Critical Evaluation

V.   Power Beyond the Rules
    A.   Revolution
    B.   Terrorism

PART II: LEARNING OBJECTIVES

- To recognize the difference between power and authority.
- To be able to identify, define, and illustrate the different types of authority.
- To be able to compare the four principal kinds of political systems.
- To be able to describe the nature of the American political system of government, and discuss the principal characteristics of the political spectrum of the U.S.
- To be able to compare the pluralist and power-elite models of political power.
- To be able to describe the types of political power that exceed, or seek to eradicate, established politics.
- To be able to identify the factors which increase the likelihood of war.
- To recognize the historical pattern of militarism in the United States and around the world, and to consider factors which can be used in the pursuit of peace.

PART III: KEY CONCEPTS

Fill in the blank spaces below with the appropriate concepts.

1. _____ refers to the social institution that distributes power, sets society's agenda, and makes decisions.
2. _____ is the ability to achieve desired ends despite the resistance of others.
3. A _____ is a formal organization that directs the political life of a society.
4. _____ refers to power that people perceive as legitimate rather than coercive.
5. Power legitimated through respect for long-established cultural patterns is known as _____ _____.
6. Power legitimated by legally enacted rules and regulations refers to _____ _____.
7. _____ _____ refers to power legitimated through extraordinary personal abilities that inspire devotion and obedience.
8. The _____ ____ _____ is the transformation of charismatic authority into some combination of traditional and bureaucratic authority.
9. A _____ is a type of political system in which a single family rules from generation to generation.
10. A _____ is a type of political system that gives power to the people as a whole.

11. _____ is a political system that denies popular participation in government.

12. _____ refers to a highly centralized political system that extensively regulates people's lives.

13. A _____ _____ refers to a range of government agencies and programs that provides benefits to the population.

14. A _____ _____ is a political alliance of people interested in some economic or social issue.

15. A _____ _____ _____ is an organization formed by a political-interest group, independent of political parties, to pursue political aims by raising and spending money.

16. The _____ _____ refers to an analysis of politics that sees power as dispersed among many competing interest groups.

17. The _____ _____ refers to an analysis of politics that sees power as concentrated among the rich.

18. The _____ _____ _____ _____ is an analysis that explains politics in terms of the operation of society's economic system.

19. A _____ _____ refers to the overthrow of one political system in order to establish another.

20. _____ refers to acts of violence or the threat of such violence by by an individual or group as a political strategy.

21. _____ refers to organized, armed conflict between the peoples of various societies,

PART IV: IMPORTANT RESEARCHERS

In the space below each of the following researchers, write two or three sentences to help remind you of his or her respective contributions to sociology.

Max Weber

C. Wright Mills

Robert and Helen Lynd

Quincy Wright

Floyd Hunter

Robert Dahl

Nelson Polsby

PART V: STUDY QUESTIONS

True-False

1. T F *Authority* is power people perceive as legitimate rather than coercive.
2. T F *Traditional authority* is sometimes referred to as bureaucratic authority.
3. T F *Authoritarianism* refers to a political system that denies popular participation in government.
4. T F In the United States today, tax revenue, as a share of gross domestic product, is higher than in any other industrialized society.
5. T F For every eleven U.S. citizens, there is one government employee.
6. T F *Voter apathy* is a problem, as evidenced by the fact that eligible citizens in the U.S. are less likely to vote today than they were a century ago.
7. T F Research by *Robert* and *Helen Lynd* in Muncie, Indiana (the Middletown study) supported the *pluralist model* concerning how power is distributed in the United States.
8. T F One of the four insights offered concerning *terrorism* is that democracies are especially vulnerable to it because these governments afford extensive civil liberties to their people and have limited police networks.
9. T F More U.S. soldiers were killed during *World War II* than in all other wars in which the U.S. has ever participated.
10. T F In recent years, defense has been the largest single expenditure by the U.S. government, accounting for sixteen percent of federal spending.

Multiple Choice

1. Power that people perceive as being *legitimate* rather than coercive is the definition for

    (a) a monarchy.
    (b) totalitarianism.
    (c) government.
    (d) politics.
    (e) authority.

2. Which of the following is *not* one of the general contexts in which power is commonly defined as authority?

    (a) traditional
    (b) charismatic
    (c) rational-legal
    (d) democratic

3. Power that is legitimated by respect for long-established cultural patterns is called

   (a) traditional.
   (b) sacred.
   (c) political.
   (d) charismatic.
   (e) power-elite.

4. According to *Max Weber*, the survival of a charismatic movement depends upon

   (a) pluralism.
   (b) political action.
   (c) routinization.
   (d) assimilation.

5. Norway, Spain, Belgium, Great Britain, the Netherlands, and Denmark are all contemporary examples of what form of government?

   (a) totalitarian democracies
   (b) authoritarian
   (c) constitutional monarchies
   (d) absolute monarchies

6. What percentage of humanity live in nations that are classified as being *not free*?

   (a) 14
   (b) 21
   (c) 34
   (d) 43
   (e) 50

7. _____ refers to a highly centralized political system that extensively regulates people's lives.

   (a) Authoritarianism
   (b) Totalitarianism
   (c) Absolute monarchy
   (d) State capitalism

8. Relatively speaking, which of the following nations has the largest government, based in tax revenues as a share of gross national product?

    (a)   Japan
    (b)   France
    (c)   the United States
    (d)   Canada
    (e)   Sweden

9. A _____ refers to a range of government agencies and programs that provides benefits to the population.

    (a)   socialist system
    (b)   democracy
    (c)   authoritarian government
    (d)   welfare state
    (e)   political spectrum

10. In making sense of people's *political attitudes*, analysts distinguish between two kinds of issues, including

    (a)   institutional and personal.
    (b)   economic and social.
    (c)   structural and moral.
    (d)   national and international.

11. Approximately 44.2 percent of adults in the United States identify with the *Democratic Party*. What percentage identify with the Republican Party?

    (a)   25.3
    (b)   51.9
    (c)   48.2
    (d)   33.6

12. Which of the following statements is/are accurate concerning *voting* in the United States?

    (a)   The long-term trend has been for greater eligibility to vote.
    (b)   A smaller and smaller share of eligible citizens is actually voting.
    (c)   Women and men are equally likely to cast a ballot.
    (d)   People over the age of sixty-five are three times as likely to vote as young adults aged eighteen to twenty-four.
    (a)   All of the above are accurate statements.

13. Which idea below represents the *pluralist model* of power?

    (a)   Power is highly concentrated.
    (b)   Voting cannot create significant political changes.
    (c)   The U.S. power system is an oligarchy.
    (d)   Power is widely dispersed throughout society.

14. _____ suggest voter apathy is the result of *indifference*.

    (a)   Liberals
    (b)   Marxists
    (c)   Conservatives
    (d)   Democrats

15. With which general sociological paradigm is the *power-elite model* associated?

    (a)   social-conflict
    (b)   symbolic-interaction
    (c)   structural-functional
    (d)   social-exchange

16. An analysis that explains politics in terms of the operation of society's *economic system* is referred to as

    (a)   pluralist theory.
    (b)   Marxist political-economy model.
    (c)   power-elite model.
    (d)   welfare state model.

17. According to Paul Johnson, which of the following is/are distinguishing characteristics of *terrorism*?

    (a)   Terrorists try to paint violence as a legitimate political tactic.
    (b)   Terrorism is employed not just by groups, but by governments against their own people.
    (c)   Democratic societies reject terrorism in principle, but they are especially vulnerable to terrorists because they afford extensive civil liberties.
    (d)   Terrorism is always a matter of definition.
    (e)   all of the above

18. *Quincy Wright* has identified several circumstances as conditions which lead humans to go to war? Which of the following is *not* one of these?

   (a)   perceived threat
   (b)   political objectives
   (c)   social problems
   (d)   moral objectives
   (e)   wide-ranging alternatives

19. Over one-half of all Americans *killed* in war were killed during

   (a)   World War I.
   (b)   the Vietnam War.
   (c)   the Revolutionary War.
   (d)   the Civil War.
   (e)   World War II.

20. *Military spending* accounts for _____ percent of the federal budget of the United States.

   (a)   less than 5
   (b)   10
   (c)   16
   (d)   35

Matching

1. ____   The ability to achieve desired ends despite resistance.
2. ____   Power people perceive as legitimate rather than coercive.
3. ____   A highly centralized political system that extensively regulates people's lives.
4. ____   A political system that denies popular participation in government.
5. ____   Tax revenues as a share of the gross domestic product for Sweden in 1999.
6. ____   The percentage adults in the U.S. who identify with the Republican party.
7. ____   An analysis of politics that views power as dispersed among many competing interest groups.
8. ____   An analysis of politics that views power as concentrated among the rich.
9. ____   Random acts of violence or the threat of such violence by an individual or group as a political strategy.
10. ____   Organized, armed conflict among the people of various societies, directed by their government.

   a.   power-elite model   f.   33.6
   b.   war   g.   pluralist model
   c.   authoritarianism   h.   power
   d.   authority   i.   55.4
   e.   terrorism   j.   totalitarianism

1. _____ is the social institution that distributes power, sets a social agenda, and makes decisions.

2. _____ is a formal organization that directs the political life of a society.

3. Max Weber differentiated between three types of *authority*, including _____, _____, and _____.

4. A _____ is a political system in which a single family rules from generation to generation.

5. According to the author, *socialist* countries claim to be democratic because their economies meet everyone's basic needs for housing, schooling, work, and medical care. In contrast, *capitalist* countries have an approach to political freedom that translates into _____ _____.

6. _____ refers to a highly centralized political system that extensively regulates people's lives.

7. While conservatives suggest *voter apathy* amounts to an _____ to politics, liberals counter that most non-voters are _____ from politics.

8. Analysts claim *revolutions* share a number of traits, including: rising _____, _____ government, _____ leadership by intellectuals, and establishing a new _____.

9. *Quincy Wright* cites five factors that promote *war*, including: perceived _____, social _____, _____ objectives, _____ objectives, and the absence of _____.

10. The most recent approaches to *peace* include: _____, high-technology _____, _____ and disarmament, and resolving underlying _____.

Discussion

1. Differentiate between the concepts *power* and *authority*. Further, differentiate between *Max Weber's* three types of *authority*.

2. Four types of *political systems* are reviewed in the text. Identify and describe each of these systems.

3. What are the general patterns in attitudes among U.S. citizens concerning *social* and *economic issues* as reviewed in the text?

4. What is the evidence that *voter apathy* is a problem in our society? What are its causes?

5. Discuss the *changing work place* using demographic data presented in the text. What are three changes that you think are positive? What are three changes you think are negative?

6. Differentiate between the *pluralist* and *power-elite* models concerning the distribution of power in the United States.

7. Several approaches to reducing the chances for *nuclear war* are addressed in the text. Identify these approaches.

8. In what three ways has politics gone global?

9. What are the five insights presented in the text concerning *terrorism*?

10. Discuss how the concepts of *democracy* and *freedom* are understood within the economic systems of *capitalism* and *socialism*.

PART VI: ANSWERS TO STUDY QUESTIONS

Key Concepts

1.   Politics (p. 435)
2.   Power (p. 435)
3.   government (p. 435)
4.   Authority (436)
5.   traditional authority (p. 436)
6.   rational-legal authority (p. 436)
7.   Charismatic authority (p. 436)
8.   routinization of charisma (p. 437)
9.   monarchy (p. 437)
10. democracy (p. 438)
11. Authoritarianism (p. 440)
12. Totalitarianism (p. 440)
13. welfare state (p. 443)
14. special-interest group (p. 445)
15. political action committee (PAC) (p. 445)
16. pluralist model (p. 448)
17. power-elite model (p. 448)
18. Marxist political economy model (p. 449)
19. Political revolution (p. 449)
20. Terrorism (p. 451)
21. War (p. 452)
22. military-industrial complex (p. 455)
23. Nuclear proliferation (p.455)

True-False

1.	T	(pp. 435-436)		6.	T	(p. 446)
2.	F	(p. 436)		7.	F	(p. 449)
3.	T	(p. 440)		8.	T	(p. 452)
4.	F	(p. 442)		9.	F	(p. 453)
5.	T	(p. 443)		10.	T	(p. 455)

Multiple Choice

1.	e	(p. 436)	11.	d	(p. 445)
2.	d	(p. 436)	12.	d	(p. 446)
3.	a	(p. 436)	13.	d	(p. 448)
4.	c	(p. 437)	14.	c	(p. 447)
5.	c	(p. 438)	15.	a	(p. 448)
6.	c	(p. 439)	16.	b	(p. 449)
7.	b	(p. 440)	17.	e	(pp. 451-452)
8.	e	(p. 442)	18.	e	(p. 453)
9.	d	(p. 443)	19.	d	(p. 453)
10.	b	(pp. 443-444)	20.	c	(p. 455)

Matching

1.	h	(p. 435)	6.	f	(p. 445)
2.	d	(p. 436)	7.	g	(p. 448)
3.	j	(p. 440)	8.	a	(p. 448)
4.	c	(p. 440)	9.	e	(p. 451)
5.	i	(p. 442)	10.	b	(p. 452)

Fill-In

1. Politics (p. 435)
2. Government (p. 435)
3. traditional, rational-legal, charismatic (p. 436)
4. monarchy (p. 437)
5. personal freedom (p. 438)
6. Totalitarianism (p. 440)
7. indifference, alienated (p. 447)
8. expectations, unresponsive, radical, legitimacy (p. 450)
9. threats, problems, political, alternatives (p. 453)
10. deterrence, defense, diplomacy, conflicts (pp. 455-457)

PART VII: IN FOCUS—IMPORTANT ISSUES

• Power and Authority

  How is *authority* different from *power?*

  Define and illustrate each of the following *types of authority.*

      traditional
      rational-legal
      charismatic

227

- Politics in Global Perspective

  Define and illustrate each of the following categories of *political systems.*

      monarchy

      democracy

  Discuss the differences in how capitalists and socialists understand the concepts of *democracy* and *freedom.*

      authoritarianism

      totalitarianism

- Politics in the United States

  Describe the *political spectrum* in the United States. What strikes you most about the data presented in the text?

  Generally discuss the evidence for *voter apathy* in the United States today. What are the two major explanations of voter apathy in the United States?

- Theoretical Analysis of Power in Society

  Differentiate between the following competing models of power in the United States. What is the evidence being used in support of each model?

  pluralist model

  power-elite model

  Marxist model

- Power Beyond the Rules

  What are the four traits commonly shared by *revolutions?*

  What are the four distinguishing characteristics of *terrorism?*

- War and Peace

  Identify and illustrate five factors that promote *war.*

  What are the four recent approaches to *peace* identified in the text? What are your thoughts on each in terms of promoting peace?

- Looking Ahead: Politics in the Twenty-First Century

  What are the four *global trends* being identified by the author?

Family

PART I: CHAPTER OUTLINE

I. The Family: Basic Concepts
II. The Family: Global Variations
  A. Marriage Patterns
  B. Residential Patterns
  C. Patterns of Descent
  D. Patterns of Authority
III. Theoretical Analysis of the Family
  A. Functions of the Family: Structural-Functional Analysis
  B. Inequality and the Family: Social-Conflict Analysis
  C. Constructing Family Life: Micro-Level Analysis
    1. Symbolic-Interaction Analysis
    2. Social-Exchange Analysis
IV. Stages of Family Life
  A. Courtship
    1. Romantic Love
  B. Settling In: Ideal and Real Marriage
  C. Child Rearing
  D. The Family in Later Life
V. U.S. Families: Class, Race, and Gender
  A. Social Class
  B. Ethnicity and Race
    1. Hispanic Families
    2. African American Families
    3. Mixed Marriages
  C. Gender
VI. Transitions and Problems in Family Life
  A. Divorce
    1. Who Divorces?
  B. Remarriage
  C. Family Violence
    1. Violence against Women
    2. Violence against Children

VII. Alternative Family Forms
    A.   One-Parent Families
    B.   Cohabitation
    C.   Gay and Lesbian Couples
    D.   Singlehood
VIII. New Reproductive Technology and the Family
 IX. Looking Ahead: Family in the Twenty-First Century
  X. Summary
 XI. Key Concepts
 XII. Critical-Thinking Questions
XIII. Applications and Exercises
XIV. Sites to See

PART II: LEARNING OBJECTIVES

- To be able to define and illustrate basic concepts relating to the social institutions of kinship, family, and marriage.
- To gain a cross-cultural perspectives of the social institutions of kinship, family, and marriage.
- To be able to analyze the social institutions of kinship, family, and marriage using the structural-functional, social-conflict, and symbolic-interaction perspectives.
- To be able to describe the traditional life course of the U.S. family.
- To be able to recognize the impact of social class, race, ethnicity, and gender socialization on the family.
- To be able describe the problems and transitions that seriously affect family life.
- To be able to describe the composition and prevalence of alternative family forms.
- To become aware of the impact, both technologically and ethically, of new reproductive techniques on the family.
- To be able to identify four sociological conclusions about the family as we enter the twenty-first century.

PART III: KEY CONCEPTS

Fill-in the blank spaces below with the appropriate concepts.

1. The _____ is a social institution found in all societies that unites people in cooperative groups to oversee the bearing and raising of children.
2. _____ refers to a social bond based on blood, marriage, or adoption.
3. A _____ _____ is a social group of two or more people, related by blood, marriage, or adoption, who usually live together.
4. _____ refers to a legally sanctioned relationship, usually involving economic cooperation as well as sexual activity and childbearing, that people expect to be enduring.
5. An _____ _____ is a family unit that includes parents and children as well as other kin.
6. A _____ _____ is a family unit composed of one or two parents and their children.
7. _____ refers to marriage between people of the same social category.
8. _____ refers to marriage between people of different social categories.
9. Marriage that unites two partners is known as _____.

231

10. Marriage that units three of more people refers to _____.
11. _____ refers to marriage that unites one male and two or more females.
12. Marriage that unites one female and two or more males is known as _____.
13. _____ is a residential pattern in which a marred couple lives with or near the husband's family.
14. _____ is a residential pattern in which a married couple lives with or near the wife's family.
15. A residential pattern in which a married couple lives apart from both sets of parents.
16. _____ refers to the system by which members of a society trace kinship over generations.
17. _____ _____ is a system tracing kinship through men.
18. _____ _____ is a system tracing kinship through women.
19. _____ _____ is a system tracing kinship through both men and women.
20. The _____ _____ is a norm forbidding sexual relations or marriage between certain relatives.
21. Marriage between people with the same social characteristics is known as _____.
22. _____ refers to sexual activity outside marriage.
23. _____ _____ refers to emotional, physical, or sexual abuse of one family member b y another.
24. The sharing of a household by an unmarried couple is known as _____.

PART IV: IMPORTANT RESEARCHERS

In the space provided below each of the following researchers, write two or three sentences to help you remember his or her respective contributions to sociology.

Lillian Rubin   Jessie Bernard

Paul Bohannan

PART V: STUDY QUESTIONS

True-False

1.	T	F	The family into which one is born is referred to as the *family of procreation*.
2.	T	F	Beings based on marriage, the nuclear family is also known as the *conjugal family*.
3.	T	F	Norms of *endogamy* relate to marriage between people of the same social category.
4.	T	F	*Matrilocality* occurs more commonly in societies that engage in distant warfare or in which daughters have greater economic value.

5.	T	F	*Polyandry* is much more common around the world than is *polygyny*.
6.	T	F	*Neolocality* refers to a residential pattern in which a married couple lives apart from the parents of both spouses.
7.	T	F	While the *divorce rate* is in the U.S. high; relative to other industrialized societies it is fairly low.
8.	T	F	*Blended families* are composed of children and some combination of biological parents and stepparents.
9.	T	F	Less than one-third of those couples who *cohabit* eventually marry.
10.	T	F	*Homosexual marriage* is illegal in all fifty states in the United States.

Multiple Choice

1. Which of the following concepts refers to a social bond, based on blood, marriage or adoption?

   (a) descent group.
   (b) nuclear family.
   (c) family.
   (d) kinship.

2. The *consanguine family* is also known as the

   (a) conjugal family.
   (b) family of orientation.
   (c) nuclear family.
   (d) family of procreation.
   (e) extended family.

3. What is the family unit including parents and children, as well as other kin?

   (a) a family
   (b) a kinship group
   (c) a nuclear family
   (d) an extended family

4. Marriage between people of different social categories is called

   (a) polygamy.
   (b) monogamy.
   (c) exogamy.
   (d) endogamy.

5. What is a marriage that joins *one female* with *two or more males*?

    (a) polygamy
    (b) polyandry
    (c) endogamy
    (d) polygyny

6. What is the residential pattern in which a married couple lives apart from the parents of both spouses?

    (a) neolocality
    (b) patrilocality
    (c) matrilocality
    (d) avunculocality
    (e) bilateral descent

7. What is the system by which members of a society trace kinship over generations?

    (a) descent
    (b) family
    (c) marriage
    (d) extended family

8. Which theory and theorist traced the origin of the family to the need for men to pass property on to their sons?

    (a) symbolic-interaction--George Herbert Mead
    (b) structural-functionalism--Talcott Parsons
    (c) structural functionalism--Emile Durkheim
    (d) social-conflict--Friedrich Engels

9. According to social-conflict theorists, which of the following is *not* one of the ways that families aid in the perpetuation of social inequality?

    (a) property and inheritance
    (b) bilateral descent
    (c) patriarchy
    (d) race and ethnicity

10. Which of the following is *not* one of the familial adjustments made by parents in *later life*?

    (a) adjustment to retirement and spending more time together
    (b) helping to care for grandchildren
    (c) assumption of more household responsibilities
    (d) death of a spouse

11.   Lillian Rubin focused her research on the relationship between _____ and marriage.

    (a)   social class
    (b)   race
    (c)   presence of children
    (d)   age at marriage

12.   Which of the following is *not* a finding of Jessie Bernard's study of marriage?

    (a)   married women have poorer mental health
    (b)   married women have more passive attitudes toward life
    (c)   married women report less personal happiness
    (d)   married women are not generally required to participate in the labor force

13.   The high U.S. *divorce rate* has many causes, which of the following is *not* identified in the text as being one of them?

    (a)   Individualism is on the rise.
    (b)   Women are more dependent on men.
    (c)   Many marriages today are stressful.
    (d)   Romantic love often subsides.
    (e)   Divorce is easier to get and more socially acceptable.

14.   Remarriage often creates families composed of both biological parents and stepparents and children. These families are called

    (a)   second families.
    (b)   blended families.
    (c)   focal families.
    (d)   families of orientation.

15.   In the U.S. annually, there are approximately _____ *reported cases* of child abuse and neglect?

    (a)   100,000
    (b)   6 million
    (c)   3 million
    (d)   300,000

16.   Currently in the U.S. what percentage of children are living in *single-parent families*?

    (a)   16
    (b)   45
    (c)   9
    (d)   28

17.   Which of the following statements is *least* accurate?

(a)   About fifty-four percent of African American families are headed by a single parent.
(b)   About seventy-eight percent of all one-parent families in the U.S. are headed by women.
(c)   About one-half of all children in the U.S. will live in a one-parent family at some time before their eighteenth birthday.
(d)   There are approximately 5.5 million cohabiting heterosexual couples in the U.S. today.
(e)   Children raised in one-parent families are less likely to become single-parents than are children who are raised in families with two parents.

18.   In the U.S. today, about thirty-two percent of the live births annually are to unwed mothers. The nation with the highest rate of live births to unwed mothers, at fifty-three percent, is

(a)   France.
(b)   Italy.
(c)   Sweden.
(d)   Germany
(e)   Canada

19.   Which country, in 1989, became the first nation to legalize *same-sex marriages*?

(a)   Denmark
(b)   France
(c)   the United States
(d)   Japan

20.   Which of the following statements is *not accurate* concerning *cohabitation*?

(a)   It is more popular today in the U.S. than it was in 1970.
(b)   Almost one-half of people between the ages twenty-five and forty-four have cohabited at some point in time.
(c)   Only about thirty percent of cohabiting couples eventually marry.
(d)   Over one-third of cohabiting couples have at least one child living with them.
(e)   Cohabiting tends to appeal to more independent minded individuals as well as those who favor gender equality.

Matching

1. ___ A family unit including parents, children, as well as other kin.
2. ___ People with or without legal or blood ties who feel they belong together and want to define themselves as a family.
3. ___ The system by which members of a society trace kinship over generations.
4. ___ Marriage between people of the same social category.
5. ___ A residential pattern in which a married couple lives apart from the parents of both spouses.
6. ___ A form of marriage uniting one female with two or more males.
7. ___ A system tracing kinship through both men and women.
8. ___ A form of marriage uniting one male with two or more females.
9. ___ The feeling of affection and sexual passion toward another person as the basis of marriage.
10. ___ Families composed of children and some combination of biological parents and stepparents.

a. endogamy
b. extended family
c. blended families
d. bilateral decent
e. descent

f. neolocality
g. family of affinity
h. polygyny
i. polyandry
j. romantic love

Fill-In

1. _____ is a marriage that joins one female with two or more males.
2. _____ refers to the system by which members of a society trace kinship over generations.
3. _____ *descent* is a system tracing kinship through both men and women.
4. Structural-functionalists identify several *vital tasks* performed by the family. These include: _____, _____ of sexual activity, social _____, and material and emotional _____.
5. *Social-conflict* theorists argue that families perpetuate social inequality in several ways, including: Property and _____, _____, and racial and ethnic _____.
6. More and more mothers are working outside the home in the paid labor force. For children under the age of five whose mothers work outside the home, who is caring for their children while these mothers work? The pattern breaks down as follows: _____ percent receive care by a parent, _____ percent receive care by a relative (other than a parent) in the child's home, _____ receive care by a nonrelative in the provider's home, _____ percent receive care by a nanny or babysitter in the child's home, and _____ percent are cared for in center-based child care facilities.
7. The high U.S. *divorce rate* has many causes, including: _____ is on the rise, _____ _____ often subsides, women are now less _____ on men, many of today's marriages are _____, divorce is more socially _____, and legally, divorce is _____ to obtain.
8. Family brutality often goes unreported to police. Even so, in 1999 the U.S. Bureau of Justice Statistics reported more than _____ cases of violence between *intimate partners*. Of this total _____ percent involved violence against women.

9. _____ is the sharing of a household by an unmarried couple.
10. Sociologists point our five probable *future trends* regarding the family. These include: _____ rates are likely to remain high, family life will be highly _____, men are likely to continue to play a limited role in _____ _____, we will continue to feel the effects of _____ changes in our families, and the importance of new _____ technology will increase.

Discussion

1. What are the four basic *functions* of the family according to structural-functionalists?
2. Define and describe the three patterns of *descent*.
3. Why has the *divorce rate* increased in recent decades in the United States? What are the basic demographic patterns involving divorce in our society today?
4. What are the four *stages* of the family life cycle outlined in the text? Describe the major events occurring during each of these stages.
5. In what ways are *middle-class* and *working-class* marriages different?
6. What are the arguments being made about the family by *social-conflict* theorists?
7. What are four important points made in the text concerning *family violence*?
8. Five *alternative family forms* are discussed in the text. Identify these and review the data concerning three of them. What are your opinions concerning these changes in the family?
9. What are the five conclusions being made about marriage and family life into the twenty-first century?
10. What are the dimensions of *family violence*? What are the demographic patterns concerning each of these? What three social forces in our society do you think affect the rates of family violence in our society?

PART V: ANSWERS TO STUDY QUESTIONS

Key Concepts

1. family (p. 463)
2. Kinship (p. 463)
3. family unit (p. 464)
4. Marriage (p. 464)
5. extended family (consanguine family) (p. 464)
6. nuclear family (p. 464)
7. Endogamy (p. 465)
8. Exogamy (p. 465)
9. monogamy (p. 465)
10. polygamy (p. 465)
11. Polygyny (p. 465)
12. polyandry (p. 465)
13. Patrilocality (p. 465)
14. Matrilocality (p. 465)
15. neolocality (p. 465)
16. Descent (p. 465)

17. Patrilineal descent (p. 465)
18. Matrilineal descent (p. 466)
19. Bilateral descent (p. 466)
20. incest taboo (p. 467)
21. homogamy (p. 472)
22. Infidelity (p. 473)
23. Family violence (p. 481)
24. cohabitation (p. 482)

True-False

1.	F	(p. 463)		6.	T	(p. 465)
2.	T	(p. 464)		7.	F	(p. 478)
3.	T	(p. 465)		8.	T	(p. 480)
4.	T	(p. 465)		9.	F	(p. 483)
5.	F	(p. 465)		10.	T	(p. 483)

Multiple Choice

1.	d	(p. 463)		11.	a	(pp. 474-475)
2.	e	(p. 464)		12.	d	(pp. 477-478)
3.	d	(p. 464)		13.	b	(pp. 478-479)
4.	c	(p. 465)		14.	b	(p. 480)
5.	b	(p. 465)		15.	c	(p. 473)
6.	a	(p. 465)		16.	d	(p .481)
7.	a	(p. 465)		17.	e	(p. 482)
8.	d	(p. 469)		18.	c	(p. 483)
9.	b	(p. 469)		19.	a	(p. 483)
10.	c	(p. 474)		20.	c	(p. 483)

Matching

1.	b	(p. 464)		6.	i	(p. 465)
2.	g	(p. 464)		7.	d	(p. 465)
3.	e	(p. 465)		8.	h	(p. 465)
4.	a	(p. 465)		9.	j	(p. 472)
5.	f	(p. 465)		10.	c	(p. 480)

Fill-In

1. Polyandry (p. 465)
2. Descent (p. 465)
3. Bilateral (p. 466)
4. socialization, regulation, placement, security (pp. 467-468)
5. inheritance, patriarchy, race, ethnicity (p. 470)
6. 24, 23, 16, 6, 32 (p. 475)

7.   individualism, romantic love, dependent, stressful, acceptable, easier (pp. 478-479)
8.   791,000, 85 (p. 481)
9.   Cohabitation (p. 482)
10.   divorce, variable, child rearing, economic, reproductive (p. 485)

PART VII: IN FOCUS--IMPORTANT ISSUES

- The Family: Basic Concepts

  What does the author mean by saying that there is a trend toward a more *inclusive* definition of the family?

- The Family: Global Variations

  Identify and define or illustrate the different *patterns* found around the world for each of the following.

  marriage

  residence

  descent

  authority

- Theoretical Analysis of the Family

  According to structural-functionalists, what are the *functions* performed by families? Provide one piece of evidence for each function.

  In what ways do *conflict theorists* believe the family perpetuates inequality? Illustrate or define each of these.

  Micro-level approaches explore how individuals shape and experience family life. Differentiate between the following two micro-level perspectives.

    symbolic-interaction analysis

    social-exchange analysis

- Stages of Family Life

  Briefly describe the content for each of the following stages in family life.

    courtship

settling in

child rearing

the family in later life

- U.S. Families: Class, Race, and Gender

  Summarize the findings concerning Lillian Rubin's research on the relationship between *social class* and the family.

  Identify important demographic differences between white families and the following racial and ethnic minorities.

    African Americans

    Hispanics

  Summarize the conclusions of Jessie Bernard concerning *gender* and the family.

- Transitions and Problems In Family Life

  Identify the major causes of *divorce* as listed in the text.

  What are the characteristics most associated with divorce?

  How common is *remarriage*?

  Identify three important facts concerning each of the following two types of *family violence*.

    violence against women

    violence against children

- Alternative Family Forms

  Identify two important demographic facts concerning *single-parent families* in our society today.

How common is *cohabitation* in our society today?

What are two important points being made about *gay and lesbian couples*?

How common is *singlehood* in our society today?

- New Reproductive Technology and the Family

  What is *in vitro fertilization*?

  What are you thoughts concerning the different forms of *reproductive technologies* and their impact on the lives of individuals, couples, and society as a whole?

- Looking Ahead: The Family In the Twenty-First Century

  What are the five likely trends for the family of the twenty-first century s identified by the author?

Chapter 19 Religion

PART I: CHAPTER OUTLINE

I. Religion: Basic Concepts
    A. Religion and Sociology
II. Theoretical Analysis of Religion
    A. Functions of Religion: Structural-Functional Analysis
    B. Constructing the Sacred: Symbolic-Interaction Analysis
    C. Inequality and Religion: Social-Conflict Analysis
III. Religion and Social Change
    A. Max Weber: Protestantism and Capitalism
    B. Liberation Theology
IV. Types of Religious Organization
    A. Church
    B. Sect
    C. Cult
V. Religion in History
    A. Religion In Preindustrial Societies
    B. Religion In Industrial Societies
VI. World Religions
    A. Christianity
    B. Islam
    C. Judaism
    D. Hinduism
    E. Buddhism
    F. Confucianism
    G. Religion: East and West
VII. Religion in the United States
    A. Religious Affiliation
    B. Religiosity
    C. Religion and Social Stratification
        1. Social Class
        2. Ethnicity and Race

PART II: LEARNING OBJECTIVES

- To be able to define basic concepts relating to the sociological analysis of religion.
- To be able to identify and describe the three functions of religion as developed by Emile Durkheim.
- To be able to discuss the view that religion is socially constructed.
- To be able to discuss the role of religion in maintaining social inequality.
- To be able to describe how industrialization and science affect religious beliefs and practices.
- To be able to compare and contrast the basic types of religious organization.
- To be able to distinguish between preindustrial and industrial societies in terms of religious beliefs and practices.
- To be able to identify and generally distinguish between the world's major religions.
- To be able to discuss the basic demographic patterns concerning religious affiliation, religiosity, secularization, and religious revival in the U.S. today.
- To begin to critically think about the role of religion in the world as it will unfold over the next generation, and to consider the relationship between religion and science.

PART III: KEY CONCEPTS

Fill in the blank spaces below with the appropriate concepts.

1.   The _____ refers to that which people define as an ordinary element of everyday life.
2.   The _____ refers to that which people set apart as extraordinary, inspiring a sense of awe and reverence.
3.   _____ is a social institution involving beliefs and practices based on a conception of the sacred.
4.   A _____ refers to formal, ceremonial behavior.
5.   _____ refers to belief anchored in conviction rather than scientific evidence.
6.   A _____ is an object in the natural world collectively defined as sacred.
7.   _____ _____ is a fusion of Christian principles with political activism, often Marxist in character.

8.   A _____ is a type of religious organization well integrated into the larger society.
9.   A _____ _____ is a church formally allied with the state.
10. A _____ is a church, independent of the state that accepts religious pluralism.
11. A _____ is a type of religious organization that stands apart from the larger society.
12. _____ refers to extraordinary personal qualities that can turn an audience into followers.
13. A _____ is a religious organization that is largely outside a society's cultural traditions.
14. _____ refers to the belief that elements of the natural world are conscious life forms that affect humans.
15. _____ is the belief in a single divine power.
16. _____ is the belief in many gods.
17. The importance of religion in a person's life is known as _____.
18. _____ refers to the historical decline in the importance of the supernatural and the sacred.
19. A _____ _____ is a quasi-religious loyalty binding individuals in a basically secular society.
20. _____ refers to a conservative religious doctrine that opposes intellectualism and worldly accommodation in favor of restoring traditional, otherworldly religion.

PART IV: IMPORTANT RESEARCHERS

In the space provided below each of the following researchers, write two or three sentences to help you remember his respective contributions to sociology.

Emile Durkheim   Karl Marx

Max Weber

PART V: STUDY QUESTIONS

True-False

1. T   F   According to Emile Durkheim, the *profane* refers to that, which is an ordinary element of everyday life.
2. T   F   A major criticism of Emile Durkheim's analysis of religion is that he focuses too much attention on the *dysfunctions* of religious belief and practice.
3. T   F   The symbolic-interaction approach views religion as a *social construction*.
4. T   F   Whereas a *cult* is a type of religious organization that stands apart from the larger society, a *sect* represents something almost entirely new and stands outside a society's cultural tradition.
5. T   F   *Animism* is the belief that natural objects are conscious life forms that affect humanity.
6. T   F   *Islam* is the most widespread religion in the world.
7. T   F   *Judaism* is the world's oldest religion.
8. T   F   By global standards, *North Americans* are relatively nonreligious people.
9. T   F   Science and new technologies are reducing the relevance of religion in modern society as many moral dilemmas and spiritual issues are resolved or are diminishing in significance.
10. T   F   The *Scopes Monkey Trial* of 1925 involved the prosecution of a science teacher who was teaching evolution in violation to Tennessee state law.

Multiple Choice

1. _____ refers to that which people set apart as extraordinary, inspiring a sense of awe and reverence.

    (a)   Profane
    (b)   Sacred
    (c)   Animism
    (d)   Religiosity

2. What is the term for the social institution involving beliefs and practices based upon a conception of the sacred?

    (a)   faith
    (b)   totem
    (c)   religion
    (d)   ritual

3.   Emile Durkheim referred to the ordinary elements of everyday life as

(a)   religion.
(b)   faith.
(c)   ritual.
(d)   the profane.

4.   Formal, ceremonial behavior refers to

(a)   the sacred.
(b)   ritual.
(c)   religion.
(d)   faith.

5.   The view that religion is completely *socially constructed* by a society's members and largely serves to place our fallible, brief lives within some "cosmic frame of reference" giving us "the semblance of ultimate security and permanence" is espoused by

(a)   Max Weber.
(b)   Peter Berger.
(c)   Karl Marx.
(d)   Emile Durkheim.

6.   Which of the following is an appropriate criticism of a *symbolic-interactionist's* approach to the study of religion?

(a)   It ignores religion's link to inequality.
(b)   It fails to consider the importance of rituals.
(c)   It treats reality as objective.
(d)   It ignores the social construction of religion.

7.   *Liberation theology* advocates a blending of religion with

(a)   the family.
(b)   the economy.
(c)   education.
(d)   politics.

8.   A church, independent of the state, that accepts religious pluralism is a(n)

(a)   denomination,
(b)   sect.
(c)   cult.
(d)   civil religion.

9. A religious organization that is largely outside society's cultural traditions is called a

   (a) totem.
   (b) cult.
   (c) ecclesia.
   (d) sect.

10. The belief that elements of the natural world are conscious life forms that affect humanity refers to

   (a) animism.
   (b) cults.
   (c) a totem.
   (d) sects.

11. Which religion is the most *widespread* in the world?

   (a) Islam
   (b) Buddhism
   (c) Christianity
   (d) Judaism

12. The followers of *Islam* are called

   (a) Buddhists.
   (b) animists.
   (c) Hindus.
   (d) Muslims.

13. A distinctive concept of *Judaism* is the _____, a special relationship with God by which Jews become the "chosen people".

   (a) covenant
   (b) Torah
   (c) dharma
   (d) Passover

14. Which of the following is the *oldest* of all the world's religions?

   (a) Christianity
   (b) Judaism
   (c) Hinduism
   (d) Islam

15. Which world religion is so intertwined with one nation that it cannot be diffused widely to other nations?

    (a)   Judaism
    (b)   Confucianism
    (c)   Hinduism
    (d)   Buddhism

16. Which of the following is the largest *Protestant denomination*?

    (a)   Baptist
    (b)   Presbyterian
    (c)   Methodist
    (d)   Episcopalian
    (e)   Lutheran

17. The strength of a person's emotional ties to a religion is called

    (a)   ideological religiosity.
    (b)   ritualistic religiosity.
    (c)   experiential religiosity.
    (d)   intellectual religiosity.

18. What is *secularization*?

    (a)   the ecumenical movement
    (b)   the historical decline in the importance the supernatural and the sacred
    (c)   the increase in religiosity in postindustrial society
    (d)   fundamentalism

19. Which of the following is *not* identified in the text as a distinction of *religious fundamentalism*?

    (a)   Fundamentalists interpret sacred texts literally.
    (b)   Fundamentalists promote religious pluralism.
    (c)   Fundamentalists pursue the personal experience of God's presence.
    (d)   Fundamentalism opposes "secular humanism".
    (e)   Many fundamentalists endorse conservative political goals.

20. In the *Scopes trial* of 1925, the state of Tennessee prosecuted a man for

    (a)   polygamy.
    (b)   profanity.
    (c)   cohabitation.
    (d)   teaching evolution.

Matching

1. ___ The social institution involving beliefs and practices based upon a conception of the sacred.
2. ___ Belief anchored in conviction rather than scientific evidence.
3. ___ An object in the natural world collectively defined as sacred.
4. ___ A type of religious organization well integrated into the larger society.
5. ___ A church, independent of the state, that accepts religious pluralism.
6. ___ Extraordinary personal qualities that can turn an audience into followers.
7. ___ A type of religious organization that stands apart from the larger society.
8. ___ The belief in many gods.
9. ___ The importance of religion in a person's life.
10. ___ The historical decline in the importance of the supernatural and the sacred.

a.	denomination	f.	church
b.	polytheism	g.	faith
c.	religiosity	h.	totem
d.	religion	i.	secularization
e.	charisma	j.	sect

Fill-In

1. *Emile Durkheim* labeled the ordinary elements of everyday life the _____.
2. According to Emile Durkheim, three major *functions of religion* include: Social _____, social _____, and providing _____ and _____.
3. According to *Max Weber*, industrial capitalism developed in the wake of _____.
4. A _____ is a type of religious organization well integrated into the larger society.
5. _____ refers to extraordinary personal qualities that can turn audiences into followers.
6. _____ is the belief that natural objects are conscious forms of life that can affect humanity.
7. Of special importance to Jewish people are the Bible's first five books, known as the _____.
8. The *Hindu principle* of _____ is a belief in the spiritual progress of the human soul.
9. Charles Glock proposed five distinct *dimensions of religiosity*, including: _____, _____, _____, _____, and _____.
10. *Religious fundamentalism* is distinctive in five ways, including: interpreting sacred texts _____, rejecting religious _____, pursuing the personal experience of God's _____, opposition to secular _____, and endorsement of _____ political goals.

Discussion

1. According to *structural-functional* analysis, what are three major functions of religion? Provide an example for each from U.S. society.
2. Discuss *Max Weber's* points concerning the historical relationship between Protestantism and capitalism.
3. How do theorists operating from the *social conflict* perspective understand religion and how it operates in society? Provide two examples to illustrate.
4. In a one-page written discussion, debate the issue of whether science threatens or strengthens religion in society.
5. Discuss the issue concerning the extent of *religiosity* in the United States today.
6. Discuss the relationship between *religion* and *social stratification* in the United States today.
7. What are the two major differences between *Eastern* and *Western* religions?
8. Briefly describe the history and dominant religious beliefs for two of the following religions: Christianity, Islam, Judaism, Hinduism, Buddhism, Confucianism.
9. Differentiate between the nature of religion in *preindustrial* and *industrial* societies.
10. Differentiate between *civil religion* and *religious fundamentalism*.

PART VI: ANSWERS TO STUDY QUESTIONS

Key Terms

1. profane (p. 491)
2. sacred (p. 491)
3. Religion (p. 491)
4. ritual (p. 491)
5. Faith (p. 492)
6. totem (p. 492)
7. Liberation theology (p. 495)
8. church (p. 496)
9. state church (p. 496)
10. denomination (p. 496)
11. sect (p. 496)
12. Charisma (p. 497)
13. cult (p. 497)
14. Animism (p. 498)
15. Monotheism (p. 500)
16. Polytheism (p. 500)
17. religiosity (p. 506)
18. Secularization (p. 508)
19. Civil religion (p. 509)
20. Fundamentalism (p. 510)

True-False

1.	T	(p. 491)	6.	F	(p. 499)
2.	F	(p. 491)	7.	F	(p. 503)
3.	T	(p. 493)	8.	F	(p. 504)
4.	T	(pp. 496-497)	9.	F	(p. 512)
5.	T	(p. 498)	10.	T	(p. 512)

Multiple Choice

1.	b	(p. 491)	11.	c	(p. 499)
2.	c	(p. 491)	12.	d	(p. 500)
3.	d	(p. 491)	13.	a	(p. 501)
4.	b	(p. 491)	14.	c	(p. 503)
5.	b	(p. 493)	15.	b	(p. 504)
6.	a	(p. 493)	16.	a	(p. 505)
7.	d	(p. 495)	17.	c	(p. 506)
8.	a	(p. 496)	18.	b	(p. 508)
9.	b	(p. 497)	19.	b	(pp. 510-511)
10.	a	(p. 498)	20.	d	(p. 512)

Matching

1.	d	(p. 491)	6.	e	(p. 496)
2.	g	(p. 492)	7.	j	(p. 496)
3.	h	(p. 492)	8.	b	(p. 500)
4.	f	(p. 496)	9.	c	(p. 506)
5.	a	(p. 496)	10.	i	(p. 508)

Fill-In

1. profane (p. 491)
2. cohesion, control meaning, purpose (p. 493)
3. Calvinism (p. 494)
4. church (p. 496)
5. Charisma (p. 497)
6. Animism (p. 498)
7. Torah (p. 5019)
8. karma (p. 503)
9. experimental, ritualistic, ideological, consequential, intellectual (p. 506)
10. literally, pluralism, presence, humanism, conservative (pp. 510-511)

PART VII: IN FOCUS--IMPORTANT ISSUES

- Religion: Basic Concepts

  How do sociologists conceptualize and understand the place of *faith* and *ritual* in the institution of religion?

  Provide an illustration for Emile Durkheim's distinction between the *profane* and the *sacred*.

- Theoretical Analysis of Religion

  According to *structural-functionalist* Emile Durkheim, what are the three basic *functions of religion*?

  What points are being made by *symbolic-interactionist* Peter Berger concerning religion?

  How did *conflict theorist* Karl Marx understand religion?

- Religion and Social Change

  What is Max Weber's point concerning the relationship between *Protestantism* and *capitalism*?

- Types of Religious Organization

  Differentiate between each of the following.

      church

      sect

      cult

- Religion in History

  How is religion different in *preindustrial societies* as compared with industrial societies? What are the similarities?

- World Religions

  Identify three important points concerning each of the following religions.

      Christianity

      Islam

      Judaism

      Hinduism

      Buddhism

      Confucianism

What are the two basic distinctions between religion in the *East* and *West*?

- Religion in the United States

How religious are we here in the United States? What is the evidence?

What is the relationship between *social stratification* and religion?

   social class

   race and ethnicity

- Religion In a Changing Society

Briefly discuss the place of each of the following patterns in the United States today.

   secularism

   civil religion

   religious revival

   religious fundamentalism

   What is meant by the term *post-denomination society*?

- Looking Ahead: Religion In the Twenty-First Century

What conclusions are being made by the author concerning the place of religion in contemporary United States society?

Chapter 20 — Education

PART I: CHAPTER OUTLINE

PART II: LEARNING OBJECTIVES

- To be able to describe the different role of education in low-income and high-income countries.
- To compare education in India, Japan, and Great Britain to that provided in the United States.
- To be able to identify and describe the functions of schooling.
- To consider how education supports social inequality.
- To be able to discuss the major issues and problems facing contemporary education in the United States today.
- To be able to identify and evaluate alternatives to the current structure of the institution of education in our society.

PART IV: KEY CONCEPTS

In the blank spaces below, write in the appropriate concept.

1.   _____ refers to the social institution through which society provides its members with important knowledge, including basic facts, job skills, and cultural norms and values.
2.   Formal instruction under the direction of specially trained teachers is known as _____.
3.   The _____ _____ is the subtle presentations of political or cultural ideas in the classroom.
4.   Assigning students to different types of educational programs is called _____.
5.   _____ refers to evaluating a person on the basis of educational degrees.
6.   _____ _____ refers to a lack of reading and writing skills needed for everyday living.
7.   _____ refers to integrating special students into the overall educational program.

PART IV: IMPORTANT RESEARCHERS

In the space provided below each of the following researchers, write two or three sentences to help you remember his or her respective contributions to the field of sociology.

David Karp and William Yoels   Randall Collins

James Coleman   Jonathan Kozol

Christopher Jencks   John Dewey

Theodore Sizer   Talcott Parsons

Samuel Bowles and Herbert Gintis

PART V: STUDY QUESTIONS

True-False

1. T   F   Today, schooling in *low-income nations* is very diverse because it reflects the local culture.
2. T   F   Japan still does not have national *mandatory education laws*.
3. T   F   The United States graduates *smaller percentage* of its students from high school than does Japan, however Japan, because of competitive examination, send a smaller percentage of students on to college.
4. T   F   The United States was among the first nations to endorse the principle of *mass education*.
5. T   F   The United States has a *smaller* percentage of its adult population holding a college than most other industrialized societies.
6. T   F   *John Dewey* was a foremost advocate of the idea that schooling should have *practical* consequences.
7. T   F   *Social conflict* theorists support *tracking* in that they believe it gives students the kind of learning that fits their abilities and motivation.
8. T   F   The *Coleman Report* determined that the amount of educational funding was the most important factor in determining education achievement.
9. T   F   Male college graduates can expect to earn about forty percent more than female college graduates in their lifetime.
10. T   F   The work *A Nation At Risk* focuses on the increasing violence in American schools.

Multiple Choice

1. The social institution guiding a society's transmission of knowledge--including basic facts, job skills, and also cultural norms and values--to its members is the definition for

    (a)   schooling.
    (b)   teaching.
    (c)   education.
    (d)   curriculum.

2. Formal instruction under the direction of specially trained teachers refers to

    (a) curriculum.
    (b) education.
    (c) schooling.
    (d) mainstreaming.

3. Which of the following is *inaccurate* concerning India?

    (a) People earn about five percent of the income standard in the United States, and poor families often depend on the earnings of children.
    (b) Less than one-half of Indian children enter secondary school.
    (c) About one-half of the Indian population is illiterate.
    (d) More girls than boys in India reach secondary school.

4. Which of the following is/are accurate concerning education and schooling in Japan?

    (a) Industrialization brought mandatory education to Japan in 1872.
    (b) In Japan, schooling reflects personal ability more than it does in the United States.
    (c) The Japanese government pays much of the costs of higher education.
    (d) More men and women graduate from high school in Japan than in the United States.
    (e) All of the above are accurate.

5. *Mandatory education* laws were found in every state in the United States by

    (a) 1781.
    (b) 1850.
    (c) 1822.
    (d) 1918.

6. Which of the following nations has the highest percentage of adults with a *college degree*?

    (a) the United States
    (b) Netherlands
    (c) Canada
    (d) Denmark
    (e) Sweden

7. Who advocated the idea that schooling should have *practical* consequences and promoted *progressive education*?

    (a) James Coleman
    (b) John Dewey
    (c) Daniel Moynihan
    (d) Christopher Jencks

8.	The percentage of students receiving a bachelor's degree in which of the following areas showed the greatest *increase* during the period 1988-1998?

(a)	engineering
(b)	library science
(c)	parks, recreation, leisure, and fitness studies
(d)	pre-law
(e)	communications and technologies

9.	Child care, establishing relationships and networks, and consuming the time and energy of teenagers are examples of

(a)	the latent functions of education.
(b)	school tracking.
(c)	social control.
(d)	mainstreaming.

10.	According to its critics, *structural-functionalists* overlook one core truth—

(a)	education serves as a form of social placement.
(b)	the quality of schooling is far greater for some than others.
(c)	schools serve several latent functions.
(d)	schooling helps forge a mass of people into a unified society.
(e)	education creates as well as transmits culture.

11.	*Social-conflict* analysis associates formal education with

(a)	student's skill enhancement.
(b)	the improvement of personal well-being.
(c)	patterns of social inequality.
(d)	global competitiveness.

12.	*Compliance, punctuality,* and *discipline* are parts of the _____ of formal education.

(a)	hidden curriculum
(b)	manifest functions
(c)	residual schooling
(d)	tracking system

13.	*Social conflict analysis* uses the term _____ to refer to the assignment of students to different types of educational programs.

(a)	hierarchical education
(b)	residual education
(c)	ability placement
(d)	competitive placement
(e)	tracking

14. The *Coleman Report* concluded that

    (a)   social inequality is not a problem in public education within our society.
    (b)   the simple answer to quality education is more funding for schools.
    (c)   minority schools are actually better than schools that are predominately white schools in terms of their student achievement.
    (d)   education is the great equalizer, and stressing the importance of differences between families is not particularly important for educational achievement.
    (e)   schools alone cannot overcome social inequality.

15. Randell Collins calls the United States a(n) _____ *society* because people regard diplomas and degrees so very highly.

    (a)   inclusive
    (b)   elitist
    (c)   credential
    (d)   passive
    (e)   bureaucratic

16. Theodore Sizer showed that bureaucratic schools are often insensitive to the cultural character of the community. He calls this pattern

    (a)   functional illiteracy.
    (b)   specialization.
    (c)   inclusiveness.
    (d)   rigid conformity.
    (e)   mainstreaming.

17. The National Commission on Excellence in Education (1983) issued a report called *A Nation At Risk*, in which it recommended:

    (a)   ending student passivity.
    (b)   increasing credentialism.
    (c)   more stringent educational requirements.
    (d)   reducing the length of time students spend in school to allow more students to learn practical skills through employment.
    (e)   reducing our educational focus on reading, writing, and arithmetic.

18. *Functional illiteracy* refers to

    (a)   an inability to read and write at all.
    (b)   an inability to read at the appropriate level of schooling based on one's age.
    (c)   an inability to effectively communicate abstract ideas.
    (d)   reading and writing skills insufficient for everyday living.

19.   The *school choice* model focuses on the idea of

    (a)   competition.
    (b)   consensus.
    (c)   science.
    (d)   integration.

20.   One form of *school choice* involves a school providing special facilities and programs to promote educational excellence in a particular are. This is known as:

    (a)   schooling for profit.
    (b)   magnet schools.
    (c)   charter schools.
    (d)   inclusion.

Matching

1.   ____   The percentage of high school graduates in the U.S. who go on to college.
2.   ____   The percentage of U.S. adults aged 25-64 with a college degree.
3.   ____   Championed progressive education.
4.   ____   Schooling in the U.S. reflects the value of _____.
5.   ____   The assignment of students to different types of educational programs.
6.   ____   The percentage of the 51 million primary and secondary school children attending state-funded public schools in 1998.
7.   ____   The percentage of students bused outside their neighborhoods.
8.   ____   Confirmed that predominately minority schools suffer problems, but cautioned that money alone will not magically improve academic quality.
9.   ____   Evaluating people on the basis of education degrees.
10.   ____   A 1983 study on the quality of schooling.

    a.   tracking   f.   5
    b.   63   g.   James Coleman
    c.   practical learning   h.   John Dewey
    d.   credentiaism   i.   A Nation at Risk
    e.   26   j.   90

Fill-In

1.   The social institution through which society provides its members with important knowledge, including basic facts, job skills, and cultural values and norms is termed _____.
2.   Schooling in the United States attempts to promote _____ *education,* _____ *opportunity* and _____ *learning.*
3.   *Functions* served by schooling include: _____, *cultural* _____, *social* _____, *social* _____, and several _____ *functions.*
4.   The assignment of students to different types of educational programs is referred to as _____.
5.   Although only _____ percent of U.S. school children are *bused to schools outside their neighborhoods for racial balance purposes,* this policy has generated heated controversy.

6. The most crucial factor affecting access to U.S. higher education is _____.
7. *Theodore Sizer* identified through his research five ways in which large, _____ schools undermine education, including rigid conformity, numerical rating, rigid expectations, specialization, and little individual responsibility.
8. Recent studies have linked higher levels of *student participation* to four teaching strategies, including: calling students by _____ when they volunteer, positively _____ student participation, asking _____ rather than factual questions and giving students time to answer, and asking for students' _____ even when they do not volunteer.
9. Four alternative approaches to increasing *school choice* include giving _____ to families with school-aged children and allow them to spent that money on any school they want, _____ schools, schooling for _____, and _____ schools.
10. _____ refers to the integrating of special students into the overall educational program.

Definition and Short-Answer

1. Describe the four basic *functions* of education as reviewed in the text. To what extent do you think these are being fulfilled in the United States today? What do you think can be done to improve education in the United States?
2. What were the basic findings of the *Coleman Report*? How should these findings be interpreted?
3. How do *annual earnings* differ for men and women given the same levels of education achievement?
4. What are the five serious problems with the *bureaucratic* nature of our educational system?
5. What recommendations were made in the report *A Nation at Risk*?
6. Differentiate between the educational systems of the U.S., India, Great Britain, and Japan. What are the relative advantages and disadvantages of each system?
7. What are the major *problems* in U.S. education? Identify the specific factors involved in each problem identified. What is one recommendation you have for solving each of the problems?
8. What are the three alternative approaches identified as ways of increasing *school choice*? What are your opinions on each of these?
9. What impact on education, positive and negative, do you think advances in *information and computer technology* is having today?
10. How do you think *achievement* should be measured in our education system in the United States?

PART VII: ANSWERS TO STUDY QUESTIONS

Key Concepts

1. Education (p. 517)
2. schooling (p. 517)
3. hidden curriculum (p. 524)
4. tracking (p. 413)
5. Credentialism (p. 528)
6. Functional illiteracy (p. 533)
7. Mainstreaming (p. 535)

True-False

1.	T	(p. 518)	6.	T	(p. 522)
2.	F	(p. 520)	7.	F	(p. 524)
3.	T	(p. 520)	8.	F	(p. 527)
4.	T	(p. 521)	9.	T	(p. 529)
5.	F	(p. 521)	10.	F	(p. 533)

Multiple Choice

1.	c	(p. 517)	11.	c	(p. 523)
2.	c	(p. 517)	12.	a	(p. 524)
3.	d	(p. 520)	13.	e	(p. 524)
4.	e	(p. 520)	14.	e	(p. 527)
5.	d	(p. 521)	15.	c	(p. 528)
6.	a	(p. 521)	16.	d	(p. 530)
7.	b	(p. 522)	17.	c	(p. 533)
8.	c	(p. 522)	18.	d	(p. 533)
9.	a	(p. 523)	19.	a	(p. 534)
10.	b	(p. 523)	20.	b	(p. 535)

Matching

1.	b	(p. 520)	6.	j	(p. 525)
2.	e	(p. 521)	7.	f	(p. 527)
3.	h	(p. 522)	8.	g	(p. 527)
4.	c	(p. 522)	9.	d	(p. 528)
5.	a	(p. 524)	10.	i	(p. 533)

Fill-In

1. education (p. 517)
2. mandatory, equal, practical (pp. 521-522)
3. socialization, innovation, integration, placement, latent (pp. 522-523)
4. tracking (p. 524)
5. 5 (p. 527)
6. money (p. 527)
7. bureaucratic (pp. 530-531)
8. name, reinforcing, analytical, opinions (p. 532)
9. vouchers, magnet, profit, charter (pp. 534-535)
10. mainstreaming (p. 535)

PART VII: IN FOCUS--IMPORTANT ISSUES

- Education: A Global Survey

  Briefly characterize *schooling* in each of the following countries.

  India

  Japan

  Great Britain

  United States

- The Functions of Schooling

  Illustrate each of the following *functions of schooling*.

  socialization

  cultural innovation

  social integration

  social placement

  Identify three *latent functions* of schooling.

- Schooling and Social Inequality

  In what ways do social-conflict theorists believe each of the following lead to social inequality in schooling?

  social control

  standardized testing

  school tracking

Briefly summarize the findings of the *Coleman Report*. How should these finding be interpreted for the purposes of educational policy?

- Problems In the Schools

    What is the evidence that schools have problems in the following areas?

        discipline and violence

        student passivity

        dropping out

        academic standards

    What were the findings and conclusions of the study *A Nation at Risk*? What do you think needs to be done in terms of educational reform based on these findings?

- Recent Issues In U.S. Education

    Describe each of the following alternatives for *school choice*.

        vouchers

        magnet schools

        schooling for profit

        charter schools

    What are the arguments for and against these *school choice* alternatives?

- Looking Ahead: Schooling In the Twenty-First Century

    What are three important issues confronting schools over the next generation?

Chapter 21 — Health and Medicine

V. Theoretical Analysis of Health and Medicine
  A. Structural-Functional Analysis
     1. The Sick Role
     2. The Physicians Role
  B. Symbolic-Interaction Analysis
     1. The Social Construction of Illness
     2. The Social Construction of Treatment
  C. Social Conflict Analysis
     1. Access to Care
     2. The Profit Motive
     3. Medicine as Politics
VI. Looking Ahead: Health and Medicine in the Twenty-First Century
VII. Summary
VIII. Key Concepts
IX. Critical-Thinking Questions
X. Applications and Exercises
XI. Sites to See

PART II: LEARNING OBJECTIVES

- To become aware of the ways in which the health of a population is shaped by society.
- To develop a global and historical perspective on health and illness.
- To recognize how race, social class, and age affect the health of individuals in our society.
- To be able to discuss cigarette smoking, eating disorders, and sexually transmitted diseases as serious health problems in our society.
- To be able to recognize and evaluate ethical issues surrounding dying and death.
- To be able to compare and evaluate the relative effectiveness of scientific medicine and holistic medicine.
- To be able to compare and evaluate the relative effectiveness of medicine in socialist and capitalists societies.
- To be able to differentiate between the viewpoints being provided by the three major sociological perspectives.

PART III: KEY CONCEPTS

In the blank spaces below, write in the appropriate concept.

1. _____ is a state of complete physical, mental, and social well-being.
2. _____ _____ is the study of how health and disease are distributed throughout a society's population.
3. An _____ _____ is an intense form of dieting or other unhealthy method of weight control driven by the desire to be very thin.
4. _____ refers to assisting in the death of a person suffering from an incurable disease.
5. _____ refers to the social institution that focuses on combating disease and improving health.

6. _____ _____ is an approach to health care that emphasizes prevention of illness and takes into account a person's entire physical and social environment.

7. _____ _____ is a medical care system in which the government owns and operates most medical facilities and employs most physicians.

8. A _____ _____ is a medical care system in which patients pay directly for the services of physicians and hospitals.

9. A _____ _____ _____ is an organization that provides comprehensive medical care to subscribers for a fixed fee.

10. The _____ _____ refers to patterns of behavior defined as appropriate for those who are ill.

PART IV: IMPORTANT RESEARCHERS

In the space provided below each of the following researchers, write two or three sentences to help you remember his respective contributions to the field of sociology.

Erving Goffman   Talcott Parsons

PART V: STUDY QUESTIONS

<u>True-False</u>

1.	T	F	The World Health Organization defines *health* as simply the absence of disease.
2.	T	F	*Kwashiorkor* is a negative health condition found in West Africa caused by protein deficiency.
3.	T	F	The top five *causes of death* in the U.S. have changed very little since 1900.
4.	T	F	Approximately seventy percent of all global *HIV cases* are recorded in sub-Saharan Africa.
5.	T	F	HIV is both *infectious* and *contagious*.
6.	T	F	In 1997, the Supreme Court decided that under the U.S. Constitution, there is no "right to die"
7.	T	F	*Holistic medicine* stresses that physicians have to take the primary responsibility for health care in society.
8.	T	F	One criticism of the *symbolic-interaction* paradigm is that this approach seems to deny that there are any objective standards of well-being.
9.	T	F	Most surgery in the U.S. is *elective*, or not prompted by a medical emergency.
10.	T	F	The most common objection to the *conflict approach* is that it minimizes the gains in U.S. health brought about by scientific medicine and higher living standards.

Multiple Choice

1.   The *health* of any population is shaped by

      (a)   the society's cultural standards.
      (b)   the society's technology.
      (c)   the society's social inequality.
      (d)   all of the above

2.   During the first half of the nineteenth century in Europe and the United states, the improvement in health was primarily due to

      (a)   the rising standard of living.
      (b)   medical advances.
      (c)   changes in cultural values toward medicine.
      (d)   immigration.

3.   In 1900, _____ caused one-fourth of deaths in the U.S. Today, however, most deaths are caused by

      (a)   chronic diseases/infectious diseases.
      (b)   accidents/crime.
      (c)   infectious diseases/chronic diseases.
      (d)   cancer/accidents.
      (e)   crime/accidents.

4.   _____ is the study of how health and disease are distributed throughout a society's population.

      (a)   Demography
      (b)   Social epidemiology
      (c)   Epistomolgy
      (d)   Medicalization

5.   Which of the following were the *leading causes of death* in the U.S. in 1900?

      (a)   accidents and heart disease
      (b)   cancer and diphtheria
      (c)   influenza and pneumonia
      (d)   lung disease and kidney disease
      (e)   homicide and diabetes

6. Which of the following is *true* concerning age, sex, and health in the United States?

    (a) Across the life course, men are healthier than women.
    (b) Males have a slight biological advantage that renders them less likely than females to die before or immediately after birth.
    (c) Socialization aids men's health to a greater degree than it does women's health.
    (d) Young women are more likely to die than young men.
    (e) Across the life course, women are healthier than men.

7. According to medical experts, about how many people die prematurely in the U.S. each year as a direct result of *smoking*?

    (a) 100,000
    (b)   50,000
    (c) 200,000
    (d) 1 million
    (e) 430,000

8. Which of the following statements is *inaccurate*?

    (a) Ninety-five percent of people who suffer from anorexia nervosa and bulimia (eating disorders) are female.
    (b) Research shows that college-age women believe that being thin is critical to physical attractiveness.
    (c) Research shows that college-age women believe guys like thin girls.
    (d) Most men, like women, think that their body shape is not close to what they want it to be.
    (e) Our idealized image of beauty leads many young women to diet to the point of risking their health.

9. Of the reported cases of *gonorrhea* and *syphilis* in the United States, the vast majority involved

    (a) whites.
    (b) African Americans.
    (c) Hispanics.
    (d) Asians.

10. Worldwide, *heterosexual relations* accounts for about _____ percent of transmitted cases of *AIDS*.

    (a) less than 5
    (b) 11
    (c) 27
    (d) 48
    (e) over two-thirds

11. Assisting in the death of a person suffering from an incurable disease is known as

(a) annihilation.
(b) amniocentesis.
(c) genocide.
(d) euthanasia.

12. The institutionalization of *scientific medicine* by the AMA resulted in

(a) expensive medical education.
(b) domination of medicine by white males.
(c) an inadequate supply of physicians in rural areas.
(d) all of the above

13. *Holistic medicine* is a reaction to scientific medicine. Which of the following is *not* an emphasis advocates of holistic medicine share?

(a) an emphasis upon the environment in which the person exists
(b) an emphasis upon the responsibility of society for health promotion and care
(c) an emphasis upon optimum health for all
(d) an emphasis upon the home setting for medical treatment

14. _____ refers to a health-care system in which the government owns and operates most medical facilities and employs most physicians.

(a) A health maintenance organization
(b) Socialized medicine
(c) A direct-fee system
(d) Holistic medicine

15. *European* governments pay about ____ percent of medical costs, whereas in the *United States*, the government pays about ____ percent of medical costs.

(a) 80/less than half
(b) 100/10
(c) 25/50
(d) 40/60
(e) less than half/more than half

16. Which country does not offer a comprehensive health program to the entire population?

(a) Sweden
(b) Great Britain
(c) the United States
(d) Canada

17. An association that provides comprehensive medical care for a fixed fee is termed a(n)

    (a) WHO.
    (b) DFS.
    (c) AMA.
    (d) HMO.

18. Medical expenditures in the U.S. today amount to more than _____ per person annually, more than any other nation in the world.

    (a) $4,000
    (b) $1,200
    (c) $9,350
    (d) $2,450
    (e) $6,100

19. Which of the following *theoretical paradigms* in sociology utilizes concepts like *sick role* and *physician's role* to help explain health behavior?

    (a) social-conflict
    (b) social-exchange
    (c) symbolic-interaction
    (d) cultural materialism
    (e) structural-functional

20. Which of the following *theoretical paradigms* in sociology focuses on the issues of *access* and *profits* in the study of health care?

    (a) social-conflict
    (b) structural-functional
    (c) symbolic-interaction
    (d) social-exchange

Matching

1. ____ The number one cause of death in the U.S. today.
2. ____ The number two cause of death in the U.S. today.
3. ____ The study of how health and disease are distributed throughout a society's population.
4. ____ The percentage of adults in the U.S. who are smokers.
5. ____ The social institution that focuses on combating disease and improving health.
6. ____ An approach to health care that emphasizes prevention of illness and takes account of the person's entire physical and social environment.
7. ____ Percentage of physicians in Russia who are women.
8. ____ A medical-care system in which the government owns most facilities and employs most physicians.

9. ___ The percentage of health care expenditures in our society paid by the U.S. government.
10. ___ Patterns of behavior defined as appropriate for those who are ill.

a. sick role   f. 45
b. cancer   g. medicine
c. socialized medicine   h. heart disease
d. 70   i. 25
e. social epidemiology   j. holistic medicine

Fill-In

1. Society shapes the *health* of people in five major ways. These include: cultural patterns define _____. What is "healthy" is often the same as what people define as _____ good. Cultural _____ of health change over time. A society's _____ affects people's health. And, social _____ affects people's health.
2. *Social* _____ is the study of how health and disease are distributed throughout a society's population.
3. The leading cause of death today in the U.S. is _____.
4. Death is now rare among young people, with two notable exceptions: a rise in mortality resulting from _____ and, more recently, from _____.
5. _____ percent of people who suffer from *anorexia nervosa* or *bulimia* are women.
6. Specific behaviors put people at high risk for *HIV* infection. These include _____ sex, sharing _____, and using any _____.
7. _____ is assisting in the death of a person suffering from an incurable disease.
8. The _____ refers to patterns of behavior defined as appropriate for those who are ill.
9. One strength of the _____ *paradigm* lies in revealing that what people view as healthful or harmful depends on numerous factors, many of which are not, strictly speaking, medical.
10. *Social-conflict* analysis focuses attention on three main issues concerning health care--_____ to health care, the effects of the _____ motive, and the _____ of medicine.

Definition and Short-Answer

1. It is pointed out in the text that the *health* of any population is shaped by important characteristics of the society as a whole. What are three general characteristics and an example of each?
2. How have the *causes of death* changed in the U.S. over the last century?
3. What is *social epidemiology*? Provide two illustrations of patterns found in the United States.
4. What is *HIV*? What is *AIDS*? How is it transmitted?
5. What is meant by the *sick role*?
6. Describe the three basic characteristics of *holistic medicine*.

7.   How does the health-care system of the U.S. differ from those in other capitalist systems?
8.   What are *social-conflict* analysts' arguments about the health care system in the United States?
9.   What factors are identified for why the U.S. does not have a *national health-care system*?
10.   What do *symbolic-interactionists* mean by *socially constructing illness* and *socially constructing treatment*?

PART VI: ANSWERS TO STUDY QUESTIONS

Key Concepts

1.   Health (p. 541)
2.   Social epidemiology (p. 545)
3.   eating disorder (p. 549)
4.   Euthanasia (mercy killing) (p. 553)
5.   Medicine (p. 554)
6.   Holistic medicine (p. 555)
7.   Socialized medicine (p. 557)
8.   direct-fee system (p. 557)
9.   health maintenance organization (HMO) (p. 558)
10.   sick role (p. 558)

True-False

1.	F	(p. 541)	6.	T	(p. 553)
2.	T	(p. 543)	7.	F	(p. 552)
3.	F	(p. 545)	8.	F	(p. 552)
4.	T	(pp. 550-551)	9.	T	(p. 553)
5.	T	(pp. 550-551)	10.	T	(p. 555)

Multiple Choice

1.	d	(pp. 541-542)	11.	d	(p. 553)
2.	a	(p. 545)	12.	d	(p. 554)
3.	c	(p. 545)	13.	b	(p. 555)
4.	b	(p. 545)	14.	b	(p. 557)
5.	c	(p. 545)	15.	a	(p. 557)
6.	e	(p. 546)	16.	c	(p. 557)
7.	e	(p. 548)	17.	d	(p. 558)
8.	d	(p. 549)	18.	a	(p. 558)
9.	b	(p. 549)	19.	e	(p. 558-559)
10.	e	(p. 552)	20.	a	(pp. 560-561)

Matching

1.	h	(p. 545)	6.	j	(p. 555)
2.	b	(p. 545)	7.	d	(p. 556)
3.	e	(p. 545)	8.	c	(p. 557)
4.	i	(p. 548)	9.	f	(p. 557)
5.	g	(p. 554)	10.	a	(pp. 558-559)

Fill-In

1. health, morally, standards, technology, inequality (pp. 541-542)
2. epidemiology (p. 545)
3. heart disease (p. 545)
4. accidents, AIDS (p. 545)
5. Ninety-five (p. 549)
6. anal, needles, drugs (pp. 551-552)
7. Euthanasia (p. 553)
8. sick role (pp. 558-559)
9. symbolic-interaction (p. 560)
10. access, profit, politics (p. 560)

PART VII: IN FOCUS--IMPORTANT ISSUES

- What is Health?

What are the five major ways in which society shapes people's *health*?

1.

2.

3.

4.

5.

- Health: A Global Survey

Generally describe the health of people living in *low-income countries*.

What was the impact of *industrialization* on health in the U.S. and Europe?

- Health in the United States

Briefly discuss the health patterns found in the United States using the following variables.

    age and sex

    social class and race

How significant a health problem are the each of the following? Provide demographic evidence of illness and disease each as discussed in the text.

    cigarette smoking

    eating disorders

    sexually transmitted diseases

According to legal and medical experts, how is *death* defined?

Do people have the *right to die*?

What are the laws in the United States concerning *euthanasia*? What is your opinion on this issue?

- The Medical Establishment

Describe impact of the rise of *scientific medicine* on health care in the United States.

What are the components of *holistic medicine*?

Briefly summarize how medical care is paid for in the following *socialist societies*.

the People's Republic of China

the Russian Federation

Briefly summarize how medical care is paid for in the following *capitalist societies*.

Sweden

Great Britain

Canada

Japan

How expensive is medical care in the United States? How do we pay for this medical care?

- Theoretical Analysis of Health and Medicine

  According to structural-functionalist analysis, what are the components of the *sick role*?

  What is the *physician's role*?

  What do symbolic-interactionist's mean by the *social construction of illness*?

  According to social-conflict analysts, what are the three ways in which health care is related to *social inequality*? Describe and illustrate each of these.

- Looking Ahead: Health and Medicine In the Twenty-First Century

Identify and describe the four *trends* identified by the author concerning health and health care in the U.S. over the next several decades.

Chapter 22

Population, Urbanization, and Environment

PART I: CHAPTER OUTLINE

I. Demography: The Study of Population
    A.   Fertility
    B.   Mortality
    C.   Migration
    D.   Population Growth
    E.   Population Composition

II. History and Theory of Population Growth
    A.   Malthusian Theory
    B.   Demographic Transition Theory
    C.   Global Population Today: A Brief Survey
        1.   The Low-Growth North
        2.   The High-Growth South

III. Urbanization: The Growth of Cities
    A.   The Evolution of Cities
        1.   The First Cities
        2.   Preindustrial European Cities
        3.   Industrial European Cities
    B.   The Growth of U.S. Cities
        1.   Colonial Settlement: 1624-1800
        2.   Urban Expansion: 1800-1860
        3.   The Great Metropolis: 1860-1950
        4.   Urban Decentralization: 1950-Present
    C.   Suburbs and Urban Decline
    D.   Postindustrial Sunbelt Cities
    E.   Megalopolis: Regional Cities
    F.   Edge Cities

IV. Urbanization As A Way of Life
    A.   Ferdinand Tönnies: Gemeinschaft and Gesellschaft
    B.   Emile Durkheim: Mechanical and Organic Solidarity
    C.   Georg Simmel: The Blase' Urbanite
    D.   The Chicago School: Robert Park and Louis Wirth

PART II: LEARNING OBJECTIVES

- To learn the basic concepts used by demographers to study populations.
- To be able to compare Malthusian theory and demographic transition theory.
- To be able to recognize how populations differ in industrial and nonindustrial societies.
- To gain an understanding of the worldwide urbanization process, and to be able to put it into historical perspective.
- To be able to describe demographic changes in the U.S. throughout its history.
- To consider urbanism as a way of life as viewed by several historical figures in sociology.
- To consider the idea of urban ecology.
- To gain an appreciation for the global dimension of the natural environment.
- To develop an understanding of how sociology can help us confront environmental issues.
- To be able to discuss the dimensions of the "logic of growth" and the "limits to growth" as issues and realities confronting our world.
- To be able to identify and discuss major environmental issues confronting our world today.
- To begin to develop a sense about the ingredients for a sustainable society and world in the century to come.

PART III: KEY CONCEPTS

In the blank spaces below, write in the appropriate concept.

1. _____ is the study of human population.
2. _____ refers to the incidence of childbearing in a country's population.
3. The _____ _____ _____ refers to the number of live births in a given year for every thousand people in the population.
4. _____ refers to the incidence of death in a country's population.
5. The _____ _____ _____ refers to the number of deaths in a given year for every thousand people in a population.
6. The _____ _____ _____ refers to the number of deaths among infants under one year of age for each thousand live births in a given year.
7. _____ _____ refers to the average life span of a country's population.
8. The movement of people into and out of a specified territory is known as _____.
9. The _____ _____ refers to the number of males for every hundred females in a nation's population.
10. An _____ _____ is a graphic representation of the age and sex of a population.
11. _____ _____ _____ is the thesis that population patterns reflect a society's level of technological development.
12. _____ _____ _____ refers to the level of reproduction that maintains population at a steady state.
13. The concentration of humanity into cities refers to _____.
14. A _____ is a large city that socially and economically dominates an urban area.
15. The _____ are urban areas beyond the political boundaries of a city.
16. A _____ is a vast urban region containing a number of cities and their surrounding suburbs.
17. _____ is a type of social organization by which people are closely tied by kinship and tradition.
18. _____ is a type of social organization by which people come together only on the basis of self-interest.
19. _____ _____ is the study of the link between the physical and social dimensions of cities.
20. _____ is the study of the interaction of living organisms and the natural environment.
21. The _____ _____ refers to the earth's surface and atmosphere, including living organisms, air, water, soil, and other resources necessary to sustain life.
22. An _____ is a system composed of the interaction of all living organisms and their natural environment.
23. _____ _____ refers to to profound and long-term harm to the natural environment caused by humanity's focus on short-term material affluence.
24. _____ _____ are regions of dense forestation, most of which circle the globe close to the equator.
25. _____ _____ refers to a rise in the Earth's average temperature caused by an increasing concentration of carbon dioxide and other gases in the atmosphere.

26. _____ _____ refers to the pattern by which environmental hazards are greatest for poor people, especially minorities.

27. An _____ _____ _____ is a way of life that meets the needs of the present generation without threatening the environmental legacy of future generations.

PART IV: IMPORTANT RESEARCHERS

In the space provided below each of the following researchers, write two or three sentences to help you remember his or her respective contributions to the field of sociology.

Ferdinand Tönnies   Emile Durkheim

Robert Park   Louis Wirth

Georg Simmel   Thomas Malthus

Donella Meadows

PART V: STUDY QUESTIONS

True-False

1. T   F   A significantly larger percentage of the U.S. population over the next two decades will be comprised of *childbearing aged women* than at any other period in our nation's history.

2. T   F   *Malthusian theory* predicted that while population would increase in a *geometric progression*, food supplies would increase only by an *arithmetic progression*.

3. T   F   According to *demographic transition theory*, population patterns are linked to a society's level of technological development.

4.	T	F	In the mid-eighteenth century, the *Industrial Revolution* triggered a *second urban revolution*.
5.	T	F	Most of the ten *largest cities* in the U.S. (by population) are in the *Sunbelt*.
6.	T	F	The cultural values of material comfort, progress, and science form the foundation for the *logic of growth* thesis.
7.	T	F	The limits to growth theorists are also referred to as *neo-Malthusians*.
8.	T	F	The United States is being characterized in the text as a *disposable society*.
9.	T	F	Households around the world account for more *water use* than does industry.
10.	T	F	The *greenhouse effect* is the result of too little carbon dioxide in the atmosphere.

Multiple-Choice

1.   How many people are added to the planet *each year*?

    (a)   5 million
    (b)   23 million
    (c)   51 million
    (d)   77 million

2.   The incidence of childbearing in a country's population refers to

    (a)   fertility.
    (b)   fecundity.
    (c)   demography.
    (d)   sex ratio.
    (e)   life expectancy.

3.   *Fecundity,* or maximum possible childbearing is sharply reduced in practice by

    (a)   cultural norms.
    (b)   finances.
    (c)   personal choice.
    (d)   all of the above

4.   Which region of the world has the *highest* birth rate, death rate, and infant mortality rate.

    (a)   Latin America
    (b)   Asia
    (c)   Europe
    (d)   Oceania
    (e)   Africa

5.   The movement of people into and out of a specified territory is

      (a)   demographic transition.
      (b)   migration.
      (c)   fecundity.
      (d)   mortality.
      (e)   fertility.

6.   The *sex ratio* in the U.S. is

      (a)   85.
      (b)   100.
      (c)   90.
      (d)   105.
      (e)   96.

7.   During the twentieth century, the world's population has increased _____-fold.

      (a)   two
      (b)   three
      (c)   seven
      (d)   five
      (e)   six

8.   *Demographic transition theory* links population patterns to a society's:

      (a)   religious beliefs and practices.
      (b)   technological development.
      (c)   natural resources.
      (d)   sexual norms.

9.   The *first city* to have ever existed is argued to be

      (a)   Athens.
      (b)   Cairo.
      (c)   Tikal.
      (d)   Jericho.

10.   According to the text, the *second urban revolution* was triggered by

      (a)   the fall of Rome.
      (b)   the post-World War II baby boom.
      (c)   the Industrial Revolution.
      (d)   the discovery of the New World.
      (e)   the fall of Greece.

11. The period of *1950 to the present* is described in the text as

    (a)   urban decentralization.
    (b)   the metropolitan era.
    (c)   urban expansion.
    (d)   the second urban revolution.

12. A vast urban region containing a number of cities and their surrounding suburbs is known as a:

    (a)   metropolis.
    (b)   suburb.
    (c)   Gemeinschaft.
    (d)   megalopolis.

13. The link between the *physical* and *social* dimensions of cities is known as

    (a)   Gesellschaft.
    (b)   urban ecology.
    (c)   organic solidarity.
    (d)   mechanical solidarity.
    (e)   demography.

14. This model of urbanization claims that city life is defined by people with power, and that capitalism turns cities into real estate to be traded for profit.

    (a)   concentric zone
    (b)   ecological
    (c)   urban political economy
    (d)   urban renewal strategy

15. _____ is the study of the interaction of living organisms and the natural environment.

    (a)   Environmentalism
    (b)   Sociobiology
    (c)   Ecosystem
    (d)   Ecology

16. Which of the following is *not* a projection for the next century using the *limits of growth thesis*?

    (a)   a stabilizing, then declining population
    (b)   declining industrial output per capita
    (c)   declining resources
    (d)   increasing, then declining pollution
    (e)   increasing food per capita

17. Which type of solid waste represents about *one-half* of all household trash in the U.S?

    (a)   metal products
    (b)   yard waste
    (c)   paper
    (d)   plastic

18. While industry accounts for 25 percent of water usage globally, individuals account for _____ percent of usage.

    (a)   90
    (b)   65
    (c)   50
    (d)   25
    (e)   10

19. *Rain forests* cover approximately _____ percent of the earth's land surface.

    (a)   1
    (b)   7
    (c)   2
    (d)   11

20. A way of life that meets the needs of the present generation without threatening the environmental legacy of future generations refers to

    (a)   ecologically sustainable culture.
    (b)   the Green Revolution.
    (c)   environmental racism.
    (d)   the greenhouse effect.

Matching—Population and Urbanization

1. ___   The incidence of childbearing in a society's population.
2. ___   Maximum possible childbearing.
3. ___   The concentration of humanity into cities.
4. ___   1860-1950.
5. ___   Developed the concepts Gemeinschaft and Gesellschaft.
6. ___   A type of social organization by which people stand apart from one another in pursuit of self-interest.
7. ___   Developed the concepts of mechanical and organic solidarity.
8. ___   Social bonds based on common sentiments and shared moral values.
9. ___   Argued that urbanites develop a blasé attitude, selectively tuning out much of what goes on around them.
10. ___   Saw the city as a living organism, truly a human kaleidoscope.

a.	Ferdinand Tönnies	f.	Robert Parks
b.	metropolitan era	g.	Georg Simmel
c.	fertility	h.	Emile Durkheim
d.	Gesellschaft	i.	fecundity
e.	mechanical solidarity	j.	urbanization

Matching—Environment

1. ___ The earth's surface and atmosphere, including living organisms as well as the air, soil, and other resources necessary to sustain life.
2. ___ The study of the interaction of living organisms and the natural environment.
3. ___ The system composed of the interaction of all living organisms and their natural environment.
4. ___ Profound and negative long-term harm to the natural environment caused by humanity's focus on short-term material affluence.
5. ___ The number of gallons of water consumed by a person in the U.S. over a lifetime.
6. ___ Regions of dense forestation most of which circle the globe close to the equator.
7. ___ A rise in the earth's average temperature due to an increasing concentration of carbon dioxide in the atmosphere.
8. ___ The pattern by which environmental hazards are greatest in proximity to poor people and especially minorities.
9. ___ The number of people added to the world each year (net gain) in low-income societies.
10. ___ The number of people added to the world's population each year (net gain).

a.	natural environment	f.	ecology
b.	global warming	g.	environmental deficit
c.	10 million	h.	rain forests
d.	77 million	i.	environmental racism
e.	74 million	j.	ecosystem

Fill-In—Population and Urbanization

1. _____ is the incidence of childbearing in a society's population.
2. _____ refers to the incidence of death in a country's population.
3. The *crude death rate* in Africa in 2000 was _____. For North America this figure was _____.
4. Movement out of a territory--or _____--is measured in terms of an *out-migration rate*.
5. The _____ _____ refers to the number of males for every hundred females in a given population.
6. *Thomas Malthus* saw population increasing according to _____ progression, and food production increasing in _____ progression.
7. _____ *theory* is the thesis that population patterns are linked to a society's level of technological development.
8. _____ _____ _____ refers to the level of reproduction that maintains population at a steady state.

9. The *Bureau of the Census* recognizes 276 urban areas in the U.S. in the year 2001 which they call MSAs, or _____.

10. In 1950, only seven cities in the world had populations over five million, and only two of these were in low-income countries. By 2000, _____ cities has passed this mark, and _____ were in low-income countries.

Fill-In—Environment

1. The _____ _____ refers to the earth's surface and atmosphere, including living organisms, air, water, soil, and other resources necessary to sustain life.

2. An _____ is defined as the system composed of the interaction of all living organisms and their natural environment.

3. The concept of *environmental deficit* implies three important ideas. First, the state of the environment is a _____ _____. Second, much environmental damage is _____. And third, in some respects environmental damage is _____.

4. Core values that underlie cultural patterns in the U.S. include progress, material comfort, and science. Such values form the foundation for the _____ *thesis*.

5. The _____ *thesis* states that humanity must implement policies to control the growth of population, material production, and the use of resources in order to avoid environmental collapse.

6. It is estimated that fifty percent of household trash is _____.

7. In the U.S. only about _____ percent of *solid waste* is recycled.

8. The earth naturally recycles water and refreshes the land through what scientists call the _____ *cycle*.

9. We need to curb *water consumption* by industry, which uses _____ percent of the global total, and by farming, which consumes _____ of the total for irrigation.

10. Strategies for creating an *ecologically sustainable culture* include bringing _____ _____ under control, _____ of finite resources, and reducing _____.

Discussion

1. What are the three basic factors which determine the *size* and *growth rate* of a population? Define each of these concepts.

2. Differentiate between *Malthusian theory* and *demographic transition theory* as perspectives on population growth. What are the three stages in the *demographic transition theory*? Describe each.

3. Identify and describe the five *periods of growth* of U.S. cities.

4. What are three factors that are causing *urban growth* in poor societies?

5. What are the three *urban revolutions*? Briefly describe each.

6. Differentiate between the concepts *ecology* and *natural environment*.

7. What three important ideas are implied by the concept *environmental deficit*?

8. Briefly describe the pattern of word *population growth* prior to an after the Industrial Revolution.

9.   Critically differentiate between the *logic of growth* and the *limits to growth* views concerning the relationship between human technology and the natural environment.

10.   What is meant by the term *disposable society*? What evidence is being presented to support this view of the U.S?

PART VI: ANSWERS TO STUDY QUESTIONS

Key Concepts

1.   Demography (p. 569)
2.   Fertility (p. 570)
3.   crude birth rate (p. 570)
4.   Mortality (p. 570)
5.   crude death rate (p. 570)
6.   infant mortality rate (p. 571)
7.   Life expectancy (p. 571)
8.   migration (p. 571)
9.   sex ratio (p. 573)
10.   age-sex pyramid (p. 573)
11.   Demographic transition theory (p. 575)
12.   Zero population growth (p. 576)
13.   urbanization (p. 578)
14.   metropolis (p. 580)
15.   suburbs (p. 580)
16.   megalopolis (p. 581)
17.   Gemeinschaft (p. 582)
18.   Gesellschaft (p. 582)
19.   Urban ecology (p. 584)
20.   Ecology (p. 586)
21.   natural environment (p. 586)
22.   ecosystem (p. 585)
23.   Environmental deficit (p. 587)
24.   Rain Forests (p. 593)
25.   Global warming (p. 593)
26.   Environmental racism (p. 594)
27.   ecologically sustainable culture (p. 595)

True-False

1.	F	(pp. 573-574)	6.	T	(p. 588)
2.	T	(p. 574)	7.	T	(p. 589)
3.	T	(p. 575)	8.	T	(p. 589)
4.	T	(p. 579)	9.	F	(p. 592)
5.	T	(p. 580)	10.	F	(p. 593)

Multiple-Choice

1.	d	(p. 569)	11.	a	(p. 580)
2.	a	(p. 570)	12.	d	(p. 581)
3.	d	(p. 570)	13.	b	(p. 584)
4.	e	(pp. 571-573)	14.	c	(p. 585)
5.	b	(p. 571)	15.	d	(p. 585)
6.	e	(p. 573)	16.	e	(p. 586)
7.	b	(p. 574)	17.	c	(p. 588)
8.	b	(p. 575)	18.	e	(p. 592)
9.	d	(p. 578)	19.	b	(p. 593)
10.	c	(p. 579)	20.	a	(p. 595)

Matching--Population and Urbanization

1.	c	(p. 570)	6.	d	(p. 582)
2.	i	(p. 570)	7.	h	(p. 583)
3.	j	(p. 578)	8.	e	(p. 583)
4.	b	(p. 580)	9.	g	(p. 583)
5.	a	(p. 582)	10.	f	(p. 583)

Matching--Environment

1.	a	(p. 586)	6.	h	(p. 593)
2.	f	(p. 586)	7.	b	(p. 593)
3.	j	(p. 587)	8.	i	(p. 594)
4.	g	(p. 587)	9.	e	(p. 595)
5.	c	(p. 592)	10.	d	(p. 596)

Fill-In—Population and Urbanization

1. Fertility (p. 570)
2. Mortality (p. 570)
3. 38, 14 (570)
4. emigration (p. 571)
5. sex ratio (p. 573)
6. geometric, arithmetic (p. 574)
7. Demographic transition (p. 575)
8. Zero population growth (p. 580)
9. metropolitan statistical areas (p. 580)
10. 48, 32 (p. 586)

Fill-In—Environment

1.   natural environment (p. 586)
2.   ecosystem (p. 586)
3.   social issue, unintended, reversible (p. 587)
4.   logic of growth (p. 588)
5.   limits of growth (p. 588)
6.   paper (p. 589)
7.   33 (p. 590)
8.   hydological (p. 590)
9.   25, two-thirds (p. 592)
10.   population growth, conservation, waste (p. 595)

PART VII: IN FOCUS--IMPORTANT ISSUES

- Demography: The Study of Population

   Define each of the following factors that affect *population size*.

      fertility

            crude birth rate
            fecundity

      mortality

            crude death rate
            life expectancy

      migration

            immigration
            emigration

   What is the *natural growth rate* of the United States? How does it compare to the comparable rate in other parts of the world like Asia and Africa? Explain.

   In what ways is the *age-sex pyramid* an important measure of population growth?

- History and Theory of Population growth

  Briefly describe the components of each of the following theories of population growth.

    Malthusian theory

    demographic transition theory

  What is meant by the *low-growth North*?

  What is meant by the *high-growth South*?

- Urbanization: The Growth of Cities

  Identify and describe the three *urban revolutions*.

    first

    second

    third

Describe each of the following periods in the *growth of cities* in the United States.

colonial settlement

urban expansion

the metropolitan era

urban decentralization

- Urbanization As a Way of Life

  How did each of the following theorists characterize cities and the process of *urbanization*?

  Ferdinand Tönnies

  Emile Durkheim

  Georg Simmel

  the Chicago School

  Robert Park

  Louis Wirth

What is *urban ecology*?

How is the *urban political economy model* different than the ecological model in term of understanding urban issues?

- Urbanization in Poor Societies

  Briefly describe the *third urban revolution.*

- Environment and Society

  Differentiate between each of the following views concerning environmental issues.

  the logic of growth

  the limits to growth

  What are two important points being made in the text concerning each of the following?

  solid waste

  water

  air

299

Why are the *rain forests* so important to the world and all living things?

- Looking Ahead: Toward a Sustainable World

What are the three recommendations being made for establishing an *ecologically sustainable culture*?

What specific ideas would you recommend implementing to encourage each of these?

Chapter	Collective Behavior
23	and Social Movements

PART I: CHAPTER OUTLINE

PART II: LEARNING OBJECTIVES

- To be able to identify and discuss the specific problems associated with studying collective behavior from a sociological perspective.
- To be able to identify and describe the basic characteristics of collectivities, and to be able to distinguish them from groups.
- To be able to differentiate between localized and dispersed collectivities, and to be able to provide examples for each.
- To be able to identify and distinguish between the different theories used to explain the nature of collectivities.
- To be able to identify and describe the four basic types of social movements.
- To be able to compare and critique the six different theories used to describe the nature of social movements.
- To be able to identify and illustrate the four stages of a social movement.
- To be able to discuss the relationship between social movements and social change from a sociological perspective.

PART IV: KEY CONCEPTS

1. _____ _____ refers to activity involving a large number of people, often spontaneous and sometimes controversial.
2. A _____ is a large number of people whose minimal interaction occurs in the absence of well-defined and conventional norms.
3. A _____ is a temporary gathering of people who share a common focus of attention and who influence one another.
4. A _____ is a highly emotional crowd that pursues a violent of destructive goal.
5. A _____ refers to a social eruption that is highly emotional, violent, and undirected.
6. _____ _____ is collective behavior among people dispersed over a wide geographical area.
7. _____ refers to unsubstantiated information spread informally, often by word of mouth.
8. _____ refers to rumor about people's personal affairs.
9. _____ _____ refers to widespread attitudes about controversial issues.
10. Information presented with the intention of shaping public opinion is known as _____.
11. _____ is a form of localized collective behavior
12. _____ _____ or _____ _____ refers to a form of dispersed collective behavior by which people react to a real or imagined event with irrational and even frantic fear.
13. _____ refers to a social patterned favored by a large number of people.
14. A _____ is an unconventional social pattern that people embrace briefly but enthusiastically.
15. A _____ _____ refers to organized activity that encourages or discourages social change.
16. _____ _____ is a perceived disadvantage arising from a specific comparison.

PART IV: IMPORTANT RESEARCHERS

Gustave Le Bon   Ralph Turner and Lewis Killian

Charles Horton Cooley   Thorstein Veblen

Herbert Blumer   Alexis de Tocqueville

William Kornhauser   Neil Smelser

Fredrick Miller

PART V: STUDY QUESTIONS

True-False

1.   T   F   *Collective behavior* is difficult to study because it is wide-ranging, complex, and transitory.

2.   T   F   People gathered at a beach or observing an automobile accident are used in the text to illustrate *conventional crowds*.

3.   T   F   Using *contagion theory*, it is argued that people lose their individual identities and surrender personal will and responsibility to a collective mind.

4.   T   F   *Emergent-norm theory* is linked to the social-conflict perspective.

5.   T   F   According to the text, *social movements* are rare in preindustrial societies.

6.   T   F   *Reformative social movements* have greater depth, but less scope than *redemptive social movements*.

7.   T   F   The rise of the Ku Klux Klan and passage of Jim Crow laws by whites intent on enforcing segregation in the South after the Civil War illustrate *deprivation theory*.

8.   T   F   Using *mass-society theory*, social movements are *personal* as well as *political*.

9.   T   F   According to *structural-strain theory*, people form social movements because of a shared concern about the inability of society to operate as they believe it should.

10. T   F   One clear strength of *new social movements theory* is its recognition that social movements have increased in scale in response to the development of a global economy and international political connections.

1. Which of the following is *not* identified as a difficulty in researching *collective behavior* using the sociological perspective?

    (a) the concept of collective behavior is wide-ranging
    (b) collective behavior is complex
    (c) collective behavior is often transitory
    (d) collective behavior tends to be localized to historical context

2. A large number of people whose minimal interaction occurs in the absence of well-defined and conventional norms refers to a

    (a) collectivity.
    (b) group.
    (c) secondary group.
    (d) category.

3. Herbert Blumer identified several *types of crowds* based on their level of emotional intensity. Which of the following is *not* a type of crowd identified by Blumer?

    (a) casual
    (b) conventional
    (c) expressive
    (d) acting
    (e) emergent

4. A _____ is a temporary gathering of people who share a common focus of attention and who influence one another.

    (a) group
    (b) crowd
    (c) dispersed collectivity
    (d) category

5. A _____ is a highly emotional crowd that pursues a violent or destructive goal.

    (a) riot
    (b) protest
    (c) mob
    (d) aggregate

6. A *theory of crowds* which claims that the motives that drive collective action do not originate within a crowd, but rather are carried into the crowd by particular individuals is called _____ *theory*.

    (a) contagion
    (b) reactive
    (c) convergence
    (d) subversive

7. One of the first theories of *crowds*, developed by French sociologist Gustave Le Bon, is called _____ *theory*, which focuses on how anonymity in a crowd causes people to lose their identities and surrender personal will and responsibility to a collective mind.

    (a) mob
    (b) convergence
    (c) retreative
    (d) contagion

8. A theory which argues that crowds are not merely irrational collectivities, nor are they always deliberately arranged and organized is _____ *theory*.

    (a) consensual
    (b) emergent-norm
    (c) structural
    (d) reactive

9. *Emergent-norm theory* represents a _____ approach to crowd dynamics.

    (a) social-conflict
    (b) symbolic-interaction
    (c) structural-functional
    (d) functionalism

10. Which of the following is *not* an example of a *dispersed collectivity*?

    (a) rumor
    (b) gossip
    (c) propaganda
    (d) public opinion
    (e) riots

11. Which of the following is *not* an essential characteristic of *rumor*?

    (a) it thrives in a climate of ambiguity
    (b) it is unstable
    (c) it is difficult to stop
    (d) all are characteristics of rumor

12.   The radio broadcast by H.G. Wells "War of the Worlds" is used to illustrate

   (a)   gossip.
   (b)   rumor.
   (c)   mass hysteria or moral panic.
   (d)   panic.

13.   An unconventional social pattern that people embrace briefly, but enthusiastically refers to

   (a)   a fad.
   (b)   gossip.
   (c)   fashion.
   (d)   mass hysteria.
   (e)   rumor.

14.   What *type* of social movement seeks limited social change for the entire society?

   (a)   revolutionary
   (b)   redemptive
   (c)   deprivation
   (d)   alternative
   (e)   reformative

15.   The following points--people join social movements as a result of experiencing relative deprivation; social movements are a means of seeking change that brings participants greater benefits; social movements are especially likely when rising expectations are frustrated, best fit which *theory of social movements*?

   (a)   deprivation
   (b)   resource-mobilization
   (c)   structural-strain
   (d)   mass-society

16.   _____ *theory* suggests social movements attract socially isolated people who feel personally insignificant.

   (a)   Mass-society
   (b)   Structural-strain
   (c)   Resource-mobilization
   (d)   New social movements

17.   _____ *theory* identifies six factors that encourage the development of a social movement, including structural conductiveness, structural strain, growth and spread of an explanation, precipitating factors, mobilization for action, and lack of social control.

    (a)   Resource-mobilization
    (b)   Deprivation
    (c)   Structural-strain
    (d)   Conductive order

18.   Addressing the changing character of social movements, this theory focuses on the globalization of social movements and a focus on cultural change for the improvement of social and physical surroundings.

    (a)   global-resource theory
    (b)   new social movements theory
    (c)   mass-society theory
    (d)   modernization theory

19.   *Emergence* is identified as *stage 1* of a social movement. Which of the following is *not* identified as a stage in the evolution of a social movement?

    (a)   bureaucratization
    (b)   coalescence
    (c)   decline
    (d)   realignment

20.   It is being argued that social movements in the United States and the problems they address are always

    (a)   related to money.
    (b)   short-lived.
    (c)   political.
    (d)   counter productive to cultural norms.
    (e)   related to a feeling of relative deprivation.

Matching

1.   ____   Activity involving a large number of people, often spontaneous, and sometimes controversial.
3.   ____   A collectivity motivated by an intense, single-minded purpose.
4.   ____   A theory that suggests crowds exert hypnotic influence over their members.
5.   ____   Holds that crowd behavior is not a product of the crowd itself, but is carried into the crowd by particular individuals.
6.   ____   Collective behavior among people dispersed over a wide geographic area.
7.   ____   A form of localized collective behavior by which people react to a threat or other stimulus with irrational, frantic, and often self-destructive behavior.

8.   ___   A form of dispersed collective behavior by which people react to a real or imagined event with irrational, frantic, and often self-destructive behavior.
9.   ___   A perceived disadvantage arising from some specific comparisons.
10. ___   A theory that sees social movements as personal and political.

a.	acting crowd	f.	relative deprivation
b.	panic	g.	mass hysteria
c.	mass-society theory	h.	mass behavior
d.	contagion theory	i.	collective behavior
e.	convergence theory	j.	expressive crowd

Fill-In

1. *Collective behavior* is difficult for sociologists to study for the following reasons: it is _____, _____, and _____.

2. Collectivities are of two kinds. A _____ collectivity, referring to people in physical proximity to one another, and a _____ collectivity, or mass behavior.

3. Four types of *crowds* are identified in the text, including _____, _____, _____, _____, and _____.

4. _____ *theory* holds that crowd behavior is not a product of the crowd itself, but is carried into the crowd by particular individuals.

5. Representing a symbolic-interaction approach, _____ *theory* suggests that crowd behavior reflects the desires of participants, but is also guided by norms that emerge as the situation unfolds.

6. *Rumor* has three essential characteristics, including: thriving on _____, being _____, and _____ to stop.

7. Four *types of social movements* are identified in the text. The least threatening is termed an _____ social movement. There is also _____ social movements which are selective, but seek radical change. _____ social movements aim for only limited social change--but target everyone. Finally, _____ social movements are the most extreme.

8. According to Neil Smelser's *structural-strain theory* there are six factors that foster social movements, including: structural _____, structural _____, growth and spread of an _____, precipitating _____, mobilization for _____, and lack of social _____.

9. _____ _____ *theory* points out that no social movement is likely to succeed--or even get off the ground--without substantial resources.

10. Three reasons why the scope of social movements is likely to increase. First, protest should increase as _____, _____, and other historically excluded categories gain a greater political voice. Second, the _____ _____ is increasing awareness of global issues. Third, new technology and the emerging global _____ means social movements are now uniting people around the world.

Discussion

1. What are the basic characteristics of *dispersed collectivities*?
2. What are the four *types of crowds* identified by Herbert Blumer? Briefly describe each of these. What is the fifth type of crowd identified by our author?
3. Differentiate between *contagion theory, convergence theory,* and *emergent-norm theory* in terms of how each explains crowd behavior.
4. Differentiate between the concepts *rumor* and *gossip*.
5. Identify and describe the six characteristics that foster social movements according to *structural-strain theory*.
6. What are the six theories of social movements? Discuss how each of these helps us explain social movements. What is one criticism of each theory.
7. What are the four *stages* of a social movement? Describe each. Identify a social movement in U.S. history and explain how it fits these stages.
8. Differentiate between the concepts *mass hysteria* and *panic*.
9. Identify and describe the four *types* of social movements, providing an illustration for each.
10. Why are social movements expected to increase in *scope* over the next few decades? Do you agree? Why?

PART VII: ANSWERS TO STUDY QUESTIONS

Key Concepts

1. Collective behavior (p. 601)
2. collectivity (p. 602)
3. crowd (p. 602)
4. mob (p. 603)
5. riot (p. 604)
6. Mass behavior (p. 606)
7. Rumor (p. 607)
8. Gossip (p. 608)
9. Public opinion (p. 608
10. Propaganda (p. 608)
11. Panic (p. 609)
12. Mass hysteria, moral panic (p. 609)
13. Fashion (p. 609)
14. fad (p. 609)
15. social movement (p. 610)
16. Relative deprivation (p. 612)

True-False

1.	T	(pp. 601-602)	6.	F	(p. 611)
2.	F	(p. 603)	7.	T	(p. 612)
3.	T	(p. 605)	8.	T	(p. 613)
4.	F	(p. 606)	9.	T	(p. 613)
5.	T	(p. 611)	10.	T	(p. 616)

Multiple-Choice

1.	d	(pp. 601-602)	11.	d	(p. 607)
2.	a	(p. 602)	12.	c	(p. 609)
3.	e	(p. 603)	13.	a	(p. 610)
4.	b	(p. 603)	14.	e	(p. 611)
5.	c	(p. 603)	15.	a	(pp. 611-612)
6.	c	(p. 605)	16.	a	(p. 613)
7.	d	(p. 605)	17.	c	(pp. 613-614)
8.	b	(p 606)	18.	b	(p. 616)
9.	b	(p. 606)	19.	d	(pp. 617-618)
10.	e	(pp. 606-608)	20.	c	(p. 618)

Matching

1.	1	(p. 601)	6.	h	(pp. 606-607
2.	j	(p. 603)	7.	b	(p. 609)
3.	a	(p. 603)	8.	g	(p. 609)
4.	d	(p. 605)	9.	f	(p. 612)
5.	e	(p. 605)	10.	c	(p. 613)

Fill-In

1. wide-ranging, complex, transitory (pp. 601-602)
2. localized, dispersed (p. 602)
3. casual, conventional, expressive, acting (p. 603)
4. Convergence (p. 605)
5. Emergent-norm (p. 606)
6. ambiguity, unstable, difficult (pp. 606-607)
7. alternative, redemptive, reformative, revolutionary (p. 611)
8. conduciveness, strain, explanation, factors, action, control (pp. 613-614)
9. Resource-mobilization (p. 614)
10. women, African Americans, Information Revolution, economy (p. 619)

PART VII: IN FOCUS--IMPORTANT ISSUES

- Studying Collective Behavior

  What are three reasons why *collective behavior* is difficult for sociologists to study?

  1.

  2.

  3.

  What are the three important ways that collectivities are distinguished from social groups?

  1.

  2.

  3.

- Localized Collectivities: Crowds

  Differentiate between the following types of crowds as identified by Herbert Blumer.

  casual crowd

  conventional crowd

  expressive crowd

  acting crowd

  Briefly describe the following explanations of *crowd behavior*.

  contagion theory

  What is a criticism of this theory?

convergence theory

What is a criticism of this theory?

emergent-Norm theory

What is a criticism of this theory?

- Dispersed Collectivities: Mass Behavior

Provide an illustration for each of the following.

rumor

gossip

public opinion

propaganda

panic

mass hysteria

fashions

fads

- Social Movements

  Describe each of the following theories of *social movement.*

  deprivation theory

  What is one criticism of this theory?

  mass-society theory

  What is one criticism of this theory?

  structural-strain theory

  What is one criticism of this theory?

  resource-mobilization theory

  What is one criticism of this theory?

  cultural theory

  What is one criticism of this theory?

  new social movements theory

  What is one criticism of this theory?

- Looking Ahead: Social Movements In the Twenty-First Century

  What is the future of social movements as projected by the author?

<table>
<tr><td>Chapter</td></tr>
<tr><td>24</td></tr>
</table>

Social Change: Traditional, Modern, and Postmodern Societies

PART I: CHAPTER OUTLINE

PART II: LEARNING OBJECTIVES

- To be able to identify and describe the four general characteristics of social change.
- To be able to identify and illustrate the different sources of social change.
- To be able to discuss the perspectives on social change as offered by Ferdinand Tönnies, Emile Durkheim, Max Weber, and Karl Marx.
- To be able to identify and describe the general characteristics of modernization.
- To be able to identify the key ideas of two major interpretations of modern society: mass society and class society.
- To be able to discuss the ideas of postmodernist thinkers and critically consider their relevance for our society.

PART III: KEY CONCEPTS

Fill in the blank spaces below with the appropriate concept.

1. _____ _____ refers to the transformation of culture and social institutions over time.
2. _____ refers to social patterns resulting from industrialization.
3. The process of social change begun by industrialization is known as _____.
4. A _____ _____ is a society in which industry and bureaucracy have eroded traditional social ties.
5. A _____ _____ is a capitalist society with pronounced social stratification.
6. _____ _____ refers to personality patterns common to members of a particular society.
7. _____-_____ refers to a rigid conformity to time honored ways of living.
8. _____-_____ refers to a receptiveness to the latest trends and fashions, often expressed by imitating others.
9. _____ refers to social patterns characteristic of postindustrial societies.

PART IV: IMPORTANT RESEARCHERS

In the space provided below each of the following researchers, write two or three sentences to help you remember his or her respective contributions to the field of sociology.

Karl Marx   Max Weber

Emile Durkheim   Ferdinand Tönnies

William Ogburn   David Reisman

Herbert Marcuse   William Bennett

PART V: STUDY QUESTIONS

True-False

1. T   F   *Max Weber* argued that technology and conflict are more important than ideas in transforming society.
2. T   F   Overall, only about nine percent of U.S. residents have not moved during the last thirty years.
3. T   F   Sociologist *Peter Berger* suggests that a important characteristic of modernization is the expression of personal choice.
4. T   F   According to our author, *Emile Durkheim's* view of modernity is both more complex and more positive than that of *Ferdinand Tönnies*.
5. T   F   Compared to *Emile Durkheim, Max Weber* was more critical of modern society, believing that the rationalization of bureaucracies would cause people to become alienated.
6. T   F   A *mass society* is one in which industry and bureaucracy have enhanced social ties.
7. T   F   *Class society theory* maintains that persistent social inequality undermines modern society's promise of individual freedom.
8. T   F   According to *David Reisman*, a type of social character he labels *other-directedness* represents rapidly changing industrial societies.
9. T   F   *Postmodernity* refers to the recent trend in industrialized societies of a return to tradition values and practices.
10. T   F   The *communitarianism movement* rests on the simple premise that "strong rights presume strong responsibilities".

Multiple Choice

1. The transformation of culture and social institutions over time refers to

    (a) social statics.
    (b) social change.
    (c) cultural lag.
    (d) modernity.

2. *William Ogburn's* theory of _____ states that material culture changes faster than nonmaterial culture.

    (a) modernity
    (b) cultural lag
    (c) modernization
    (d) anomie
    (e) rationalization

3. _____ is the process of social change begun by industrialization.

    (a) Postmodernity
    (b) Anomie
    (c) Mass society
    (d) Modernization
    (e) Gemeinschaft

4. Developed the theory of *Gemeinschaft* and *Gesellschaft*, arguing that the Industrial Revolution weakened the social fabric of family and tradition by introducing a business-like emphasis on facts, efficiency, and money.

    (a) Karl Marx
    (b) Emile Durkheim
    (c) Emile Durkheim
    (d) Ferdinand Tönnies

5. For *Emile Durkheim*, modernization is defined by the increasing _____ of a society.

    (a) mechanical solidarity
    (b) alienation
    (c) division of labor
    (d) conspicuous consumption

6.   In contrast to Ferdinand Tönnies who saw industrialization as amounting to a loss of solidarity, _____ viewed modernization not as a loss of community but as a change from community based on bonds of likeness to community based on economic interdependence.

    (a)   Emile Durkheim
    (b)   Karl Marx
    (c)   Max Weber
    (d)   Peter Berger

7.   Which of the following is most *accurate?*

    (a)   Emile Durkheim's concept of organic solidarity refers to social bonds of mutual dependency based on specialization.
    (b)   Ferdinand Tönnies saw societies as changing from the social organization based on Gesellschaft to the social organization based on Gemeinschaft.
    (c)   Karl Marx was a strong proponent of mass-society theory.
    (d)   Emile Durkheim's concept of mechanical solidarity is very similar in meaning to Ferdinand Tönnies' concept of Gesellschaft.

8.   Structural-functionalist *Emile Durkheim's* concepts of *mechanical solidarity* and *organic solidarity* are similar in meaning to the concepts

    (a)   mass society and class society.
    (b)   tradition-directedness and other-directedness.
    (c)   anomie and progress.
    (d)   Gemeinschaft and Gesellschaft.
    (e)   none of the above

9.   For *Max Weber*, modernity means replacing a traditional world view with a _____ way of thinking.

    (a)   alienated
    (b)   marginal
    (c)   mechanical
    (d)   organic
    (e)   rational

10.   *Karl Marx's* theory underestimated the dominance of _____ in modern society.

    (a)   inequality
    (b)   alienation
    (c)   power
    (d)   bureaucracy
    (e)   false consciousness

11. _____ *theory* focuses on the expanding scale of social life and the rise of the state in the study of modernization.

   (a) Dependency
   (b) Modernization
   (c) Social class
   (d) Rationalization
   (e) Mass-society

12. _____ *theory* views the process of modernization as being linked to the rise of capitalism, and sees its effects as involving the persistence of social inequality.

   (a) Mass-society
   (b) Class-society
   (c) Modernity
   (d) Cultural lag

13. Which social scientist described *modernization* in terms of its affects on *social character*?

   (a) Peter Berger
   (b) William Ogburn
   (c) David Reisman
   (d) Herbert Marcuse
   (e) David Klein

14. _____ refers to personality patterns common to members of a particular society.

   (a) Mass-society
   (b) Class-society
   (c) Traditionalism
   (d) Social character
   (e) Autonomy

15. _____ *theory* argues that persistent social inequality undermines modern society's promise of individual freedom.

   (a) Mass-society
   (b) Modernization
   (c) Traditional-rational
   (d) Mechanical
   (e) Class-society

16. David Reisman suggests that _____ is representative of modern societies.

(a) other-diectedness
(b) self-directedness
(c) mechanical-directedness
(d) anomic-directedness

17. _____ suggested that we be critical of *Max Weber's* view that modern society is rational because technological advances rarely empower people; instead, we should focus on the issue of how technology tends to reduce people's control over their own lives.

(a) Emile Durkheim
(b) Herbert Spencer
(c) David Reisman
(d) Herbert Marcuse
(e) Ferdinand Tönnies

18. The *Kaiapo*

(a) are a people living in a tribal society in Brazil.
(b) is a ritual among the Mbuti of the Ituri forest.
(c) is a sacred tradition involving animal sacrifices which has been made illegal by the Canadian government.
(d) are a people of Asia who represent the Gesellschaft concept developed by Ferdinand Tönnies.
(e) is a ritualistic war pattern of the Maring, a New Guinea culture of horticulturalists.

19. According to public opinion polls, in which of the following modern societies does the largest percentage of the population believe that *scientific advances* are helping society.

(a) Great Britain
(b) Japan
(c) the United States
(d) Canada
(e) Mexico

20. The bright light of "progress" is fading; science no longer holds the answers; cultural debates are intensifying; in important respects, modernity has failed; and social institutions are changing--are all themes running through _____ *thinking*.

(a) class society
(b) postmodern
(c) mass society
(d) social movements

Matching

1. ___ The transformation of culture and social institutions over time.
2. ___ Social patterns resulting from industrialization.
3. ___ Developed the concepts of Gemeinschaft and Gesellschaft.
4. ___ Developed the concepts of mechanical and organic solidarity.
5. ___ Argued that modern society was dominated by rationality.
6. ___ Understood modern society as being synonymous with capitalism.
7. ___ A society in which industry and bureaucracy have eroded traditional social ties.
8. ___ A capitalist society with pronounced social stratification.
9. ___ Personality patterns common to members of a particular society.
10. ___ The premise that strong rights presume strong responsibilities.

a. mass society
b. social change
c. Max Weber
d. Ferdinand Tönnies
e. modernity
f. social character
g. Emile Durkheim
h. communitarian
i. class society
j. Karl Marx

Fill-In

1. The process of *social change* has four major characteristics, including: social change is _____ social change is sometimes _____ but often _____, social change is _____, and some changes matter more than _____.

2. Focusing on culture as a source, *social change* results from three basic processes: _____, _____, and _____.

3. According to Peter Berger, four major characteristics of *modernization* include: The decline of small, _____ communities, the _____ of personal choice, increasing social _____, and future orientation and growing awareness of _____.

4. _____ is a condition in which society provides little moral guidance to individuals.

5. For *Max Weber*, modernity amounts to the progressive replacement of a traditional world-view with a _____ way of thinking.

6. *Mass society theory* draws upon the ideas of _____, _____, and _____.

7. A _____ *society* is a society in which industry and expanding bureaucracy have eroded traditional social ties.

8. _____ *society* is a capitalist society with pronounced social stratification.

9. *David Reisman* argues that preindustrial societies promote _____-directedness, or rigid personalities based on conformity to time-honored ways of living.

10. Five themes have emerged as part of *postmodern thinking*. These include that in important respects, _____ has failed; the bright promise of "_____" is fading; _____ no longer holds the answers; cultural debates are _____; and, social institutions are _____.

Discussion

1. What are four characteristics of *social change*? Further, five general domains which are involved in *causing* social change are identified and discussed in the text. List these and provide an example for each.
2. *Peter Berger* identifies four important general characteristics of *modern societies*. What are these characteristics?
3. Differentiate between *Ferdinand Tönnies*, *Emile Durkheim*, *Max Weber*, and *Karl Marx's* perspective on modernization.
4. What factors of *modernization* do theorists operating from the *mass society* theory focus upon?
5. What are the two types of *social character* identified by *David Reisman*? Define each of these.
6. What are the arguments being made by *postmodernists* concerning social change in modern society? What do critics of this view say?
7. Referring to *Table 24-1*, select a nonindustrialized society and compare it to the U.S. on four elements of society identified in the table. Provide a specific illustration representing a relative comparison for each element.
8. Four general types of *social movements* are discussed in the text. Identify, define, and illustrate each of these.
9. Four explanations of *social movements* are discussed in the text. Identify and describe each of these.
10. *Peter Berger* has identified four major characteristics of modernization. What are these? Provide an illustration for each of these.

PART VII: ANSWERS TO STUDY QUESTIONS

True-False

1.	F	(p. 628)	6.	T	(p. 633)
2.	T	(p. 628)	7.	T	(p. 636)
3.	T	(p. 629)	8.	T	(p. 637)
4.	T	(p. 631)	9.	T	(p. 641)
5.	T	(p. 633)	10.	T	(p. 644)

Multiple Choice

1.	b	(p. 626)	11.	e	(p. 634)
2.	b	(p. 626)	12.	b	(p. 636)
3.	d	(p. 629)	13.	c	(pp. 637)
4.	d	(p. 630)	14.	d	(p. 637)
5.	c	(p. 631)	15.	e	(p. 637)
6.	a	(p. 631)	16.	a	(p. 638)
7.	a	(pp. 631-632)	17.	d	(p. 639)
8.	d	(p. 631)	18.	a	(p. 640)
9.	e	(p. 632)	19.	c	(p. 640)
10.	d	(p. 633)	20.	b	(p. 641)

Matching

1.	b	(p. 626)
2.	e	(p. 629)
3.	d	(p. 630)
4.	g	(p. 631)
5.	c	(p. 632)

6.	j	(p. 633)
7.	a	(p. 633)
8.	i	(p. 636)
9.	f	(p. 637)
10.	h	(p. 644)

Fill-In

1. inevitable, intentional, unplanned, controversial, others (pp. 626-627)
2. invention, discovery, diffusion (p. 627)
3. tradition, expansion, diversity, time (p. 629-630)
4. Anomie (p.632)
5. rational (p. 633)
6. Tönnies, Durkheim, Weber (p. 633)
7. mass (p. 633)
8. Class (p. 636)
9. tradition (p. 637)
10. modernity, progress, science, intensifying, changing (p. 641)

PART VII: IN FOCUS--IMPORTANT ISSUES

- What Is Social Change?

  What are the four major characteristics of the process of *social change*?

- Causes of Social Change

  Provide an illustration for each of the following *causes of social change.*

  culture and change

  invention

  discovery

  diffusion

conflict and change

ideas and change

demographic change

- Modernity

What are the four major characteristics of *modernization*?

Briefly summarize the view of modernity as expressed by each of the following theorists.

Ferdinand Tönnies

Emile Durkheim

Max Weber

Karl Marx

- Theoretical Analysis of Modernity

  According to structural-functionalists, what are the essential characteristics of *mass-society*?

  What is the major problem associated with mass-society? Illustrate.

  What are the major criticisms of mass-society theory?

  According to conflict theorists, what are the essential characteristics of *class-society*?

  What is the major problem associated with class-society? Illustrate this problem.

  What are the major criticisms of class-society theory?

- Postmodernity

  What are the five themes shared by *postmodern* thinkers?

  Provide evidence for two of these themes.

- Looking Ahead: Modernization and Our Global Future

  How do *modernization theory* and *dependency theory* shed light on issues raised in this chapter concerning modernization?